Tokyo TDC, Vol.24

The Best in International
Typography & Design

東京タイプディレクターズクラブ編集

Azur Corporation

Tokyo TDC, Vol.24
The Best in International Typography & Design

Art Direction
Takahisa Nakajima

Design
Yuko Sekine / Ryota Sugahara / Kyohei Mizutani　(ntD)

Editing & Program
The Tokyo Type Directors Club
Takako Terunuma (TDC Secretarial Director, Curator)
Misa Kawaguchi (TDC Staff)

First Published in overseas edition in 2013
by AZUR Corporation
5F Aikusu Building, 1-44-8, Jimbo-Cho, Kanda Chiyoda-ku,
Tokyo 101-0051 Japan
Tel:+81-3-3292-7601 / Fax:+81-3-3292-7602
E-mail: azur@galaxy.ocn.ne.jp

Distributed by :
Worldwide except Japan = AZUR Corporation

Acknowledgements
We express deep appreciation to all those who provided their full cooperation in holding the exhibition and producing this annual.
We also extend our sincere gratitude to the companies who advertised in the Japanese edition.

Special Thanks to
Ginza Graphic Gallery / ddd Gallery / Samwon Paper Gallery / The Oct Art And Design Gallery /
Tokyo Design Center / Seiichi Kazunaga / Katsumi Asaba Design Office / Azusa Ozawa / Marki Kimura / Toru Yoshikawa

目次　　Contents

Noisy Heaven

こんな話を聞いた。日本に精通している外国人が、「日本は静かな天国」だが、うるさい地獄の方がいい時もあると言う。ぼくが一番心配しているのは、日本が静かな地獄に近づいているのでは…ということだ。やはり「うるさい天国」が一番いいと思う。そこには未来が見える。

2013年3月2日、中国深圳OCTアート＆デザインギャラリーで東京TDC 2012展が、王序（ワン・シュー）さんの招待で盛大に開催された。香港から車で45分の深圳は、花が咲き、鳥が鳴き、蜂の巣の様な六角形のパターンの黒いビルにTDCのネオンが輝き、目の前の池に写り揺れていた。入口を入るとホワイ・ノット・アソシエイツとゴードン・ヤングによるTDC賞2012のグランプリ作品。イングランド北西部海岸沿いのブラックプールという町に敷かれているのと同じように、見る者に向かって大声で呼びかけるタイポグラフィを、皆が踏みしめている。2階、3階と王序がみごとに展示してくれた。2日は講演会。なんとスタンリー・ウォンが香港から浅葉のために長い卓球台を用意してくれた。香港・中国各地から仲間が大勢来てくれた。中国のヤングデザイナーが700名も集まり、うるさい天国になった。

東京TDCは今年も「うるさい天国」をめざすぞ。

A foreigner familiar with Japan once said that "Japan is a quiet heaven," but sometimes a noisy hell can be better. What I am most worried about is that Japan may be heading toward being a "quiet hell." A "noisy heaven" certainly is the best, in my opinion. That's where you can get a glimpse of the future.

On March 2, 2013, the Tokyo TDC 2012 exhibition, curated by Wang Xu, was held at the OCT Art & Design Gallery in Shenzhen, China. In Shenzhen, a 45-minute drive from Hong Kong, I found flowers in bloom, birds singing, and a "TDC" neon sign on a hexagonal, beehive-like black building reflected in the swaying surface of a pond in front of me. Upon entering the building, visitors were greeted by TDC 2012 Grand Prize-winning works by Why Not Associates and Gordon Young. The typography, laid out like originally done in the northwestern English seashore town of Blackpool, loudly appealed to those who viewed it — while stepping on it. On the second and third floors, art director Wang Xu had put together some excellent displays. The program on March 2 included a lecture. Stanley Wong even brought a long ping-pong table for me all the way from Hong Kong. With countless friends coming together from Hong Kong and various parts of China, the gathering of 700 Chinese young designers was quite a "noisy heaven."

I hope we can have such a "noisy heaven" again at Tokyo TDC this year.

浅葉克己
Katsumi Asaba

NPO法人 東京タイプディレクターズクラブ 理事長
Chairman, Tokyo Type Directors Club (NPO)

Potential of Typography

初期の頃より東京TDCの活動に大きな関心を抱いていた。文字を一切使わないポスターを目にしたことはなく、またタイポグラフィだけでデザインされたポスターには優れた作品が数多くある。タイポグラフィに特別な可能性があるに違いないという強い思いが私にあった。TDCは毎年この可能性を認識させてくれる。その活動は決して独善的になることなく、全てのメディア、カテゴリーを通じて行われる。毎年の展覧会や年鑑が国際的なハイライトになっているのはそうした理由からだ。

TDC展2013のためのポスターを制作した。ラテン文字を使う場合、文字同様に重要なのが文字と文字の間にある空間であり、このポスターではTDCという文字がポジとネガの両方から構成され、どこからが文字なのか、どこからが間なのかはっきりしない。このような形で3つの文字を一筆書きのように一つの線から形成できたのは偶然で、文字がこのような順で並んでいたことも偶然だった。運が良かったのは、角張ったラインが一様に、左から右へ曲線に変化していること。このラインの二つの端部は、展覧会の開催地である東京と大阪の地理を表したもので、これだけが意図して主張したものである。

I've been following the activities of TDC Tokyo with great interest almost from the very beginning.
The fact that I know few posters that do without letters, but that there are many outstanding ones that are exclusively composed of typographical elements, affirms my supposition that typography must be holding a special kind of potential.
This is exactly the potential that the TDC Tokyo showcases book every year.
The club does this in a refreshingly undogmatic fashion and presents it across a variety of media — and thanks to this, the exhibition and the annual book are an international highlight year after year.

To design a poster for this year's edition of the TDC Tokyo's annual exhibition was a great honor and challenge for me. When typesetting Roman letters, the intervals are just as important as the letters themselves. The letters "TDC" are made from the positive mold as well as from the negative, making it unclear which is a letter and which is an interval.
Coincidentally, one can write these three letters in one line, whereas the order of the letters is another aspect that benefits this coincidence.
That the angular line homogeneously morphs from left to right into a curved one is a lucky factor, while the terminal points' geographical reference to the two exhibition venues in Tokyo and Osaka is merely a proposition.

ラルフ・シュライフォーゲル
Ralph Schraivogel

グラフィックデザイナー
Graphic Designer

掲載作家一覧 [国内]
Type Directors' Index From Japan

相澤千晶　Chiaki Aizawa
409
chiaki.aizawa@me.com
http://www.chiakiaizawa.com/

青木克憲　Katsunori Aoki
044　136　246
バタフライ・ストローク・株式会社　butterfly・stroke inc.
shintomi@btf.co.jp
http://www.butterfly-stroke.com/
http://www.shopbtf.com/

秋山具義　Gugi Akiyama
221
デイリーフレッシュ株式会社　Dairy Fresh
info@d-fresh.com
http://www.d-fresh.com/gugi/

浅葉克己　Katsumi Asaba
013　022　023　031　038　051　195　196　216
223　348　390　426
株式会社浅葉克己デザイン室　Asaba Design Co., Ltd.
info@asaba-d.co.jp
http://www.asaba-design.com/

artless Inc.
363
info@artless.co.jp
http://www.artless.co.jp/

安部洋佑　Yosuke Abe
328　344
yosuke.abe1001@gmail.com

天野裕一　Yuichi Amano
079
Amano Graphics
amano@amano-g.com
http://amano-g.com/

安齋朋恵　Tomoe Anzai
435
anzaitomoe111@yahoo.co.jp

池上直樹　Naoki Ikegami
191　249
コトホギデザイン　Kotohogi Design
info@kotohogidesign.com
http://www.kotohogidesign.com/

石川 耕　Ko Ishikawa
371　416
株式会社サムライ　Samurai Inc.
ishikawa@samurai.sh
http://kashiwasato.com/

石黒篤史　Atsushi Ishiguro
410

石黒 潤　Jun Ishiguro
066

怡土希帆　Kiho Ito
298
株式会社アサツー ディ・ケイ　Asatsu-DK Inc.
itokihokitoi@gmail.com
http://kihoito.com/

伊東友子　Tomoko Ito
437
tomoco.ito@gmail.com

稲田尊久　Takahisa Inada
077
ネイティブグラフィック　naitive graphic
inada@nativegraphic.net
http://www.nativegraphic.net/

井上嗣也　Tsuguya Inoue
056　059
ビーンズ　BEANS

今村 浩　Hiroshi Imamura
400

居山浩二　Koji Iyama
359
株式会社イヤマデザイン　iyamadesign inc.
info@iyamadesign.jp
http://iyamadesign.jp/

色部義昭　Yoshiaki Irobe
016　201　270
日本デザインセンター　色部デザイン研究室
Irobe Design Institute, Nippon Design Center Inc.
irobedesign@ndc.co.jp
http://irobe.ndc.co.jp/

岩崎悦子　Etsuko Iwasaki
088　151
有限会社イー　E. Co., Ltd.
iwasaki@e-ltd.co.jp
http://e-ltd.co.jp/

岩田勇紀　Yuki Iwata
419
株式会社オールレイド　Allraid Inc.
iwata@allraid.jp
http://www.allraid.jp/

石見俊太郎　Shuntaro Iwami
115　116
iwami@north-design.me
http://north-design.me/

上田真未　Mami Ueda
393
mamiueda1054@gmail.com

上西祐理　Yuri Uenishi
231　387
uenishi.yuri@dentsu.co.jp
http://www.uenishiyuri.com/

植原亮輔　Ryosuke Uehara
179　203　204　205　206　218　229　289　322
349　353　354　368　370
株式会社キギ　KIGI co., ltd.
ue@ki-gi.com
http://www.ki-gi.com/

後 智仁　Tomohito Ushiro
084
株式会社 White Design
info@whitedesign.jp

内田真弓　Mayumi Uchida
114　238
10 inc.
kaki@tuba.ocn.ne.jp
http://www.10inc.jp/

浦田高史　Koushi Urata
076

永樂雅也　Masaya Eiraku
101
アムズィー　AMSY
amsivee@gmail.com
http://www.amsy.jp/

えぐちりか　Rika Eguchi
400

大塚南海子　Namiko Otsuka
234
info@namikootsuka.com
http://www.namikootsuka.com/

大原健一郎　Kenichiro Ohara
294　351
NIGN（株式会社ナイン）　NIGN Co., Ltd.
info@nign.co.jp
http://www.nign.co.jp/

大原大次郎　Daijiro Ohara
190　332　442
オモンマ　omomma
ohara@omomma.in
http://omomma.in/

大森 剛　Tsuyoshi Omori
318　350
トリプレットデザイン　triplet design inc.
tsuyoshi@triplet.jp
http://triplet.jp/

大八木 翼　Tsubasa Oyagi
448

大来 優　Yu Orai
441
株式会社電通　Dentsu Inc.
orai.yu@dentsu.co.jp

大澤悠大　Yudai Osawa
277
osawayudai@gmail.com

奥村靫正　Yukimasa Okumura
094　149
TSTJ inc.
oua@tstj-inc.co.jp
http://www.tstj-inc.co.jp/

尾﨑友則　Tomonori Ozaki
017
ozaki_tomonori@hotmail.co.jp

折形デザイン研究所　Origata Design Institute
265
info@origata.com
http://www.origata.com/

葛西 薫　Kaoru Kasai
003　012　029　142　178　185　188　197　198
240　267　273　325　352　388　408
株式会社サン・アド　SUN-AD Co., Ltd.

柏倉瑛子　Eiko Kashiwakura
311
mail@eikokashiwakura.com
http://eikokashiwakura.com/

加瀬 透　Toru Kase
220
toru.kase.1209@gmail.com
http://kstrw.tumblr.com/

川村真司　Masashi Kawamura
444　445
PARTY
http://prty.jp/

菊井美沙希　Misaki Kikui
110
kikuiiii0808@gmail.com

菊地敦己　Atsuki Kikuchi
123　127　145　150　164　244　335　357　412
415
株式会社菊地敦己事務所　Atsuki Kikuchi Ltd.
studio@akltd.jp
http://atsukikikuchi.com/

菊地和広　Kazuhiro Kikuchi
248
バックヤード　Backyard
kiku@thebackyard.biz
http://www.thebackyard.biz/

岸 さゆみ　Sayumi Kishi
109
sayumi630@gmail.com

北林 誠　Makoto Kitabayashi
111
マトインク　Mato Inc.
kitabayashi@matoinc.jp
http://matoinc.jp/

木村高典　Takanori Kimura
018
株式会社たき工房　TAKI Corporation
takanori_kimura@taki.co.jp
http://chokushanikko.tumblr.com/

草谷隆文　Takafumi Kusagaya
383　384
有限会社草谷デザイン　Kusagaya Design Inc.
kusagaya@kt.rim.or.jp
http://www.kusagayadesign.com/

栗林和夫　Kazuo Kuribayashi
007　215　392
クリとグラフィック　Kuri + Graphic
kurivo.1@jcom.home.ne.jp
http://kuri-graphic.com/

黒栁 潤　Jun Kuroyanagi
367　375　378
kjdh@kjdh.jp

軍司匡寛　Tadahiro Gunji
153

河野 智　Satoshi Kohno
081　225
satoshikohno.com@gmail.com

小杉幸一　Koichi Kosugi
247　252　336　337
koichi.kosugi@hakuhodo.co.jp

小松洋一　Yoichi Komatsu
265
yoichi.komatsu@dentsu.co.jp

小山秀一郎　Shuichirow Koyama
052
株式会社バスキュール　Bascule inc.
s.h.u@bascule.co.jp

齋藤 浩　Hiroshi Saito
233
有限会社トンプー・グラフィクス　tong-poo graphics
saito@tongpoographics.jp
http://tongpoographics.jp/

榮 良太　Ryota Sakae
358　389
ryota.sakae@hakuhodo.co.jp

佐古田英一　Eiichi Sakota
078
レックセカンド　REC2nd
rec2nd@io.ocn.ne.jp
http://rec2nd.com/

佐々木 俊　Shun Sasaki
050　067
nuhsikasas@gmail.com
http://sasakishun.tumblr.com/

佐藤亜沙美　Asami Sato
168　174
コズフィッシュ　cozfish
sato@cozfish.jp

佐藤大介　Daisuke Sato
214

佐藤 卓　Taku Satoh
143　320　440
株式会社佐藤卓デザイン事務所
Taku Satoh Design Office
tsdo@tsdo.co.jp
http://www.tsdo.co.jp/

佐野研二郎　Kenjiro Sano
024　183　317　396　401　402　410
MR_DESIGN
info@mr-design.jp
http://www.mr-design.jp/

SUNDAY PROJECT
431
sketch@sundayproject.jp
http://sundayproject.jp/

市東 基　Motoi Shito
024　037　269　296
info@motoishito.jp
http://www.motoishito.jp/

柴田賢蔵　Kenzo Shibata
323

澁谷克彦　Katsuhiko Shibuya
034　035　385
株式会社資生堂　Shiseido Co., Ltd.
http://www.shiseido.co.jp/

清水幹太　Qanta Shimizu
444　445
PARTY
http://prty.jp/

白澤真生　Masao Shirasawa
154
株式会社オープンエンズ　OPENENDS Inc.
masao@openends.org
http://www.openends.org/

シラスノリユキ　Noriyuki Shirasu
020
株式会社カラー　color.inc.
info@color-81.com
http://www.color-81.com/

新世界タイポ研究会（岡澤慶秀・塚田哲也・秀親）
Shinsekai Type Study Group
(Yoshihide Okazawa, Tetsuya Tsukada, Hidechika)
004
shinsekai@type.org
http://shinsekai.type.org/

杉山耕太　Kota Sugiyama
212　285
株式会社ドラフト　Draft Co., Ltd.
sugiyama@draft.jp
http://www.draft.jp/

鈴木信輔　Shinsuke Suzuki
278
トンネル　Tunnel
info@tunnel-p.com
http://tunnel-p.com/

鈴木壮一　Soichi Suzuki
148
souichi517@hotmail.com

瀬尾 大　Masaru Seo
265
masaru.seo@dentsu.co.jp

関 和亮　Kazuaki Seki
445

関本明子　Akiko Sekimoto
228　377
sekimoto@draft.jp
http://www.draft.jp/

髙井 薫　Kaoru Takai
347
takai@sun-ad.co.jp

田頭慎太郎　Shintaro Tagashira
046　070　339
shintarotagashira@gmail.com

高田 唯　Yui Takada
224　237　324
オールライトグラフィックス　All Right Graphics
all@allrightgraphics.com
http://www.allrightgraphics.com/

髙谷 廉　Ren Takaya
213　222　413
AD & D
takaya@ad-and-d.jp
http://www.ad-and-d.jp/

滝本 圭　Kei Takimoto
058
keitakimoto.work@gmail.com

竹内佐織　Saori Takeuchi
093　241　243　282　331　369　422
株式会社博報堂　Hakuhodo Inc.
SAORI.TAKEUCHI@hakuhodo.co.jp

竹田麻衣子　Maiko Takeda
194
リム　Lim
info@lim-tm.com

竹村真太郎　Shintaro Takemura
397
株式会社ADKアーツ　ADK Arts Inc.
takemura@adk-arts.jp
http://www.adk-arts.jp/

田中良治　Ryoji Tanaka
443　447
セミトランスペアレント・デザイン
Semitransparent Design
info@semitransparentdesign.com
http://www.semitransparentdesign.com/

谷岡茂樹　Shigeki Tanioka
439
tanishi@z-est.jp
http://www.z-est.jp/

玉置太一　Taichi Tamaki
398
株式会社電通　Dentsu Inc.
taichi.tamaki@dentsu.co.jp

千葉菜々子　Nanako Chiba
434
chi_ba7_6975@yahoo.co.jp

千原徹也　Tetsuya Chihara
026　279
株式会社れもんらいふ　Lemonlife & Co.
chihara@lemonlife.jp
http://www.lemonlife.jp/

塚本 陽　Kiyoshi Tsukamoto
036
tkmt@xf6.so-net.ne.jp
http://eraplatonico.tumblr.com/

塚本哲也　Tetsuya Tsukamoto
265
tetsuya.tsukamoto@dentsu.co.jp

対馬 肇　Hajime Tsushima
404
対馬デザイン事務所　Tsushima Design
info@tsushima-design.com
http://www.tsushima-design.com/

堤 裕紀　Yuki Tsutsumi
288
y.tsutsumi@dentsu.co.jp

常橋恵美　Emi Tsunehashi
293
info@emitsunehashi.jp
http://emitsunehashi.jp/

寺島響水　Kyosui Terashima
369

寺島賢幸　Masayuki Terashima
250
有限会社寺島デザイン制作室　Terashima Design Co.
tera@tera-d.net
http://www.tera-d.net/

土居裕彰　Hiroaki Doi
099
info@dddoi.com
http://www.dddoi.com/

豊島 晶　Aki Toyoshima
260
Akipon Design House Inc.
aki@akipon.com
http://www.akipon.com/

永井裕明　Hiroaki Nagai
160
株式会社エヌ・ジー　N.G. inc.
ng@nginc.jp
http://www.nginc.jp/

中島英樹　Hideki Nakajima
057　121　130　132　133　165　177　208　209
355
有限会社中島デザイン　Nakajima Design Inc.
info@nkjm-d.com
http://www.nkjm-d.com/

長嶋りかこ　Rikako Nagashima
211　283　291　361　386　403
rikako.nagashima@hakuhodo.co.jp
http://rikako-nagashima.com/

仲條正義　Masayoshi Nakajo
002　030　125　139　158　202　330
株式会社仲條デザイン事務所　Nakajo Design Office

中田卓志　Takushi Nakada
342
ラディッグルーバー　LUDWIGROOVER
info@ludwigroover.com
http://www.ludwigroover.com/

長友啓典　Keisuke Nagatomo
060
株式会社ケイツー　K2 Inc.
k-two@k2-d.co.jp
http://www.k2-d.co.jp/

中野豪雄　Takeo Nakano
175
株式会社中野デザイン事務所
Nakano Design Office Co., Ltd.
info@nakano-design.com
http://nakano-design.com/

中村至男　Norio Nakamura
040　141
中村至男制作室　Norio Nakamura Studio
contact@nakamuranorio.com
http://nakamuranorio.com/

中村勇吾　Yugo Nakamura
320　440
tha ltd.
yugo@tha.jp
http://tha.jp/

中本陽子　Yoko Nakamoto
199　366

中山智裕　Tomohiro Nakayama
098
株式会社サン・アド　SUN-AD Co., Ltd.
tomohiro_nakayama@sun-ad.co.jp

根岸明寛　Akitomo Negishi
117　119

野村勝久　Katsuhisa Nomura
276
野村デザイン制作室　Nomura Design Factory
nomukatsu@nifty.com
http://www.nomura-design.com/

白村玲子　Reiko Hakumura
082
HB スタジオ　HB studio
hb.hakumura@gmail.com

服部一成　Kazunari Hattori
011　100　137　138　166　167　171　235　411
421
有限会社服部一成　Kazunari Hattori Inc.
hattori@flyingcake.com

林 規章　Noriaki Hayashi
064　103　112　134　227
Hayashi Design
hayashid@me.com

原 健三　Kenzo Hara
239　319　343

原田祐馬　Yuma Harada
107　144
UMA / design farm
uma@umamu.jp
http://www.umamu.jp/

樋口寛人　Hiroto Higuchi
041　176　278　341
ミネラル　mineral
higuchi@mineraldo.com
http://www.mineraldo.com/

平井秀和　Hidekazu Hirai
083
ピース グラフィックス　Peace Graphics
peace_hide@guitar.ocn.ne.jp
http://peacegraphics.jp/

平野篤史　Atsushi Hirano
074　075　173　290　345
株式会社ドラフト　DRAFT Co., Ltd.
hirano@draft.jp
http://www.draft.jp/

廣村正彰　Masaaki Hiromura
356　379
株式会社廣村デザイン事務所
Hiromura Design Office
http://www.hiromuradesign.com/

広本理絵　Rie Hiromoto
065
hinekure design
joydesign@me.com
http://hiro.webcrow.jp/

福岡南央子　Naoko Fukuoka
242　338
woolen
fukuoka@woolen2010.com
http://woolen2010graphic.blogspot.com/

福澤卓馬　Takuma Fukuzawa
212　285
株式会社ドラフト　Draft Co., Ltd.
fukuzawa@draft.jp
http://www.draft.jp/

藤田純平　Junpei Fujita
424　425
JUNPEI.FUJITA@hakuhodo.co.jp

藤巻洋紀　Hiroki Fujimaki
069
hirokifujimaki@gmail.com

干場邦一　Kunikazu Hoshiba
309　310

細島雄一　Yuichi Hosojima
373
サンクディレクションズ　CINQ Directions
hoso@39d.co.jp
http://www.tottemoinc.com

本田千尋　Chihiro Honda
047
honda@ki-gi.com
http://hondachihiro.tumblr.com/

前川景介　Keisuke Maekawa
406
トレモロランプ　Tremololamp
contact@tremololamp.com
http://www.tremololamp.com/

前原翔一　Shoichi Maehara
212　285　308
株式会社ドラフト　Draft Co., Ltd.
maehara@draft.jp
http://www.draft.jp/

正光亜実　Ami Masamitsu
236
iMasaMi2@gmail.com

増永明子　Akiko Masunaga
333　372　376
マスナガデザイン部　masunaga design team
masunaga@masdb.jp
http://www.masdb.jp/

松田洋和　Hirokazu Matsuda
147
matsuda@hekichi.info
http://matsudahirokazu.com/

松永 真　Shin Matsunaga
395

松永美春　Miharu Matsunaga
053
miharu.matsunaga@dentsu.co.jp
http://miharumatsunaga.com/

松原秀祐　Shusuke Matsubara
321　374
shuu168@gmail.com
http://s-matsubara.com/

松本健一　Kenichi Matsumoto
268
株式会社モトモト　MOTOMOTO inc.
matsumoto@moto-moto.jp

松本幸二　Koji Matsumoto
096
株式会社グランドデラックス　Grand Deluxe inc.
matsumoto@grand-deluxe.com
http://grand-deluxe.com/

間宮伊吹　Ibuki Mamiya
085

丸橋 桂　Katsura Marubashi
189　360
株式会社資生堂 宣伝制作室
Advertising Division, Shiseido Co., Ltd.
marubashikatsura@gmail.com

丸山 建　Ken Maruyama
045　062　418
maruyama@neos-design.co.jp

三浦 遊　Yu Miura
272
株式会社資生堂 宣伝制作部
Advertising Division, Shiseido Co., Ltd.
miura@ad-shiseido.com

三木 健　Ken Miki
304
三木健デザイン事務所　Ken Miki & Associates
http://www.ken-miki.net/

宮川和之　Kazuyuki Miyakawa
329
miyakawa@prdx.co.jp
http://www.prdx.co.jp/

宮川 宏　Hiroshi Miyakawa
155　316

三宅宇太郎　Utaro Miyake
334
info@utaromiyake.com
http://utaromiyake.com/

宮田絵里子　Eriko Miyata
427
eriko.m.net@gmail.com

宮田裕美詠　Yumiyo Miyata
019　039　245
STRIDE
s@stride.me
http://www.stride.me/

村松里紗　Lisa Muramatsu
236
lisamramats@gmail.com

目時綾子　Ayako Metoki
054
有限会社バウ広告事務所　BAU Advertising Office
metoki@bau-ad.co.jp
http://bau-ad.co.jp/

杢谷吉也　Yoshinari Mokutani
157
モクタニデザイン　Mokutani Design
mokutani_d@h05.itscom.net

森 和之　Kazuyuki Mori
080
株式会社ルーク　Luke Inc.
info@luke-inc.jp

八木義博　Yoshihiro Yagi
399
yagi.y@dentsu.co.jp

矢後直規　Naonori Yago
086　281
NAONORI.YAGO@hakuhodo.co.jp

山口 馨　Kaoru Yamaguchi
429
有限会社バウ広告事務所　BAU Advertising Office
yamaguchi@bau-ad.co.jp
http://www.bau-ad.co.jp/
http://www.e-ykj.com/

山下ともこ　Tomoko Yamashita
032　033　126　200
yamashita@flyingcake.com
http://www.tomokoyamashita.net/

山田和寛　Kazuhiro Yamada
131
yamada@nipponia.in
http://www.nipponia.in/

山本和久　Kazuhisa Yamamoto
326
ドニー・グラフィクス　Donny Grafiks
info@donnygrafiks.com
http://www.donnygrafiks.com/

ユーフラテス　Euphrates
（山本晃士ロバート / 貝塚智子 / 佐藤 匡 / うえ田みお /
石川将也 / 米本弘史 / 時田亜希夫 / 菅 俊一 / 湧川晶子 /
廣瀬隼也 / 大島 遼）
（Kohji Robert Yamamoto / Tomoko Kaizuka /
Masashi Sato / Mio Ueta / Masaya Ishikawa /
Hirofumi Yonemoto / Akio Tokita / Syun'ichi Suge /
Masako Wakigawa / Junya Hirose / Ryo Oshima）
446
euph@euphrates.co.jp
http://euphrates.jp/

よつやなつみ　Natsumi Yotsuya
438
tsunashi0921@gmail.com

若杉智也　Tomoya Wakasugi
102
有限会社イー　E. Co., Ltd.
w.tom118@gmail.com

和久井裕史　Hiroshi Wakui
364　365

渡邉良重　Yoshie Watanabe
124　179　206　210　217　218　346　354　370
株式会社キギ　KIGI co., ltd.
http://www.ki-gi.com/

Tim Ahrens [Germany]
258
Just Another Foundry
askme@justanotherfoundry.com
http://justanotherfoundry.com/

Cara Ang [Singapore]
300
Asylum
cara@theasylum.com.sg
http://www.theasylum.com.sg/

Philippe Apeloig [France]
381 391
Studio Philippe Apeloig
info@apeloig.com
http://www.apeloig.com/

Atelier mit Meerblick [Germany]
118 295 312
brief@atelier-mit-meerblick.de
http://www.atelier-mit-meerblick.de/

Benny Au [Hong Kong, China]
315
Amazing Angle Design Co., Ltd.
benny@amazingangle.com
http://www.amazingangle.com/

Mehtap Avci [Germany]
312
contact@mehtapavci.de
http://www.mehtapavci.de/

Andre Baldinger [France]
042 302
Baldinger • Vu-Huu
info@baldingervuhuu.com
http://www.baldingervuhuu.com/

Gene Bawden [Australia]
048
Deputy Head, Design, Monash University
Art Design & Architecture
gene.bawden@monash.edu
http://www.artdes.monash.edu.au/design/people.php#!

Till Beckmann [Germany]
193
Rimini Berlin
post@rimini-berlin.de
http://www.rimini-berlin.de/

Chris Bolton [Finland]
380
chris@chrisbolton.org
http://designbychrisbolton.tumblr.com/

Mark Boule [Germany]
090 092

Erich Brechbühl [Switzerland]
006
Erich Brechbühl [Mixer]
erich@mixer.ch
http://www.mixer.ch/

Brighten the Corners [UK]
(Billy Kiosoglou, Frank Philippin)
049 122
contact@brightenthecorners.com
http://www.brightenthecorners.com/

Ilya Bryabrin [Russian Federation]
073
ilya@bryabrin.ru
http://www.bryabrin.ru/

Veronika Burian [Czech Republic]
254
TypeTogether s.r.o.
info@type-together.com
http://www.type-together.com/

Fabienne Burri [Switzerland]
015 104 105
C2F : Cybu Richli & Fabienne Burri
to@c2f.to
http://www.c2f.to/

Theseus Chan [Singapore]
146 152 182
WORK
http://www.workwerk.com/

Pu-Hui Chang [Taiwan]
219
P : Chang Design
pchangdesign@gmail.com
http://cargocollective.com/P_

Kuokwai Cheong [Macao, China]
170
Joaquim Cheong Design
info@jocdesign.com
http://www.jocdesign.com/

Ivan Chermayeff [USA]
417
Chermayeff & Geismar & Haviv
info@cghnyc.com
http://www.cgstudionyc.com/

Lin Chi Tai [Taiwan]
161
TAIGRAPHIC Design Studio
linchitai.design@gmail.com
http://cargocollective.com/chitailin

Matthias Christ [Germany]
091
mail@matthiaschrist.net
http://www.matthiaschrist.net/

Cohen Van Balen [UK]
010
http://www.cohenvanbalen.com/

Zhang Dali [China]
284
Zhangdali Design / Elephant Space
elephant_space@163.com
zhangdali@vip.sina.com
http://www.zhangdali.com/

Leslie David [France]
187
Leslie David Studio
http://www.leslie-david.com/

Sonya Dyakova [UK]
186
Atelier Dyakova
sonya@atelierdyakova.com
http://www.atelierdyakova.com/

Vanessa Eckstein [Canada]
314
Blok Design
disinfo@blokdesign.com
http://www.blokdesign.com/

Ding Fan [China]
055
United Design lab
http://u-d-l.com/

Fraser Muggeridge Studio [UK]
156
info@pleasedonotbend.co.uk
http://pleasedonotbend.co.uk/

Friederike Gaigl [Germany]
307
ZWO rundum kommunikation
info@agenturzwo.de
http://www.agenturzwo.de/

Stephen Gilmore [UK]
305
North
info@northdesign.co.uk
http://www.northdesign.co.uk/

Lia Gordon [USA]
280
Landor Associates
schmia00@yahoo.com

tino grass [Germany]
414
tino grass visuelle kommunikation
info@tinograss.de
http://www.tinograss.de/

Guo Guo Guang [China]
340

Stefan Guzy [Germany]
382
Zwölf
mail@zwoelf.net
http://www.zwoelf.net/portfolio/

Nicolas Haeberli [Switzerland]
163
Büro Haeberli Zürich, Visual Communication
hello@buerohaeberli.ch
http://www.buerohaeberli.ch/

Tosh Hall [USA]
280
Landor Associates
th@toshhall.com

Ma Hao [China]
327
thorsdays@gmail.com
http://www.markds.com.cn/

Jenny Hasselbach [Germany]
193
Rimini Berlin
post@rimini-berlin.de
http://www.rimini-berlin.de/

Carolin Himmel [Germany]
362

Hong Hun Hun [China]
274
day day up design consultants
hwttxs@163.com
http://www.dduhw.com/

Ean-Hwa Huang [Malaysia]
423
Mccann Worldgroup /
Mccann Erickson Malaysia
hwa@merdekalhs.com
http://mccann.com/

Jianping He [Germany]
106
hesign (Berlin)
info@hesign.com
http://www.hesign.com/

He Jun [China]
162   230

Ignatius Hernawan Tanzil [Indonesia]
095
LeBoYe
info@leboyedesign.com
http://www.leboyedesign.com/

Pedro Inoue [Brazil]
180
pedro@coletivo.org
http://www.coletivo.org/pedro/
http://cargocollective.com/pedroinoue

Olaf Jäger [Germany]
275
Jäger & Jäger
info@jaegerundjaeger.de
http://www.jaegerundjaeger.de/

Jeong In-gee [Korea]
014   063
ordinarypeople.kr@gmail.com
http://www.ordinarypeople.kr/

Fang Jianping [China]
055
United Design lab
http://U-D-L.com/

Michael Johnson [UK]
428

Juanjo Justicia [Spain]
192
info@underbau.com
http://www.underbau.com/

Miki Kadokura [Germany, Tokyo]
226
The Simple Society　シンプル組合
yes@thesimplesociety.jp
http://thesimplesociety.com/

Jason Kedgley [UK]
113
tomato
kedge@tomato.co.uk
http://www.tomato.co.uk/

Sean Kelvin Khoo [Singapore]
068
Pupilpeople
info@pupilpeople.com
http://www.pupilpeople.com/

Dylan Kendle [UK]
113   433
tomato
http://www.tomato.co.uk/

Seán Kennedy [Switzerland]
163
Büro Haeberli Zürich, Visual Communication
hello@buerohaeberli.ch
http://www.buerohaeberli.ch/

Do-Hyung Kim [Korea]
061   097
grayoval
http://www.grayoval.com/

Grace Kim [New Zealand]
436
grace@altgroup.net

Benjamin Kivikoski [Germany]
072
kivikoski@kivikoski-staege.de
http://www.kivikoski-staege.de/

Wing Lau [Australia]
089
atelier@winglau.net
http://www.winglau.net/

Chris Lee [Singapore]
300
Asylum
Chris@theasylum.com.sg
http://www.theasylum.com.sg/

Vince Lee [Malaysia]
423
Mccann Worldgroup / Mccann Erickson Malaysia
vince.lee@mccann.com
http://mccann.com/

Gu Lei [China]
253
TINY workshop
http://www.tinyworkshop.cn/

Deng Lihua [China]
261
CSH Design

Shaobin Lin [China]
271
Lin Shaobin Design
write000@sina.com
http://www.linshaobin.com/

Zhang Lin [China]
108
http://cargocollective.com/mohouqie

Henricus Linggawidjaja [Indonesia]
207   232
Artnivora
design@artnivora.net
http://www.artnivora.net/

Domenic Lippa [UK]
292

Liu Yong qing [China]
256   259
Shenzhen huathink Design Co., Ltd.
yongqingcn@126.com
http://www.liuyongqing.com/
http://www.huathink.net/

Boris Ljubicic [Croatia]
394
Studio International
boris@studio-international.com
http://www.studio-international.com/

Driv Loo [Malaysia]
303
LIE Design & Art Direction
hi@wearenotlie.com
http://www.wearenotlie.com/

Serge Lutens [Morocco]
364   365

MADA LAB.
021   313

Ine Meganck [Switzerland]
286
ine_meganck@hotmail.com
http://www.inemeganck.be/

Louis Mikolay [UK]
305
North
info@northdesign.co.uk
http://www.northdesign.co.uk/

Jessica Minn [USA]
280
Landor Associates
minn.jessica@gmail.com

Franziska Morlok [Germany]
193
Rimini Berlin
post@rimini-berlin.de
http://www.rimini-berlin.de/

Fraser Muggeridge [UK]
432
Fraser Muggeridge studio
info@pleasedonotbend.co.uk
http://pleasedonotbend.co.uk/

Neeser & Müller [Switzerland]
181
info@neesermueller.ch
http://www.neesermueller.ch/

Corina Neuenschwander [Switzerland]
286
mail@corinaneuenschwander.ch
http://www.corinaneuenschwander.ch/

Youji Noh [Korea]
264

選考委員　Jurors

TDC賞運営委員会　TDC Annual Awards Committee

浅葉克己　　Katsumi Asaba (TDC Chairman, Art Director)
井上嗣也　　Tsuguya Inoue (TDC Member, Art Director)
奥村靫正　　Yukimasa Okumura (TDC Member, Graphic Designer)
葛西　薫　　Kaoru Kasai (TDC Member, Art Director)
菊地敦己　　Atsuki Kikuchi (TDC Member, Graphic Designer)
佐藤　卓　　Taku Satoh (TDC Member, Graphic Designer)
澁谷克彦　　Katsuhiko Shibuya (TDC Member, Art Director)
祖父江 慎　　Shin Sobue (TDC Member, Graphic Designer)
中島英樹　　Hideki Nakajima (TDC Member, Graphic Designer, Art Director)
仲條正義　　Masayoshi Nakajo (TDC Vice Chairman, Graphic Designer, Art Director)
服部一成　　Kazunari Hattori (TDC Member, Graphic Designer, Art Director)
松本弦人　　Gento Matsumoto (TDC Member, Graphic Designer)

ゲスト審査員　Guest Jurors

青木克憲　　Katsunori Aoki (TDC Member, Art Director)
植原亮輔　　Ryosuke Uehara (Art Director, Graphic Designer)
大原大次郎　Daijiro Ohara (Graphic Designer)
小林　章　　Akira Kobayashi (Type Director / Germany)
長嶋りかこ　Rikako Nagashima (Art Director)
中嶋貴久　　Takahisa Nakajima (Art Director)
羽良多平吉　heiQuiti Harata (Graphic Designer)
John Warwicker (TDC Member, Graphic Designer / UK, Australia)
Stanley Wong (Graphic Designer, Artist / Hong Kong)

和文タイプ特別審査員　Special Jurors for Japanese Type Design

鳥海　修　　Osamu Torinoumi (Type Designer)
藤田重信　　Shigenobu Fujita (Type Designer)

RGB部門審査員　RGB Category Jurors

千房けん輔　Kensuke Sembo (Artist / exonemo)
田中良治　　Ryoji Tanaka (Web Designer)
長谷川踏太　Tota Hasegawa (Creative Director)

凡例

TD. タイプディレクター Type Director
A. アーティスト Artist
AD. アートディレクター Art Director
C. コピーライター Copy Writer
CD. クリエイティブディレクター Creative Director
CA. カリグラファー Calligrapher
D. デザイナー Designer
E. エディター Editor
I. イラストレーター Illustrator
P. フォトグラファー Photographer
T. タイプデザイナー Type Designer
W. ライター/作家 Writer
CL. クライアント Client
PT. 主な使用書体 Principal Typefaces

AG. エージェンシー Agency
CH. コピーライトホルダー Copyright Holder
CO. コーディネーター Coordinator
CC. クリエイティブコーディネーター Creative Coordinator
CON. コンストラクター Constructor
CON-DI. コントリビューティングディレクター Contributing Director
DI. ディレクター Director
E-PR. エグゼクティブプロデューサー Exective Producer
F-DI. フィルムディレクター Film Director
HM. ヘア＆メイキャップアーティスト Hair & Make-up Artist
ID. インテリアデザイナー Interior Designer
IN-D. インタラクションデザイナー Interaction Designer
IN-DI. インタラクティブディレクター Intaractive Director
MO. ムービー/映像 Movie
MO-DI. ムービーディレクター Movie Director
MU. ミュージック Music
PD. プリントディレクター Print Director
PL. プランナー Planner
PM. プロジェクトマネージャー Project Manager
PR. プロデューサー Producer
PRG. プログラマー Programmer
PRI. プリンター Printer
PRI-CO. プリンティングコーディネーター Printing Coordinator
PRO. プロダクション Production
PRO-CO. プロダクションコーディネーター Production Coordinator
ST. スタイリスト Stylist
T-DI. テクニカルディレクター Technical Director
TL. トランジスター Translator
W-DI. ウェブディレクター Web Director

Prize Winning Works

グランプリ　Grand Prix
ステファン・サグマイスター ＆ ジェシカ・ウォルシュ
Stefan Sagmeister & Jessica Walsh

特別賞　Special Prize
仲條正義　Masayoshi Nakajo

特別賞　Special Prize
葛西 薫　Kaoru Kasai

TDC賞　TDC Prize
新世界タイポ研究会（岡澤慶秀・塚田哲也・秀親）
Shinsekai Type Study Group

TDC賞　TDC Prize
フェリクス・ファエフリ　Felix Pfäffli

TDC賞　TDC Prize
エーリヒ・ブレヒビュール　Erich Brechbühl

TDC賞　TDC Prize
栗林和夫　Kazuo Kuribayashi

TDC賞　TDC Prize
スタンリー・ウォン（アナザーマウンテンマン）
Stanley Wong (anothermountainman)

タイプデザイン賞　Type Design Prize
安 三烈　アン・サムヨル　Ahn Sam-yeol

RGB賞　RGB Prize
コーエン・ヴァン・バーレン　Cohen Van Balen

Grand Prix

001 Movie
TD. Stefan Sagmeister + Jessica Walsh
CL. Non-commercial work

仲條正義展 忘れちゃってEASY思い出してCRAZY Masayoshi Nakajo : Forgetting makes things easy, remembering drives you crazy. 2012年6月23日（土）〜8月12日（日） June 23, 2012 - August 12, 2012 SHISEIDO GALLERY

Special Prize

002 Poster
TD. AD. D. 仲條正義　Masayoshi Nakajo
CL. Non-commercial work
PT. 秀英初号明朝

仲條正義展忘れちゃってEASY思い出してCRAZY　Masayoshi Nakajo : Forgetting makes things easy, remembering drives you crazy.　2012年6月23日（土）〜8月12日（日）　June 23, 2012 - August 12, 2012　SHISEIDO GALLERY

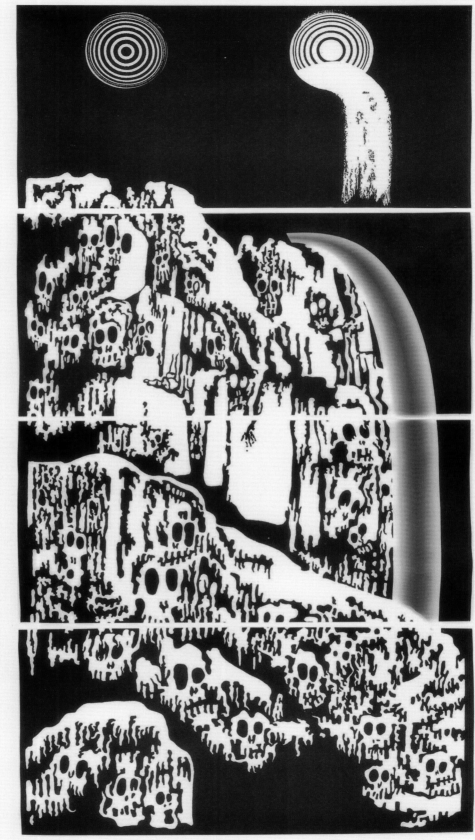

仲條正義展忘れちゃってEASY思い出してCRAZY　Masayoshi Nakajo : Forgetting makes things easy, remembering drives you crazy.　2012年6月23日(土)〜8月12日(日)　June 23, 2012 – August 12, 2012　SHISEIDO GALLERY

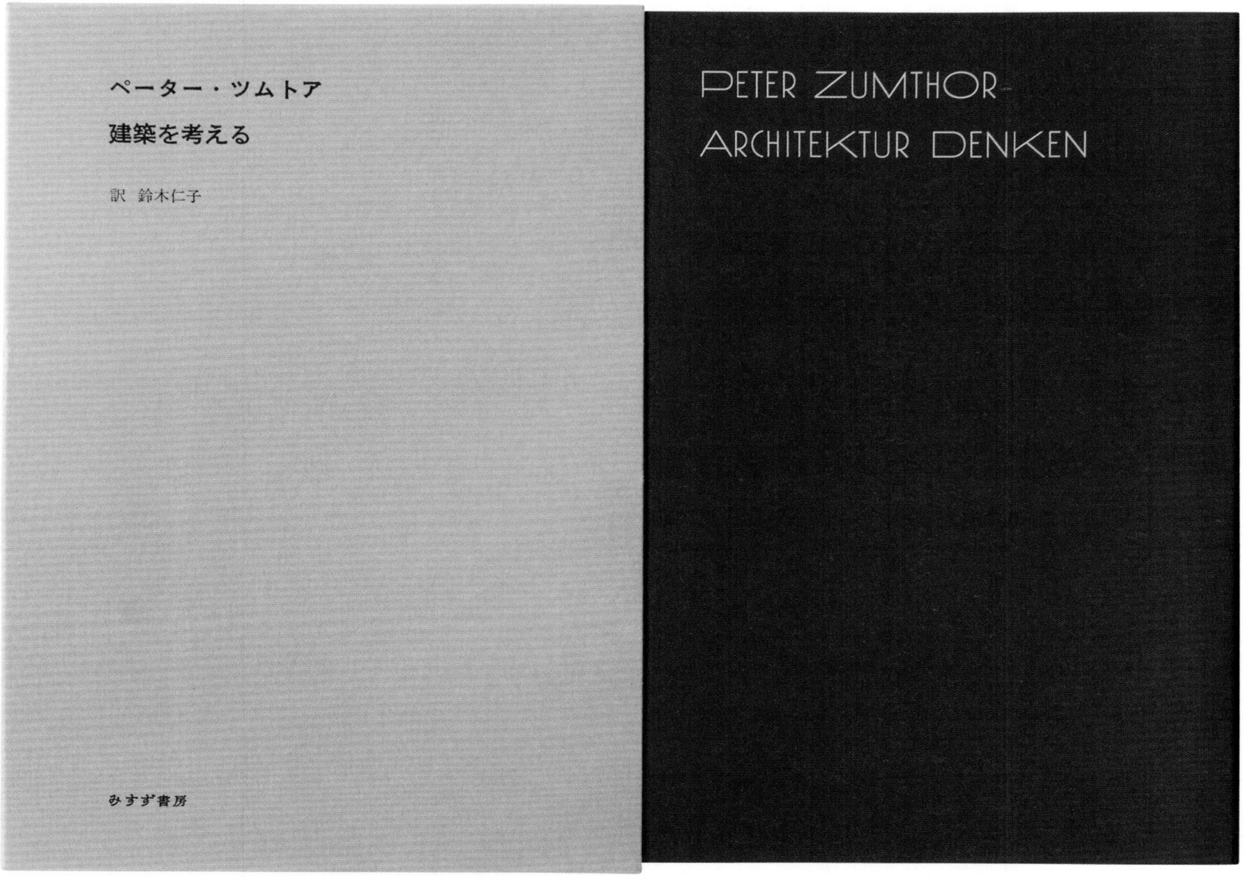

ペーター・ツムトア
建築を考える

訳 鈴木仁子

みすず書房

PETER ZUMTHOR-
ARCHITEKTUR DENKEN

Special Prize

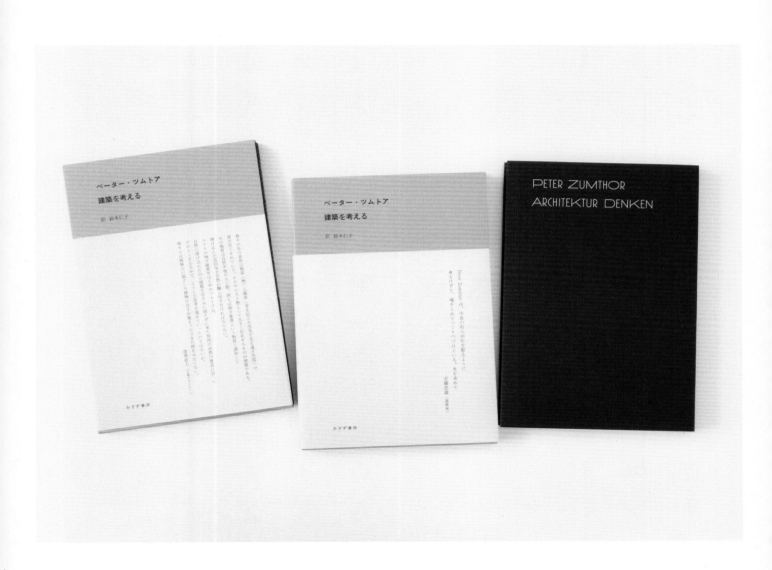

003 Book Design
TD. AD. 葛西 薫　Kaoru Kasai
D. 増田 豊　Yutaka Masuda
CL. みすず書房
Misuzu Shobo
PT. BANJO

新世界タイポ研究会 「横書き仮名」の開発

上から下に書かれる漢字をくずし今から約1,000年前に完成した「かな」は、当然、その形の中に縦書きのストロークを持っています。
上の字、下の字とのつながりを含んだ「かな」たちは、こんにち、横に並べられることなど想定していなかったのではないでしょうか。
これらの「かな」が、横書きのストロークを持って生まれてきたら、はたしてどのような形になったのか、三つの方向で探っています。

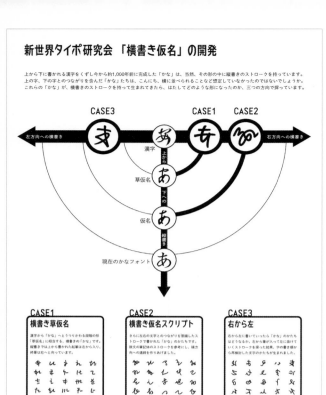

CASE1
横書き草仮名

漢字から「かな」へとうつりかわる段階の形「草仮名」に相当する、横書きの「かな」です。縦書きでは上から書かれた起筆は左から入り、終筆は右へと向っています。

CASE2
横書き仮名スクリプト

さらに左右の文字とのつながりを意識したストロークで書かれた「かな」のかたちです。欧文の筆記体のストロークを参考にし、横方向への連続をはかりました。

CASE3
右から左

右から左に書いていったら「かな」のかたちはどうなるか、右から筆が入って左に抜けていくストロークを探った結果、字の書き順から再構築した文字のかたちが生まれました。

ここでご覧いただいたのは、たとえばの可能性の、三つの例です。もちろん他にもたくさんの可能性があります。そしてその中には、おそらくひとつとして正解はありません。しかし、現在の「かな」の形に与えた影響や要因を遡って考えて、他の可能性を探るという行為は、現在の「かな」の形を改めてもう一度眺めなおし、そして新たな発見をすることのできる、とても良い機会だと思っています。

新世界タイポ研究会

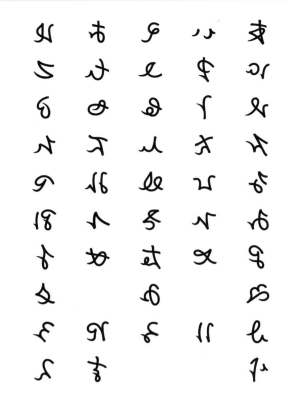

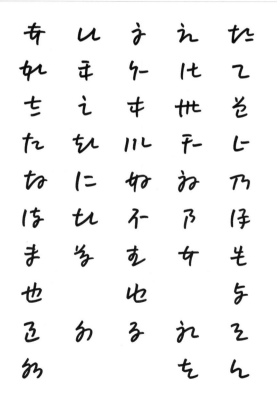

004 Experimental Work
TD. D. 新世界タイポ研究会　Shinsekai Type Study Group
（岡澤慶秀／塚田哲也／秀親）
（Yoshihide Okazawa／Tetsuya Tsukada／Hidechika）
CL. Non-commercial work
PT. Custom-made for the project
（横書き草仮名／横書きかなスプリプト／右から左）

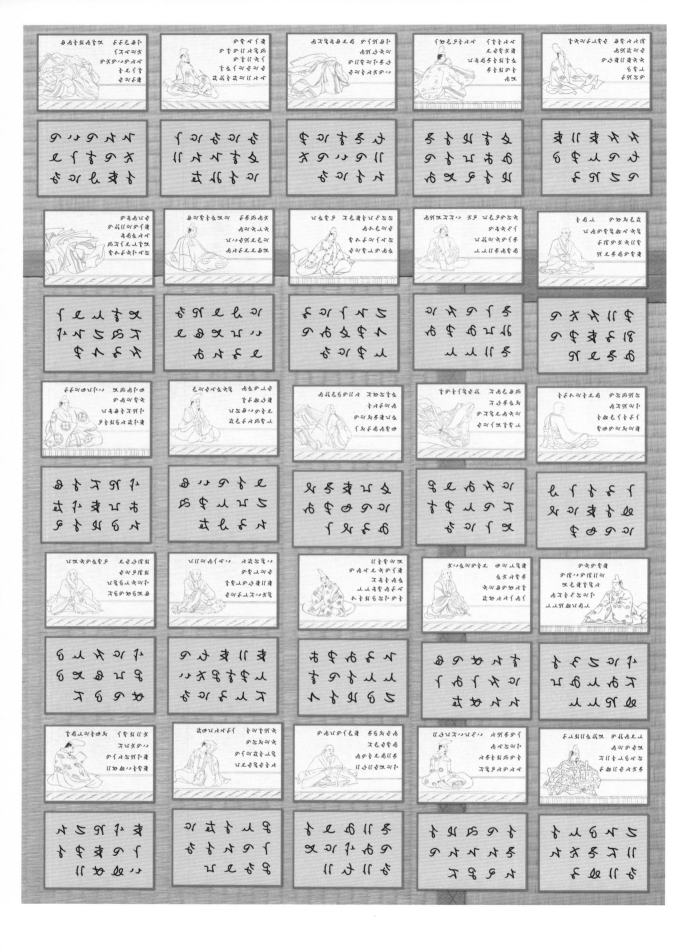

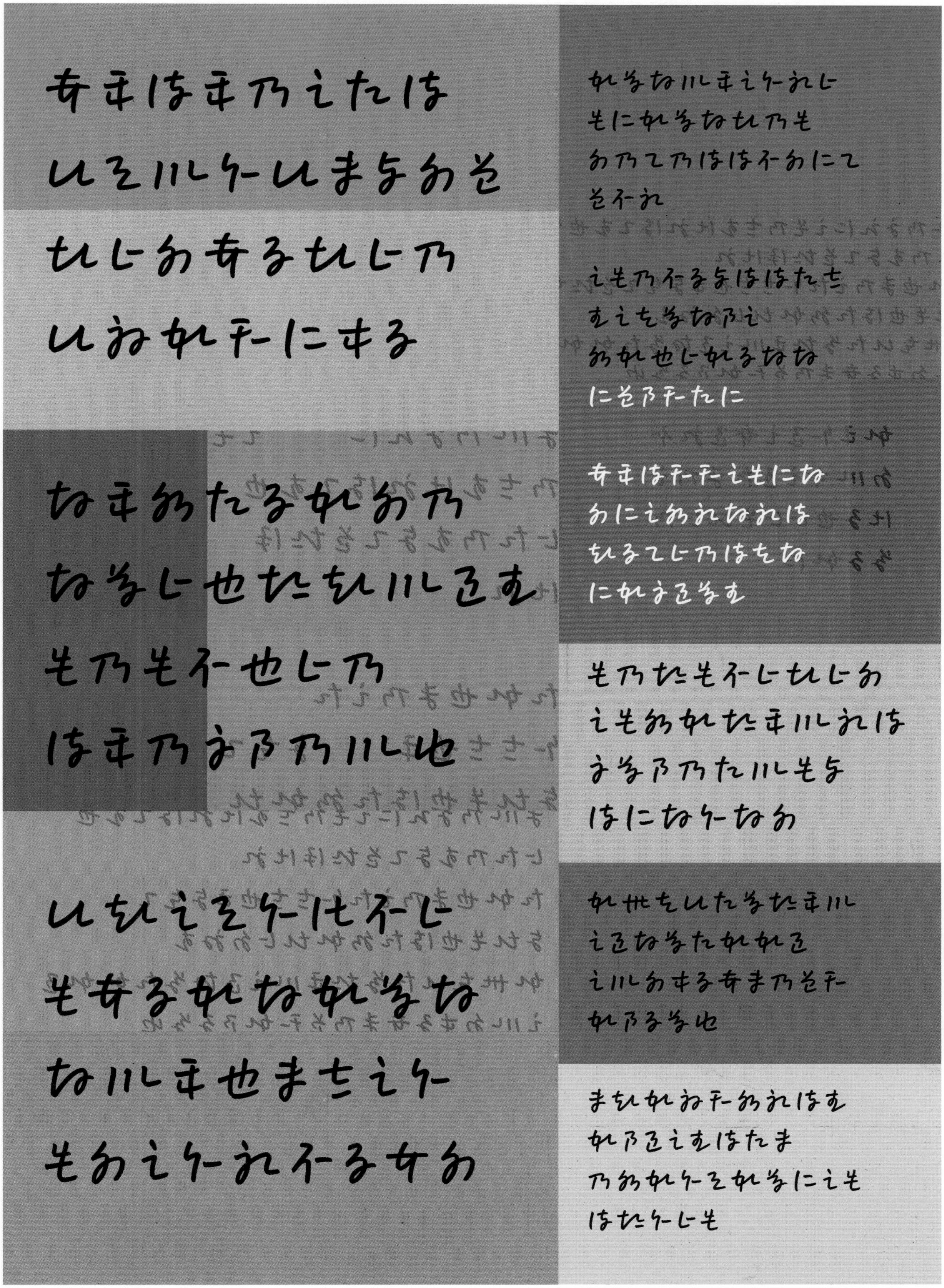

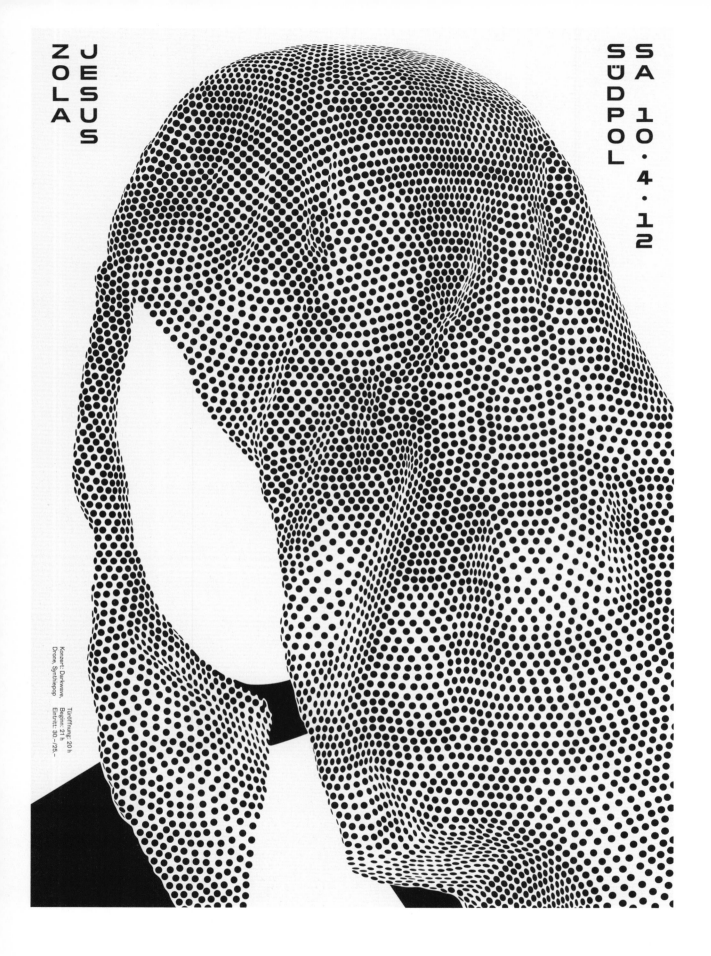

ZOLA JESUS

SÜDPOL SA 10.4.12

Konzert: Darkwave, Drone, Synthiepop

Türöffnung: 20 h
Beginn: 21 h
Eintritt: 30.–/25.–

TDC Prize

33

THERE MUST BE SOME KIND OF WAY OUT OF HERE

Luz Weibel Kuggeleyn:
There Must Be Some Kind
of Way Out of Here

Musiktheater mit Tanz:
Eine exorzistische Turnübung
Beginn: 20 Uhr
Eintritt: 25.–/18.–
www.sudpol.ch

FR SA
25. 26.5.

SÜD
POL

005 Poster
TD. Felix Pfäffli
CL. Südpol Luzern
PT. Lucarna /Ambauen Grotesk

SÜDPOL

SA 21.9.13

Saisonschluss
Doors: 22 Uhr (Ab 18 Jahren)
Eintritt: 25.– / 18.–
www.sudpol.ch

CLUB:

Bassl	Guyver & New.com		
	Faust, Zenit &	Dub Ex Machina	CH
	Raphallus Orgasmus	Bass Vandalizm	CH
Bassl	Hood Regulators	Korsett / RBMA	CH

Hosted by:
Dub Ex Machina,
Bass Vandalizm
& Korsett.

GROSSE HALLE:

GROSSE HALLE:	ACTRESS	Honest Jon's	UK
	LAUREL HALO	Hyperdub	US
	Dans La Visage	Monavale	CH
Liveacts!	Bit–Tuner	Hula Honeys	CH

Hosted by: Südpol
& Zweikommasieben

SHEDHALLE:
Electronica!
Techno!

Puzzle Keiser & Marc D'Arrigo		
Ismian Keiser & Marc D'Arrigo		
Nik & Soul	Leisure System	DE
Martin Meier	Schall&Rauch	DE/CH
	Hula Honeys	CH
	GMCA/Korsett	CH

Hosted by:
Hula Honeys,
Schall&Rauch
& Korsett

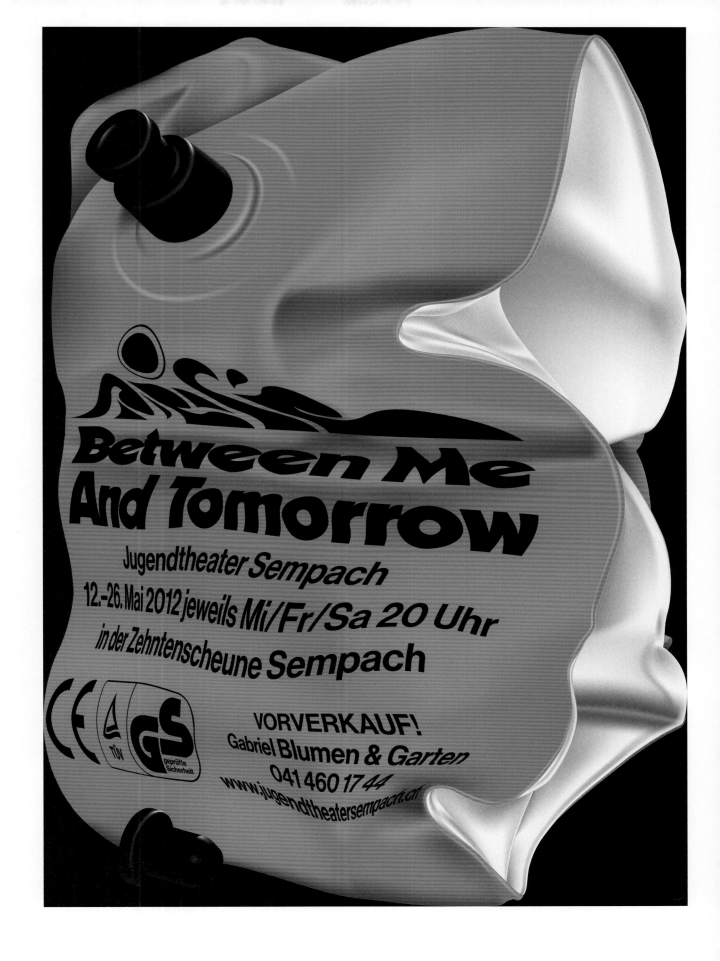

006 Poster
TD. Erich Brechbühl
CL. Jugendtheater Sempach

TDC Prize

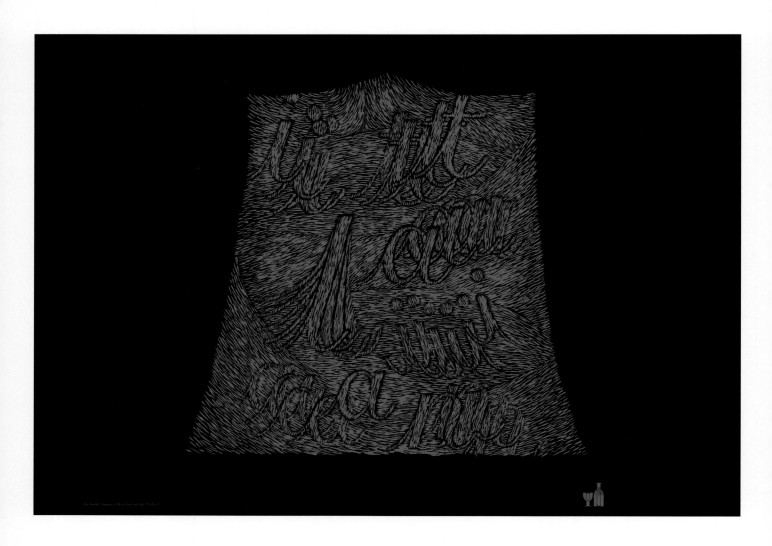

TDC Prize

007 Poster
TD. AD. D. 栗林和夫　Kazuo Kuribayashi
CL. (株)ヴィノテーク
Vinothèque Co., Ltd.
PT. Custom-made for the project

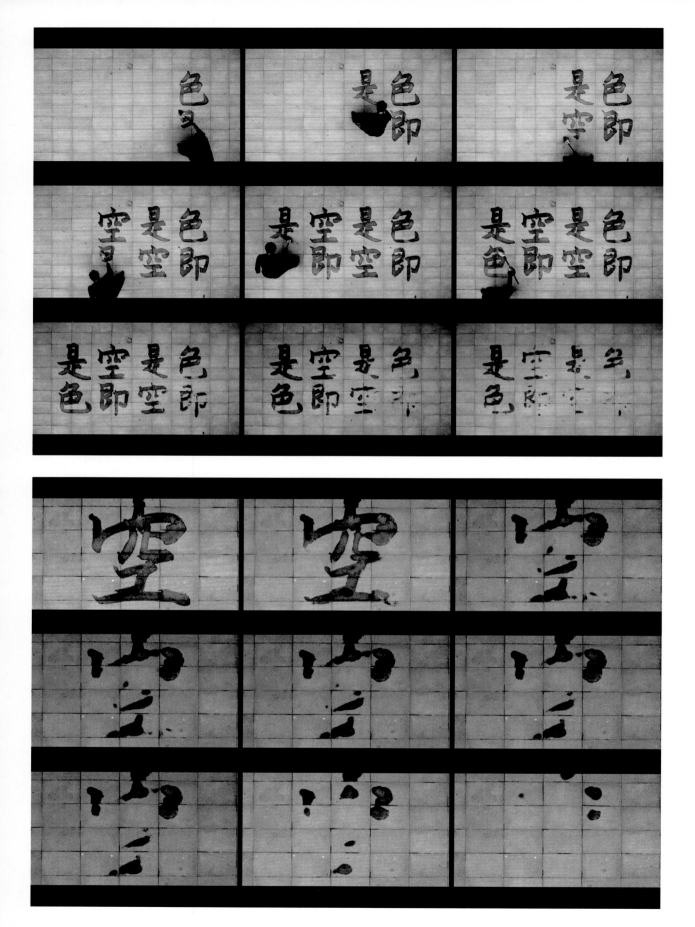

TDC Prize

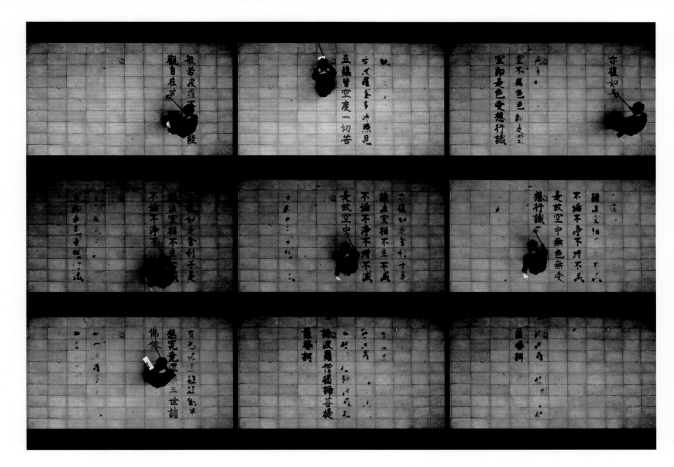

008 Experimental Work
TD. Stanley Wong (anothermountainman)
CL. Asian Culture and Arts Development Association
Ingenuity follow Nature (exhibition)

가 각 간 갇 갈 갉 갊 감 갑 값 갓 갔 강 갖 갗 같 갚 갛 개 객 갠 갤 갬 갭 갯 갰 갱 갸 갹 갼 걀 걋 걍 걔 걘 걜 거 걱 건 걷 걸 걺 검 겁 것 겄 겅 겆 겉 겊 겋 게 겐 겔 겜 겝 겟 겠 겡 겨 격 겪 견 겯 결 겸 겹 겻 겼 경 곁 계 곈 곌 곕 곗 곙 고 곡 곤 곧 골 곪 곬 곯 곰 곱 곳 공 곶 과 곽 관 괄 괆 괌 괍 괏 광 괘 괜 괠 괬 괭 괴 괵 괸 괼 굄 굅 굇 굉 교 굔 굘 굡 굣 구 국 군 굳 굴 굵 굶 굻 굼 굽 굿 궁 궂 궈 궉 권 궐 궜 궝 궤 궷 귀 귁 귄 귈 귐 귑 귓 규 균 귤 그 극 근 귿 글 긁 금 급 긋 긍 긔 기 긱 긴 긷 길 긺 김 깁 깃 깅 깆 깊 까 깍 깎 깐 깔 깖 깜 깝 깟 깠 깡 깥 깨 깩 깬 깰 깸 깹 깻 깼 깽 꺄 꺅 꺌 꺼 꺽 꺾 껀 껄 껌 껍 껏 껐 껑 께 껙 껜 껨 껫 껭 껴 껸 껼 꼇 꼈 꼉 꼍 꼐 꼬 꼭 꼰 꼲 꼴 꼼 꼽 꼿 꽁 꽂 꽃 꽈 꽉 꽐 꽜 꽝 꽤 꽥 꽹 꾀 꾄 꾈 꾐 꾑 꾕 꾜 꾸 꾹 꾼 꿀 꿇 꿈 꿉 꿋 꿍 꿎 꿔 꿜 꿨 꿩 꿰 꿱 꿴 꿸 뀀 뀁 뀄 뀌 뀐 뀔 뀜 뀝 뀨 끄 끅 끈 끊 끌 끎 끓 끔 끕 끗 끙 끝 끼 끽 낀 낄 낌 낍 낏 낑 나 낙 낚 난 낟 날 낡 낢 남 납 낫 났 낭 낮 낯 낱 낳 내 낵 낸 낼 냄 냅 냇 냈 냉 냐 냑 냔 냘 냠 냥 너 넉 넋 넌 널 넒 넓 넘 넙 넛 넜 넝 넣 네 넥 넨 넬 넴 넵 넷 넸 넹 녀 녁 년 녈 념 녑 녔 녕 녘 녜 녠 노 녹 논 놀 놂 놈 놉 놋 농 높 놓 놔 놘 놜 놨 뇌 뇐 뇔 뇜 뇝 뇟 뇨 뇩 뇬 뇰 뇹 뇻 뇽 누 눅 눈 눋 눌 눔 눕 눗 눙 눠 눴 눼 뉘 뉜 뉠 뉨 뉩 뉴 뉵 뉼 늄 늅 늉 느 늑 는 늘 늙 늚 늠 늡 늣 능 늦 늪 늬 늰 늴 니 닉 닌 닐 닒 님 닙 닛 닝 닢 다 닥 닦 단 닫 달 닭 닮 닯 닳 담 답 닷 닸 당 닺 닻 닽 닿 대 댁 댄 댈 댐 댑 댓 댔 댕 댜 더 덕 덖 던 덛 덜 덞 덟 덤 덥 덧 덩 덫 덮 데 덱 덴 델 뎀 뎁 뎃 뎄 뎅 뎌 뎐 뎠 뎡 뎨 뎬 도 독 돈 돋 돌 돎 돐 돔 돕 돗 동 돛 돝 돠 돤 돨 돼 됐 되 된 될 됨 됩 됫 됴 두 둑 둔 둘 둠 둡 둣 둥 둬 뒀 뒈 뒝 뒤 뒨 뒬 뒵 뒷 뒹 듀 듄 듈 듐 듕 드 득 든 듣 들 듦 듬 듭 듯 등 듸 디 딕 딘 딛 딜 딤 딥 딧 딨 딩 딪 따 딱 딲 딴 딷 딸 땀 땁 땃 땄 땅 땋 때 땍 땐 땔 땜 땝 땟 땠 땡 떠 떡 떤 떨 떪 떫 떰 떱 떳 떴 떵 떻 떼 떽 뗀 뗄 뗌 뗍 뗏 뗐 뗑 뗘 뗬 또 똑 똔 똘 똥 똬 똴 뙈 뙤 뙨 뚜 뚝 뚠 뚤 뚫 뚬 뚱 뛔 뛰 뛴 뛸 뜀 뜁 뜅 뜨 뜩 뜬 뜯 뜰 뜸 뜹 뜻 띄 띈 띌 띔 띕 띠 띤 띨 띰 띱 띳 띵 라 락 란 랄 람 랍 랏 랐 랑 랒 랖 랗 래 랙 랜 랠 램 랩 랫 랬 랭 랴 략 랸 럇 량 러 럭 런 럴 럼 럽 럿 렀 렁 렇 레 렉 렌 렐 렘 렙 렛 렝 려 력 련 렬 렴 렵 렷 렸 령 례 롄 롑 롓 로 록 론 롤 롬 롭 롯 롱 롸 롼 뢍 뢨 뢰 뢴 뢸 룀 룁 룃 룅 료 룐 룔 룝 룟 룡 루 룩 룬 룰 룸 룹 룻 룽 뤄 뤘 뤠 뤼 뤽 륀 륄 륌 륏 륑 류 륙 륜 률 륨 륩 륫 륭 르 륵 른 를 름 릅 릇 릉 릊 릍 릎 리 릭 린 릴 림 립 릿 링 마 막 만 많 맏 말 맑 맒 맘 맙 맛 망 맞 맡 맢 매 맥 맨 맬 맴 맵 맷 맸 맹 맺 먀 먁 먈 먕 머 먹 먼 멀 멂 멈 멉 멋 멍 멎 메 멕 멘 멜 멤 멥 멧 멨 멩 며 멱 면 멸 몃 몄 명 몇 메 모 목 몫 몬 몰 몲 몸 몹 못 몽 뫄 뫈 뫘 뫙 뫼 묀 묄 묍 묏 묑 묘 묜 묠 묩 묫 무 묵 묶 문 묻 물 묽 묾 뭄 뭅 뭇 뭉 뭍 뭏 뭐 뭔 뭘 뭡 뭣 뭬 뮈 뮌 뮐 뮤 뮨 뮬 뮴 뮷 므 믄 믈 믐 믓 미 믹 민 믿 밀 밂 밈 밉 밋 밌 밍 및 밑 바 박 밖 밗 반 받 발 밝 밞 밟 밤 밥 밧 방 밭 배 백 밴 밸 뱀 뱁 뱃 뱄 뱅 뱉 뱌 뱍 뱐 뱝 버 벅 번 벋 벌 벎 범 법 벗 벙 벚 베 벡 벤 벧 벨 벰 벱 벳 벴 벵 벼 벽 변 별 볍 볏 볐 병 볕 볘 볜 보 복 본 볼 봄 봅 봇 봉 봐 봔 봤 봬 뵀 뵈 뵉 뵌 뵐 뵘 뵙 뵤 뵨 부 북 분 붇 불 붉 붊 붐 붑 붓 붕 붙 붚 붜 붤 붰 붸 뷔 뷕 뷘 뷜 뷩 뷰 뷴 뷸 븀 븃 븅 브 븍 븐 블 븜 븝 븟 비 빅 빈 빌 빎 빔 빕 빗 빙 빚 빛 빠 빡 빤 빨 빪 빰 빱 빳 빴 빵 빻 빼 빽 뺀 뺄 뺌 뺍 뺏 뺐 뺑 뺘 뺙 뺨 뻐 뻑 뻔 뻗 뻘 뻠 뻣 뻤 뻥 뻬 뼁 뼈 뼉 뼘 뼙 뼛 뼜 뼝 뽀 뽁 뽄 뽈 뽐 뽑 뽕 뾔 뾰 뿅 뿌 뿍 뿐 뿔 뿜 뿟 뿡 쀼 쁑 쁘 쁜 쁠 쁨 쁩 삐 삑 삔 삘 삠 삡 삣 삥 사 삭 삯 산 삳 살 삵 삶 삼 삽 삿 샀 상 샅 새 색 샌 샐 샘 샙 샛 샜 생 샤 샥 샨 샬 샴 샵 샷 샹 섀 섄 섈 섐 섕 서 석 섞 섟 선 섣 설 섦 섧 섬 섭 섯 섰 성 섶 세 섹 센 셀 셈 셉 셋 셌 셍 셔 셕 션 셜 셤 셥 셧 셨 셩 셰 셴 셸 솅 소 속 솎 손 솔 솖 솜 솝 솟 송 솥 솨 솩 솬 솰 솽 쇄 쇈 쇌 쇔 쇗 쇘 쇠 쇤 쇨 쇰 쇱 쇳 쇼 쇽 숀 숄 숌 숍 숏 숑 수 숙 순 숟 술 숨 숩 숫 숭 숯 숱 숲 숴 쉈 쉐 쉑 쉔 쉘 쉠 쉥 쉬 쉭 쉰 쉴 쉼 쉽 쉿 슁 슈 슉 슐 슘 슛 슝 스 슥 슨 슬 슭 슴 습 슷 승 시 식 신 싣 실 싫 심 십 싯 싱 싶 싸 싹 싻 싼 쌀 쌈 쌉 쌌 쌍 쌓 쌔 쌕 쌘 쌜 쌤 쌥 쌨 쌩 썅 써 썩 썬 썰 썲 썸 썹 썼 썽 쎄 쎈 쎌 쏀 쏘 쏙 쏜 쏠 쏢 쏨 쏩 쏭 쏴 쏵 쏸 쐈 쐐 쐤 쐬 쐰 쐴 쐼 쐽 쑈 쑤 쑥 쑨 쑬 쑴 쑵 쑹 쒀 쒔 쒜 쒸 쒼 쓩 쓰 쓱 쓴 쓸 쓺 쓿 씀 씁 씌 씐 씔 씜 씨 씩 씬 씰 씸 씹 씻 씽 아 악 안 앉 않 알 앍 앎 앓 암 압 앗 았 앙 앝 앞 애 액 앤 앨 앰 앱 앳 앴 앵 야 약 얀 얄 얇 얌 얍 얏 양 얕 얗 얘 얜 얠 얩 어 억 언 얹 얻 얼 얽 얾 엄 업 없 엇 었 엉 엊 엌 엎 에 엑 엔 엘 엠 엡 엣 엥 여 역 엮 연 열 엶 엷 염 엽 엾 엿 였 영 옅 옆 옇 예 옌 옐 옘 옙 옛 옜 오 옥 온 올 옭 옮 옰 옳 옴 옵 옷 옹 옻 와 왁 완 왈 왐 왑 왓 왔 왕 왜 왝 왠 왬 왯 왱 외 왹 왼 욀 욈 욉 욋 욍 요 욕 욘 욜 욤 욥 욧 용 우 욱 운 울 욹 욺 움 웁 웃 웅 워 웍 원 월 웜 웝 웠 웡 웨 웩 웬 웰 웸 웹 웽 위 윅 윈 윌 윔 윕 윗 윙 유 육 윤 율 윰 윱 윳 융 윷 으 윽 은 을 읊 음 읍 읏 응 읒 읓 읔 읕 읖 읗 의 읜 읠 읨 읫 이 익 인 일 읽 읾 잃 임 입 잇 있 잉 잊 잎 자 작 잔 잖 잗 잘 잚 잠 잡 잣 잤 장 잦 재 잭 잰 잴 잼 잽 잿 쟀 쟁 쟈 쟉 쟌 쟎 쟏 쟤 쟨 쟬 저 적 전 절 젊 점 접 젓 젔 정 젖 제 젝 젠 젤 젬 젭 젯 젱 져 젼 졀 졈 졉 졌 졍 졔 조 족 존 졸 졺 좀 좁 좃 종 좆 좇 좋 좌 좍 좔 좝 좟 좡 좨 좼 좽 죄 죈 죌 죔 죕 죗 죙 죠 죡 죤 죵 주 죽 준 줄 줅 줆 줌 줍 줏 중 줘 줬 줴 쥐 쥑 쥔 쥘 쥠 쥡 쥣 쥬 쥰 쥴 쥼 즈 즉 즌 즐 즘 즙 즛 증 지 직 진 짇 질 짊 짐 집 짓 징 짖 짗 짙 짚 짜 짝 짠 짢 짤 짧 짬 짭 짯 짰 짱 째 짹 짼 쨀 쨈 쨉 쨋 쨌 쨍 쨔 쨘 쨩 쩌 쩍 쩐 쩔 쩜 쩝 쩟 쩠 쩡 쩨 쩽 쪄 쪘 쪼 쪽 쫀 쫄 쫌 쫍 쫏 쫑 쫓 쫘 쫙 쫠 쫬 쫴 쬈 쬐 쬔 쬘 쬠 쬡 쭁 쭈 쭉 쭌 쭐 쭘 쭙 쭝 쭤 쭸 쭹 쮜 쮸 쯔 쯤 쯧 쯩 찌 찍 찐 찔 찜 찝 찡 찢 찧 차 착 찬 찮 찰 참 찹 찻 찼 창 찾 채 책 챈 챌 챔 챕 챗 챘 챙 챠 챤 챦 챨 챰 챵 처 척 천 철 첨 첩 첫 첬 청 체 첵 첸 첼 쳄 쳅 쳇 쳉 쳐 쳔 쳤 쳬 쳰 촁 초 촉 촌 촐 촘 촙 촛 총 촤 촨 촬 촹 최 쵠 쵤 쵬 쵭 쵯 쵱 쵸 춈 추 축 춘 출 춤 춥 춧 충 춰 췄 췌 췐 취 췬 췰 췸 췹 췻 췽 츄 츈 츌 츔 츙 츠 측 츤 츨 츰 츱 츳 층 치 칙 친 칟 칠 칡 침 칩 칫 칭 카 칵 칸 칼 캄 캅 캇 캉 캐 캑 캔 캘 캠 캡 캣 캤 캥 캬 캭 컁 커 컥 컨 컫 컬 컴 컵 컷 컸 컹 케 켁 켄 켈 켐 켑 켓 켕 켜 켠 켤 켬 켭 켯 켰 켱 켸 코 콕 콘 콜 콤 콥 콧 콩 콰 콱 콴 콸 쾀 쾅 쾌 쾡 쾨 쾰 쿄 쿠 쿡 쿤 쿨 쿰 쿱 쿳 쿵 쿼 퀀 퀄 퀑 퀘 퀭 퀴 퀵 퀸 퀼 큄 큅 큇 큉 큐 큔 큘 큠 크 큭 큰 클 큼 큽 킁 키 킥 킨 킬 킴 킵 킷 킹 타 탁 탄 탈 탉 탐 탑 탓 탔 탕 태 택 탠 탤 탬 탭 탯 탰 탱 탸 턍 터 턱 턴 털 턺 텀 텁 텃 텄 텅 테 텍 텐 텔 템 텝 텟 텡 텨 텬 텼 톄 톈 토 톡 톤 톨 톰 톱 톳 통 톺 톼 퇀 퇘 퇴 퇸 툇 툉 툐 투 툭 툰 툴 툼 툽 툿 퉁 퉈 퉜 퉤 튀 튄 튈 튐 튑 튕 튜 튠 튤 튬 튱 트 특 튼 튿 틀 틂 틈 틉 틋 틔 틘 틜 틤 틥 티 틱 틴 틸 팀 팁 팃 팅 파 팍 팎 판 팔 팖 팜 팝 팟 팠 팡 팥 패 팩 팬 팰 팸 팹 팻 팼 팽 퍄 퍅 퍼 퍽 펀 펄 펌 펍 펏 펐 펑 페 펙 펜 펠 펨 펩 펫 펭 펴 펵 편 펼 폄 폅 폈 평 폐 폘 폡 폣 포 폭 폰 폴 폼 폽 폿 퐁 퐈 퐝 푀 푄 표 푠 푤 푭 푯 푸 푹 푼 푿 풀 풂 품 풉 풋 풍 풔 풩 퓨 퓬 퓰 퓸 퓻 퓽 프 픈 플 픔 픕 픗 피 픽 핀 필 핌 핍 핏 핑 하 학 한 할 핥 함 합 핫 항 해 핵 핸 핼 햄 햅 햇 했 행 햐 향 허 헉 헌 헐 헒 험 헙 헛 헝 헤 헥 헨 헬 헴 헵 헷 헹 혀 혁 현 혈 혐 협 혓 혔 형 혜 혠 혤 혭 호 혹 혼 홀 홅 홈 홉 홋 홍 홑 화 확 환 활 홧 황 홰 홱 홴 횃 횅 회 획 횐 횔 횝 횟 횡 효 횬 횰 횹 횻 후 훅 훈 훌 훍 훔 훗 훙 훠 훤 훨 훰 훵 훼 훽 휀 휄 휑 휘 휙 휜 휠 휨 휩 휫 휭 휴 휵 휸 휼 흄 흇 흉 흐 흑 흔 흖 흗 흘 흙 흠 흡 흣 흥 흩 희 흰 흴 흼 흽 힁 히 힉 힌 힐 힘 힙 힛 힝

abcdefghijklmnopqrstuvwxyzABCDEFGHIJKLMNOPQRSTUVWXYZ1234567890!@#$%^&*{[(⟨|⟩)]}?

생각을 담는 그릇

Type Design Prize

봄
눈
들
꽃
샛
길

108pt

옷 된 검 소 덟 천
매 류 쉰 담 솔 각
준 돗 상 올 는 다
면 효 국 늙 까 릇
삶 토 숲 진 뚫 용
닷 풀 없 겹 슭 괜
부 홅 년 않 될 령
숲 교 계 갓 뿐 닭

48pt

뿌리가 깊은 나무는 바람에
움직이지 아니하므로, 꽃이 좋고
열매가 많으니.

24pt

나랏말이 중국과 달라 문자가 서로 통하지 아니하여 이런 까닭에
어린 백성이 말하고자 하는 바가 있어도 제 뜻을 펴지 못하는
사람이 많다. 내가 이것을 가엾게 여겨 새로 스물 여덟자를
만드니, 사람들이 쉽게 익혀서 날마다 쓰는데 편하게 하고자

18pt

아궁이가 내는지 연기가 밖으로
흩어지기 시작하자 나는 아궁에
무엇이 타고 있는지를 단박에 알아낼
수 있었다. 가을걷이 지치러기인
콩깍지와 메밀대를 때고 있었다.
구수한 냄새가 바로 그것을 뜻하는
거였다. 오랜만에 맡아보는 굴뚝 냄새에
나는 불현듯 콩깍지와 메밀대를 군불
아궁이에 때어 볼 수 있었던 옛날이
그리웠다. 그 무렵은 내 손으로 직접
농사를 지어야 했던 고생스런 청소년
시절이었음에도, 호의호식하며 허리를

14pt

아궁이가 내는지 연기가 밖으로 흩어지기 시작하자
나는 아궁에 무엇이 타고 있는지를 단박에 알아낼
수 있었다. 가을걷이 지치러기인 콩깍지와 메밀대를
때고 있었다. 구수한 냄새가 바로 그것을 뜻하는
거였다. 오랜만에 맡아보는 굴뚝 냄새에 나는
불현듯 콩깍지와 메밀대를 군물 아궁이에 때어

10pt

아궁이가 내는지 연기가 밖으로 흩어지기 시작하자 나는 아궁에 무엇이
타고 있는지를 단박에 알아낼 수 있었다. 가을걷이 지치러기인 콩깍지와
메밀대를 때고 있었다. 구수한 냄새가 바로 그것을 뜻하는 거였다.
오랜만에 맡아보는 굴뚝 냄새에 나는 불현듯 콩깍지와 메밀대를 군물
아궁이에 때어 볼 수 있었던 옛날이 그리웠다. 그 무렵은 내 손으로 직접
농사를 지어야 했던 고생스런 청소년 시절이었음에도, 호의호식하며
허리를 굽실대는 수염 허연 늙은이한테 도련님도련님 하는 소리들
들었던 천부의 적의 아련한 기억보다 훨씬 찌앗이 어문 그리움이었다.

216pt

덕 수 궁
돌 담 길

70pt

기억은
가을에 씨를 뿌려
겨울에 꽃이 피고
봄이면 아지랭이 되어
날아간다.

RGB Prize

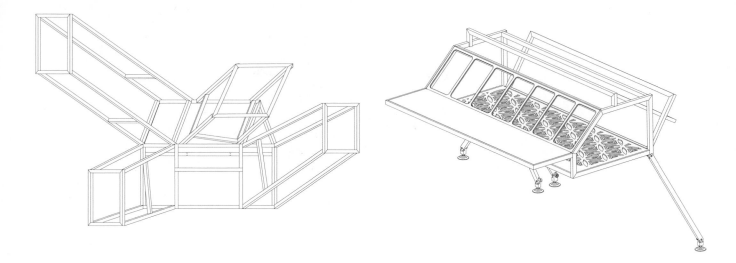

AATTGTGAGCGGATAACAATTGACATTGTGAGCGGATAACAAGATACTGAGCACATACTAGAGAAA
GAGGAGAAATACTAGATGCAAATGACGGAAGCTACCTGTTGACGCTGCTGTAAAACCGGAGCAAA
GGGGATTGTATTTGCCGGTTCTGGGAACGGGTCTTTATCTGATGCAGCCGAAAAAGGGGCGGACA
GCGCAGTCAAAAAAGGCGTTACAGTGGTGCGCTCTACCCGCACGGGAAATGGTGTCGTCACACCAAAC
CAAGACTATGCGGAAAAGGACTTGCTGGCATCGAACTCTTTAAACCCCCAAAAAGCACGGATGTTGCT
GATCGTTGCTCTTACCAAAACAAATGATCCTCAAAAAATCCAAGCTTATTTCAATGAGTATTGAAGAAA
GAAGGCGAATAAGCCTTCTTTTTTTTGGCTTTTTAGGACCAATAATGACCTCTGAATCTTAAAATTTCTT
TAAAAATAAGCCAAAATTACCCTTTACTTAATTAATTTGGTAACGTAATATAATTGGAGAATTTGTTA
CAAAAAAAGGAGGATATTATGAAATTTGTAAAAGAAGGATCATTGCACTTGTAACAATTTTGATGCT
GTCTGTTACATCGCTGTTTGCGTTGCAGCCGTCAGCAAAAGCCGCTGAACACAATCCAGTCGTTATG
GTTCACGGTATTGGAGGGGCATCATTCAATTTTGCGGGAATTAAGAGCTATCTCGTATCTCAGGGCTG
GTCGCGGGACAAGCTGTATGCAGTTGATTTTTGGGACAAGACAGGCACAAATTATAACAATGGACCG
GTATTATCACGATTTGTGCAAAAGGTTTTAGATGAAACGGGTGCGAAAAAGTGGATATTGTCGCTCACAG
CATGGGGGGCGCGAACACACTTTACTACATAAAAAATCTGGACGGCGGAAATAAAGTTGCAAACGTCGT
GACGGTTGGCGGCGCGAACCGTTTGACGACAGGCAAGGCGCTTCCGGGAACAGATCCAAATCAAAA
GATTTTATACACATCCATTTACAGCAGTGCCGATATGATTGTCATGAATTACTTATCAAGATTAGATGGTGCT
AGAAACGTTCAAATCCATGGCGTTGGACACATCGGCCTTCTGTACAGCAGCCAAGTCAACAGCCTGATTAAAG
AAGGGCTGAACGGCGGGGGCCAGAATACGAATTAATGAAAAACAAAACCTTGAAGAATGCTATTCTTC
AAGGTTATTCTGCTTTCAGCACAATGGTTTTCGCAGCCATATCATGAACGGTTTGTTTTTTCTTCGTAA
ATGCGGCAGTCAAATAGATCAGGCGGGAGAACACATGCACCCACGCTATCAGGTAACGGACAATGGC
TTGCGGGAAGGATATTTTTTTATATGTTTCGTCCCTCACGATTTGCAGCCCGATGCTTTTTTTGCCCAGTGTGCCCT
TCCAATTTGTCAGCGGCATCAGCAAAAAATACACAATCAGCATCAATATGGCGACAATAATGACACCGG
CGGACCCATCGCCAAACGTAAATCCGGCTGCCAAAATCACTGCTGCGCAATGATTACATCAAGTTAATAAT
ACTAGAGCCAGGCATCAAATAAAACGAAAGGCTCAGTCGAAAGACTGGGCCTTTCGTTTTATCTG
TTGTTTGTCGGTGAACGCTCTCTACTAGAGTCACACTGGCTCACCTTCGGGTGGGCCTTTCTGCGTTTATA

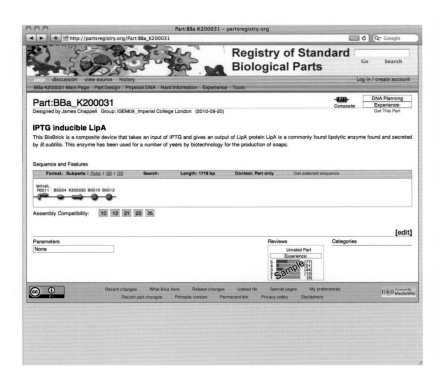

010 Project
TD. Cohen Van Balen
    (Revital Cohen + Tuur Van Balen)
http://www.cohenvanbalen.com/work/pigeon-dor

Grand Prix　グランプリ

Now Is Better

ステファン・サグマイスター & ジェシカ・ウォルシュ
Stefan Sagmeister & Jessica Walsh

他の時代ではなく、この時代に生まれて良かった。今は、世界の大部分の人々が自分の運命を自分で決められる初めての時代である。ハーバード大学の心理学者スティーブン・ピンカーによると、2度の世界大戦とホロコーストを経験した20世紀を含む過去2000年の間に、犯罪（＝他者の手による死）は確かに毎世紀減少した。私たちは、この短いタイポグラフィ映像を、フィラデルフィアの現代芸術協会で開かれる展覧会「ハッピー・ショー」のために制作した。2013年の末に公開される次のドキュメンタリー「ハッピー・フィルム」でも、この映像を取り上げることになりそうだ。

I'd much rather live now than in other time in history. This is the first time that large parts of the world population can be in charge of their own destiny. Harvard Psychologist Steven Pinker shows that crime (=death by the hand of another man) actually decreased in every single century over the last 2000 years, including the twentieth century that featured both world wars and the Holocaust. We made this little typographic film for our exhibition The Happy Show at the Institute for Contemporary Art in Philadelphia. It likely will also be featured in our upcoming documentary The Happy Film, to be published at the end of 2013.

ステファン・サグマイスター

オーストリアに生まれ、現在はニューヨークに住居とオフィスを持つ。ローリング・ストーンズ、トーキング・ヘッズ、ルー・リード、グッゲンハイム美術館、リーバイスなどの仕事に携わった。これまでにニューヨーク、フィラデルフィア、東京、大阪、ソウル、パリ、ローザンヌ、チューリッヒ、ウィーン、プラハ、ケルン、ベルリンで個展が開催された。

Stefan Sagmeister was born in Austria and lives and works in New York. He has worked for the Rolling Stones, The Talking Heads, Lou Reed, The Guggenheim Museum and Levis. Exhibitions on Sagmeister's work have been mounted in New York, Philadelphia, Tokyo, Osaka, Seoul, Paris, Lausanne, Zurich, Vienna, Prague, Cologne and Berlin.

ジェシカ・ウォルシュ

ニューヨークで活動するマルチデザイナー。作品はこれまでにNY TDC、NY ADC、SPD、プリント誌、グラフィス誌などでデザイン賞を受賞。また、コンピューター・アート誌の「デザイン界のトップスター」、NY ADCの「ヤングガン」、プリント誌の「ニュー・ビジュアル・アーティスト」など数々の有名な賞を受賞している。

Jessica Walsh is a multidisciplinary designer working in New York City. Her work has won her design awards from the Type Director's Club, Art Director's Club, SPD, Print, and Graphis. She has received various celebrated distinctions such as Computer Art's "Top Rising Star in Design," Art Director's Club "Young Gun," and Print Magazine's "New Visual Artist".

Special Prize 特別賞

忘れちゃって EASY 思い出して CRAZY（ダイジェスト A, B, C, G シリーズ／資生堂ギャラリー）
Forgetting makes things easy; remembering drives you crazy. (Digest A, B, C, G series / SHISEIDO GALLERY)

仲條正義
Masayoshi Nakajo

去年の夏事の展覧会「忘れちゃって EASY 思い出して CRAZY」の作品を思い出に 4 枚にまとめました。入賞するのも意外で期待もしていませんでした。審査員の温情を感じました。

These four posters are a digest of the exhibition titled, "Wasure-chatte EASY Omoidashite CRAZY," held last summer and consolidated as a memory. I did not expect that I could receive a prize. I felt the kindness of the judges.

仲條正義
1933年東京生まれ。1956年東京藝術大学美術学部図案科を卒業後、資生堂宣伝部、デスカを経て1961年仲條デザイン事務所設立。主な仕事に40年以上にわたった資生堂『花椿』誌のアートディレクション及びデザイン、ザ・ギンザ／タクティクスデザインのアートディレクション及びデザイン、資生堂パーラーのロゴタイプ及びパッケージデザイン、東京銀座資生堂ビルのロゴタイプ及びサイン計画、松屋銀座、スパイラル、東京都現代美術館、細見美術館のCI計画、またNHK「にほんごであそぼ」かるたの絵、『暮しの手帖』誌の表紙絵など、グラフィックデザインを中心に活動。東京TDC副理事長、東京ADC会員、JAGDA会員、TIS会員、女子美術大学客員教授。

Masayoshi Nakajo was born in Tokyo in 1933; graduated from the Department of Design, Faculty of Fine Arts, Tokyo University of the Arts in 1956; joined the PR department of Shiseido Co., Ltd. and then DESKA; and established Nakajo Design Office in 1961. His major engagements focused on graphic design, including: art direction and design for Shiseido's Hanatsubaki magazine, which lasted for over 40 years; art direction and design for Shiseido, The Ginza/Tactics Design; logotype and package design for Shiseido Parlour; logotype and sign planning for Tokyo Ginza Shiseido Building; CI planning for Matsuya Ginza, SPIRAL building, Museum of Contemporary Art Tokyo and Hosomi Museum; pictures for NHK's "Nihongo-de Asobo" karuta (picture cards); and cover painting for Kurashi-no Techo magazine. He also serves as the vice chairman of Tokyo TDC and is a member of Tokyo ADC, JAGDA, and TIS. He also serves as a guest professor of the Joshibi University of Art and Design.

Special Prize　特別賞

建築を考える　Architektur Denken

葛西 薫
Kaoru Kasai

スイスの建築家、ペーター・ツムトアの講演原稿を中心にまとめられた Peter Zumthor, Architektur Denken, Birkhäuser, 2010の邦訳本。2006年初秋、みすず書房の小川純子さんがツムトア氏のアトリエを訪ね、邦訳刊行の希望を伝えたことに始まる。帰国後、小川さんから僕に「ピーター・ズントーは知ってますか？もし出版の了解が得られたら、装丁を」と言われ、「もちろん。ぜひとも！」と。翌年の春、正式に了解の返事。「翻訳は、ドイツ語版からに（英語版は自分の言葉の感じがしないと）。名はピーター・ズントーではなくドイツ語発音のペーター・ツムトアで。そしてエッセイ集のような読む本として作ってほしいので訳者は文学畑の人に。」との要望が添えられて。以来、訳者の鈴木仁子さんと小川さんは、数年かけてツムトア自身の言葉を日本語に紡ぐ。小川さんも僕もツムトアのどこに惹かれるのか、言葉にできないでいる。その言い表せないものが、装丁という小さな建築物にならないか…という大それた目標に向かい、長い長い幸福な苦しみの時間を過ごした。

This is a Japanese edition of Architektur Denken, published by Birkhäuser in 2010. The book is compiled with a focus on the speech scripts of Peter Zumthor, a Swiss architect. In the early autumn of 2006, Ms. Junko Ogawa of Misuzu Shobo visited Mr. Zumthor at his studio and asked to let Misuzu Shobo publish a Japanese translation of the book. After returning to Japan, Ms. Ogawa asked me, "Do you know Mr. Peter Zumthor? I will ask you for bookbinding if he agrees to publishing." I answered, "Of course, I would very much like to!" In the spring of the following year, Mr. Zumthor gave an official approval with requests. He said, "The Japanese version should be translated from the German version" (because English is not his native language). He also stipulated that the name of "Peter Zumthor" should be indicated based on the German pronunciation, not on the English pronunciation, and that the translator should be someone with a literature background because the book should be made as an essay collection. After that time, Ms. Hitoko Suzuki (translator) and Ms. Ogawa tried to express Zumthor's own words in the Japanese language for several years; however, neither Ms. Ogawa nor I could verbalize what attracts us to Zumthor. I wondered if we could translate that nameless feeling into the "small structure" of bookbinding... With this ambitious goal in mind, I spent many long but happy hours of struggle.

葛西 薫

1949年札幌生まれ。（株）サン・アド アートディレクター。サントリーウーロン茶、ユナイテッドアローズの長期にわたる広告制作、虎屋のアートディレクション、六本木商店街振興組合、相模女子大学のＣＩ計画のほか、映画演劇の広告美術、装丁など活動は多岐。近作に、「サラダ好きのライオン　村上ラヂオ3」（村上春樹文・大橋歩画／マガジンハウス）、「あるカタチの内側にある、もうひとつのカタチ」（柴田文江著／ADP）の装丁、スポーツカー TOYOTA86の広告、TORAYA TOKYO の店舗計画、NHK みんなのうた「泣き虫ピエロ」の動画制作の仕事がある。著書に『図録 葛西薫 1968』（ADP）。

Kaoru Kasai was born in Sapporo in 1949 and is an art director at SUN-AD Co., Ltd., has engaged in various activities including: longstanding advertising creation for Suntory Oolong Tea and United Arrows Ltd., art direction for Toraya Confectionery Co., Ltd., CI planning for Roppongi Shopping Street Association and Sagami Women's University, advertising art for movies and plays, and bookbinding. His recent works include bookbinding for Salada Zukino Lion: Murakami Radio 3 (author: Haruki Murakami, illustrator: Ayumi Ohashi, publisher: Magazine House, Ltd.) and Aru Katachi-no Uchigawa-ni Aru Mohitotsu-no Katachi (author: Fumie Shibata, publisher: ADP), advertising for the TOYOTA86 sports car, store planning for TORAYA TOKYO, and animation for NHK's Minna-no Uta "Nakimushi Pierrot." He also published the literary work, Pictorial Record of Kaoru Kasai 1968 (publisher: ADP).

TDC Prize　TDC賞

「横書き仮名」の開発　The formation of "New" kana written holizontly

新世界タイポ研究会（岡澤慶秀・塚田哲也・秀親）
Shinsekai Type Study Group

平仮名（ひらかな）は、縦書きに書かれた漢字の簡略化から生まれた文字です。つまりそこには必然的に縦書きの動き（ストローク）が入り込んでいます。ところが現在、ウェブサイトはもちろん、会社の資料、役所に提出する書類だって、ほとんど横書きになっている。縦書きのストロークを持った平仮名が横に並ぶことなんて、そもそも成立した時代には想定もできなかったことです。それじゃあ、これら平仮名が、横書きのストロークを持って生まれてきたら、はたしてどのような形になったのだろう。仮名の成り立ちを横書きの視点から見直して、あらたな「横書きのための仮名文字」の姿を開発しようじゃないか、というのがこのプロジェクトです。まるでパラレルワールドのような書体の開発・研究に賞をいただき、とても嬉しく思うと同時に、TDCの審査範囲がそんなパラレルワールドにまで拡がったと思うと、とってもワクワクします。

Hiragana (Japanese monosyllabic characters) was created by simplifying vertically-written Chinese characters; therefore, hiragana naturally has the motion of vertical writing (strokes). Currently, however, not only websites but also most company brochures and documents to be submitted to government offices are written horizontally. The horizontal writing of hiragana, which has the stroke characteristics of vertical writing, is something that could not be assumed when hiragana was created. Then, how would hiragana appear if it was created using the strokes of horizontal writing? This project was designed to review kana formation from a horizontal writing viewpoint and to develop new "kana letters for horizontal writing." We are very happy to receive an award for this parallel universe-like typeface R&D and, at the same time, we are very excited to know that the scope of TDC review has extended to such a parallel universe.

新世界タイポ研究会
文字の持つ可能性を、グラフィカルなアイデアから歴史や専門的な観点も交えた上で考察し、「現在を生きる文字」そして「文字の未来」を研究・開発する会。http://shinsekai.type.org/
Shinsekai Type Study Group: This is a group aimed at studying the possibility of typeface from the perspectives of graphical ideas, histories, and technical matters, as well as conducting the R&D of "contemporary typefaces" and the "future of typeface." http://shinsekai.type.org/

岡澤慶秀 (中央) / フォントデザイナー。1994年字游工房入社。「ヒラギノファミリー」「游築見出し明朝体」「ヒラギノ UD ファミリー」などの開発に参画。2009年にヨコカク設立。「こどものじ」「どうろのじ」「ドットのじ」をリリース。http://yokokaku.jp/
Yoshihide Okazawa (center) is a font designer; joined Jiyu-Kobo in 1994; participated in the development of "Hiragino Family," "Yutsuki Midashi Mincho-style typeface," and "Hiragino UD Family," etc.; established Yokokaku in 2009; and released "Kodomo-no Ji," "Doro-no Ji," and "Dot-no Ji." http://yokokaku.jp/

塚田哲也 (右)・秀親 (左) / 秀親と塚田哲也で1993年に大日本タイポ組合を結成。文字を解体し、組合せ、再構築することにより新しい文字の概念を探る実験的タイポグラフィ集団。作品集に『Type Card Play Book』『大日本字』。http://dainippon.type.org/
Tetsuya Tsukada (right) and Hidechika (left) established the Dainippon Type Organization in 1993. This experimental typography group seeks a new concept for typefaces by disassembling, combining, and restructuring letters. Its works include *Type Card Play Book* and *Dainippon Ji*. http://dainippon.type.org/

TDC Prize TDC賞

Südpol Poster Series

フェリクス・ファエフリ
Felix Pfäffli

Südpolはルツェルンから近いスイスのクリエンスにある多目的文化センターで、音楽、ダンス、演劇、文学、デジタルアートなどのための劇場に加え、交響曲オーケストラ、ブラスバンド、音楽学校、レストラン、フリーマーケット、レンタルルームなどが備わっている。2010年以来、このセンターのすべてのポスターをデザインしているが、この施設の多用途性を反映するというのが当初からの考え方だった。コーポレート・デザインには消極的で、できるだけ自由なデザインとするようにした。今回のポスターは、2010年から制作された合計50枚のうちの3枚。その大半は、リソグラフを使って印刷される比較的小さいA3サイズのポスターとは異なり、シンプルな言語、多用途性、そして言うまでもなくリソグラフの鮮やかな色彩を特徴としている。常に流動的で、あらゆる物事が何度も問い直され、再考案、再構成される。これらの3枚は2012年1月から6月にかけて制作した。2枚は音楽用のポスター、1枚は演劇用のポスターだ。「There Must Be Some Kind Of Way Out Of Here」は、私自身、自分のアイデンティティ、自分の考えからは逃れられないというテーマを扱った舞台演劇用のポスターである。頭の中と同じように、終わりのない階段上を演目名がぐるぐると巡り、劇中の俳優と同様、デザインもポスター形式から逃れようと試みる。逃れられないことは明らかである。

The Südpol is a multi purpose cultural center in Kriens, Switzerland, close to Lucerne, that houses a theater, a sinfony orchestra, a brass band, a music school, a restaurant, a flea market, and rents its rooms for performances of music, dance, theater, literature, digital arts and so on. Since 2010 Felix Pfäffli designs all posters for that house. From the beginning, it was the idea that the poster series of the Südpol reflects its versatility. The corporate design is set very reluctant so that the design can be as free as possible. The three posters are three of total 50 posters which are produced since 2010. Most of the posters of the Südpol are unlike those posters printed using a Risograph to the relatively small size A3. They are characterized by their simple language, the versatility and of course the vivid colors of the risograph. The Südpol poster series is always in flux. Everything is questioned again and again, reinvented and restructured. The three selected posters are created in 2012 in the period between January and June. These are two music posters and a theater poster. The "There Must Be Some Kind Of Way Out Of Here" poster is a poster for a stage play that deals with the impossibility to escape from himself, his identity and his thoughts. Just as the actors in the play, the design tries to escape the poster format while the title of the play repeats itself, as in thought, in an endless flight of stairs over and over again. It's obvious: There is no escape.

フェリクス・ファエフリ

1986年に生まれ、2010年に学業を終えると、自身のスタジオ「Feixen」を立ち上げた。2011年の夏にルツェルン・グラフィックデザイン学校でタイポグラフィ、ナラティブデザイン、ポスターデザインを教える教師に就任。作品は、スイス・グラフィックデザイン100年展（2012年、スイス）、第23回ショーモン国際ポスター・フェスティバル（2012年、フランス）、100ベスト・ポスター(2011年、ドイツ、オーストリア、スイス)、台湾国際グラフィックデザイン賞（2011年）、第24回ブルノ国際グラフィックデザイン・ビエンナーレ（2010年、チェコ）など数々のポスター展で展示された。

Feixen is the graphic design work of Felix Pfäffli. Felix was born in 1986. In 2010 he graduated and started his own studio «Feixen». In the summer of 2011 he was appointed as teacher at the Lucerne School of Graphic Design to teach in the fields of typography, narrative design, and poster design. His works has been shown at several Poster Exhibitions like 100 Years of Swiss Graphic Design in Switzerland (2012, Switzerland), 23e Festival International de l'Affiche et du Graphisme de Chaumont (2012, France), The 100 Best Posters (2011, Germany/Austria/Switzerland), Taiwan International Graphic Design Award (2011), 24th Int. Biennal of Graphic Design Brno (2010, Czechia) and so on.

Between me and tomorrow

エーリヒ・ブレヒビュール
Erich Brechbühl

Youth Theatre Sempach は1999年に設立された。私は、共同設立者の一人として、設立当時から公演用のポスターを毎年デザインしている。私にとって、人目を引くポスターを創作するために演劇のエッセンスを理解することは、常にチャレンジである。

2012年の演目は「Between me and tomorrow」というタイトルの、若者が大人になる物語で、舞台は公共の水泳プールである。数人の若者が、彼らの年代の問題について話し合っている。

このポスターのために、私は、空気が抜けかかったアームヘルパー（子供用の腕に付けて使う浮き輪）のイメージを使って、子供から大人への過渡期をシンプルに示すことにした。写真ではあまり人目を引かないため、イラストレーターのグラデーションメッシュを使い、極めて写実的な絵を描いた。そのため、さえない CMYK カラーの代わりに蛍光オレンジ色を使うことができた。ポスターの中にイラストをできるだけ大きく配置し、近くに貼ってある他のポスターよりも、このポスターが大きく見えるようにした。

The Youth Theatre Sempach was founded in 1999. I was one of the co-founders. Since then every year I design the poster for the annual production. For me it's always a challenge to find the essence of the play to create an eye-catching poster. The 2012 production is called "Between me and tomorrow". It's a coming-of-age story located at a public swimming pool. Several young adults are talking about the problems at their age.

For the poster I decided to use an image of a single water wing losing air, showing in a simple way the transition from childhood to adulthood. Because a photograph was not very catchy, I illustrated it using the gradient mesh on Adobe Illustrator in a hyperrealistic manner. Because of that it was possible to use a luminous orange instead of dull CMYK colours. Placing the illustration as big as possible in the poster format, I made shure that the poster looks bigger than other posters hanging in the neighbourhood.

エーリヒ・ブレヒビュール

1977年生まれ、スイスのゼンバッハで育つ。ルツェルン近郊でのタイポグラフィ見習い期間（1994～1998年）、ヴィリザウの Niklaus Troxler スタジオでのグラフィックデザイン見習い期間（1998～2002年）を経てドイツに移り、メタ・デザイン・ベルリンでインターンとして勤務。その後、ルツェルンに戻り、グラフィックデザイン・スタジオ「Mixer」を設立。2007年から国際グラフィック連盟（AGI）会員。2009年、ルツェルンのポスター・フェスティバル「Weltformat」を共同で立ち上げた。韓国国際ポスター・ビエンナーレ学生部金賞（2002年）、中国国際ポスター・ビエンナーレ銅賞（2003年）、トルナヴァ・ポスター・トリエンナーレ第2位（2006年）、ラハティ・ポスター・ビエンナーレのグランプリ（2007年）、ショーモン国際ポスター・コンクール第2位（2008年）、スイス・ポスター賞グランプリ（2008年）、モスクワ国際グラフィックデザイン・ビエンナーレのゴールデン・ビー賞（2012年）など、受賞歴多数。

Erich Brechbühl was born on the 3rd of October 1977, and grew up in Sempach, Switzerland. After a typography apprenticeship near Lucerne (1994-1998) he began an apprenticeship in graphic design at the studio of Niklaus Troxler in Willisau (1998-2002). Then Erich moved to Germany where he did an internship at MetaDesign Berlin. Back in Lucerne he founded his own graphic design studio "Mixer". Since 2007 he's a member of the Alliance Graphique Internationale (AGI). 2009 he was co-founder of the poster festival "Weltformat" in Lucerne. A selection of Brechbühl's awards and honors include: Gold prize, Student Section, Korea International Poster Biennale (2002); Bronze prize, China International Poster Biennial (2003); 2nd Prize, Trnava Poster Triennial (2006); Grand Prix, Lahti Poster Biennial (2007); 2nd Prize, Concours international d'affiches, Chaumont (2008); Grand Prix, Swiss Poster Award (2008); Golden Bee Award, Moscow Global Biennale of Graphic Design (2012).

Italian wines

栗林和夫
Kazuo Kuribayashi

この作品は、ワインの月刊誌「ヴィノテーク」の特集告知用ポスターです。テーマタイトルは「イタリアワインの個性は百花繚乱」。このお題をどう料理したらよいか悩んだ末、「雑誌自体を舞台に見立て、様々な個性を誇るワインが競演する」アイディアが浮かびました。そこで一枚は「幕が開きながら、各産地の血気盛んなワインが我こそはと集まる様」を、もう一枚は「開幕後、ざわざわしながらも各ワインが整列して挨拶しようとしている様」を、それぞれアルファベットを用いて描いてみました。そんな妄想グラフィックをいつも採用して頂ける、編集長をはじめとするスタッフの方々に心より感謝いたします。

These are feature announcement posters for the monthly Vinothéque wine magazine, with a theme title of "A great variety of excellent Italian wines." After considering how to handle this title, I got the idea of "using the magazine as a stage where a variety of distinctive wines are involved in a contest." Using the alphabet, one poster shows "a scene where hot-blooded wines from across Italy gather, showing off themselves, when the stage curtain opens," while the other shows "a scene where wines line up in a buzz, in order, for a greeting after the curtain falls." I sincerely thank the chief editor and the other staff, who always adopt my daydream-like graphics.

栗林和夫

1960年東京都生まれ。1988年多摩美術大学グラフィックデザイン科卒業。東京アドバタイジング、ステューディオ・トウキョウ・ジャパン、ミノルタ・デジタル・ソリューションを経て、2001年クリとグラフィックを設立。「ヴィノテーク」は2006年12月号よりアートディレクターとして係わる。

Kazuo Kuribayashi was born in Tokyo in 1960, graduated from the Department of Graphic Design, Tama Art University in 1988, and established Kuri-to Graphic in 2001 after working for Tokyo Advertising, Studio Tokyo Japan, and Minolta Digital Solutions. He has been engaged in the production of Vinothéque magazine as the art director since the December 2006 issue.

Ingenuity / Nature.　妙法 / 自然。

スタンリー・ウォン（アナザーマウンテンマン）
Stanley Wong (anothermountainman)

色 / 空
ウォーター・カリグラフィー
オン・アンド・オフ
それは、何年も前に広州の公園で、感動的な妙義を直に経験した時からずっと私の頭の中にあった。その文化的歴史と人間性からだけでなく、その構成と環境への配慮からだけでなく、その禅の瞑想のような実践からだけでなく。それは、仏教の色（しき・存在）と空（くう）に対する最も意味のある反応である。全ては無から有へ、そして有から無へ。色そのものは空であり、空そのものが色である。

Water calligraphy.
On and off
it has been in my mind
ever since I experienced the touching feat firsthand
in a park of Guangzhou many years ago.

Not just because its cultural history and humanity,
Not just because its composition and environmental sensitive.
Not just because its zen meditation-like practice.

It is the most meaningful response to the form and emptiness of the Buddhist. Everything from absence to presence, and from presence to absence. Form itself is emptiness. Emptiness itself is form.

スタンリー・ウォン / 別名 anothermountainman（又一山人）
クリエイティブ・ディレクターとして多くの有名な広告会社の仕事をしてきた。2007年、商業・文化ブランド化と販促の仕事に集中するために、84000 Communications を設立。これまで美術、写真、グラフィックデザイン、広告分野で500以上の国内外の賞を受賞している。最近では国内外の多くの大学で客員講師を務めている。作品「Redwhiteblue」は、2005年第51回ヴェネツィア・ビエンナーレで香港からの出展作品2点のうちの1点として展示された。また、2011年香港芸術発展賞でアーティスト・オブ・ザ・イヤー（ビジュアルアート部門）に選ばれ、香港芸術館の2012年香港現代芸術賞を受賞。
Stanley Wong alias anothermountainman, had been worked as Creative Director for many renowned advertising companies. In 2007, Wong set up 84000 communications to focus on commercial, cultural branding and promotion works. Wong has won more than 500 awards in fine art, photography, graphic design and advertising at home and abroad. Recently, he presents as guest lecturer through numerous colleges and universities in local and overseas. His works "Redwhiteblue" have won critical acclaim both locally and internationally and had travelled to Venice as one of the two art works from Hong Kong presented at the 51st Venice Biennale in 2005. Wong was also just awarded the Artist of the Year 2011 (Visual Arts) from Hong Kong Arts Development Awards and the Hong Kong Contemporary Art Awards 2012 from Hong Kong Museum of Art.

Type Design Prize タイプデザイン賞

Ahn Sam-yeol (Hangul typefaces)

安 三烈 アン・サムヨル
Ahn Sam-yeol

文字というのは、その国の歴史、文化と共に成長します。しかしハングルは1900年以来の近代化の過程で、戦争という断絶があり、古活字の根を正しく引き継ぎにくい環境にありました。現在使用されているハングルの本文用書体はほとんどは、1950年代のチェ・ジョンホ（Choi Jung-ho 崔 正治）書体に根ざしたもので、手書きの慣習がだいぶ残っています。そのため私は、これを現代的な感覚で再解釈してはどうかと考えました。アンサムヨル体（Ahn Sam-yeol 安 三烈）は、チェ・ジョンホ体の美感に根を置いており、横画と縦画のコントラストと現代的解釈を加えた活字の試みです。これからも引き続き、この書体を整えていきたいと思っています。初めて作った書体で東京TDCタイプデザイン賞を受賞し、とてもうれしく思います。ありがとうございました。

Characters evolve with the history and culture of the country. However, the evolution of Hangul was discontinued by war in the process of modernization since 1900, and we were in an environment where it was difficult to correctly inherit the root of old typefaces. Most of the Hangul typefaces currently used for body text are based on the typeface designed by Choi Jung-ho in the 1950s and have considerable traces of handwriting practice. Thus, I thought of reinterpreting the typeface in a modern sense. Ahn Sam-yeol is rooted in the sense of beauty of the Choi Jung-ho typeface and is a trial with an addition of the contrast between horizontal & vertical writings and modern interpretation. I will continue to improve this typeface.
I am very happy to receive the Tokyo TDC Type Design Prize with my first typeface. Thank you.

アン・サムヨル
グラフィックデザイナー。1971年ソウル生まれ。1997年弘益大学（Hongik University）視覚デザイン科卒業。1997年〜2001年、Ahn Graphics に勤務。現在フリーランスのデザイナーとして活動。
Ahn Sam-yeol is graphic designer born (1971) and raised in Seoul, Korea. He graduated from department of visual communication design, hongik university in 1997. He worked in ahn graphics (1997~2001) and several design offices. A few years ago, he interested in typeface design, while he worked independently, and start typeface design in 2011.
http://www.310.co.kr

RGB Prize　　RGB賞

PIGEON D'OR (2011)

コーエン・ヴァン・バーレン
Cohen Van Balen

この作品は、鳩の糞から石鹸を作ることを目的とする、さまざまな規模の一連の介入で構成されている。最初の介入は、微小規模である。私たちは、生化学者 James Chappell の助けを得て、合成生物学を用い、鳩の代謝を変えることのできるバクテリアを作り出した。これを達成するために、私たちはバクテリアの遺伝情報に加えるとリパーゼを作り出す新しいバイオブリック（標準生物学的パーツ）を作った。また、ph 値を下げるバイオブリックも使用した。その結果として出来上がったのが、一種の窓用石鹸を生産する生物学的装置である。私たちはこれを、消化管にももともと存在する乳酸菌を使って作り出した。このバクテリアを鳩に与えると、鳩の糞は生物学的石鹸になる。私たちが作ったバイオブリックは、標準生物学的パーツ登録所（Standard Registry of Biological Parts）で自由に閲覧できる。（中略）映像に記録されたように、これらの微視的介入は、巨視的介入と織り合わされる。鳩の飼育家の大半は、鳩レースのために数百羽もの鳩を飼う中年男性だが、このような人々は年々減少している。彼らが習得する、言葉に表されない知識や方法の多くは、科学とはみなされず、新しいバイオテクノロジーがもたらし得る DIY 式美学と再認識されるかもしれない。微視的規模と巨視的規模の両方での相互作用と知識の移転からインスピレーションを得て、一連の創作物が出来上がった。最初の創作物は、鳩と駐車中の自動車とのインターフェースであり、生産された石鹸がフロントガラス上に落ちる仕組みになっている。2 番目の創作物は、鳩が家や建築物の一部となる仕掛けである。この鳩小屋を窓枠に取り付けることで、鳩に餌をやり、鳩を分離・選別し、別の出口から外に出るよう誘導することができる。特注の都市除菌装置としても役立つ。現在は、欧州規制があるために、私たちが作ったバクテリアを試験場の外で鳩に試すことはできない。しかし、バイオブリックを標準生物学的パーツ登録所に加えることによって、誰でもデザインを閲覧し、このバクテリアを作ることができる。合成生物学の未来において、これはレゴで遊ぶのと同じくらい容易なことになるだろう。というわけで、このバクテリアはともかくも世界に解き放たれたと私は信じたい。さらに重要なこととして、この作品は、大いに必要とされる美的・概念的多様性を道具箱に加え、いずれは人工生命の開発に利用されると信じたい。法規制以外に、政治的・倫理的・観念的考察も影響する。この作品の目的は、このグレーゾーンに接近することである。その意味でも、鳩は強力なメッセンジャーである。実際、野生の鳩は、都市部のバイオテクノロジーにとって、理想的なプラットフォームであると同時に理想的なインターフェースである。一方では、鳩は多くの人から有毒生物か空飛ぶネズミのように思われているが、他方では、実際のところ、鳩はすでにバイオテクノロジーの産物だと主張することもできる。というのも鳩は、速く飛び、見た目が良く、手紙を運び、スパイや宙返りをし、レースに参加できるよう、何世代もかけて交配・繁殖されてきたからだ。もしかすると私たちが知っている鳩は、これまでも人工的な生命体だったのではないだろうか？

This work consists of a series of interventions on different scales, in pursuit of making a pigeon defecate soap. The first intervention is on the micro-scale. With the help of biochemist James Chappell, we have used synthetic biology to design and create a bacteria that can modify the metabolism of pigeons. To achieve this, we have created a new biobrick, or standard biological part, that when added to the genetic information of the bacteria, creates lipase. We have also used a biobrick that lowers the ph. The result is a biological device that produces a kind of window-soap. We have built this device in the bacteria Lactobacillus, which is a bacteria that naturally occurs in the digestive tract. So when feeding this bacteria to a pigeon, it should produce and defecate biological soap. The biobrick we have created is freely accessible from the standard registry of biological parts. See the biobrick created for this project in the Registry of Standard Biological Parts. One can however never consider the bacteria in itself. Like the Lactobacillus bacteria is the chassis for the synthetic genetic information, so is the pigeon the carrier of the synthetic bacteria. And beyond the bacteria in the pigeon, we should consider the pigeon in the city. We should consider the city as a vast and incredibly complex metabolism in which we, the human species, are but the tiniest of fractions; tiny and yet intrinsically linked into an organic embroidery beyond our understanding. It is within this complex fabric that (future) biotechnologies will end up. Therefore, these microscopic interventions are interwoven with interventions on the macro-scale, as documented in the film. Pigeon fanciers are a dying breed of mostly middle-aged men that keep up to hundreds of pigeons in order to race them. The tacit knowledge and rituals they master might by many not be considered science but does often remind of the DIY aesthetics that new biotechnologies might bring. The interactions and knowledge transfer both on the microscopic and macroscopic scale, have inspired a series of speculative objects. The first artefact is an interface between pigeons and parked automobile, allowing the produced soap to land on the windscreen. The second artefact is a contraption that allows these pigeons to become part of your house, part of the architecture. This pigeon house is attached to your windowsill and allows you to feed the pigeons, separate and select them and direct them through different exits. It facilitates bespoke urban disinfection. Currently, European regulations make it impossible to take our created bacteria out of the lab and test it on pigeons. However by adding the biobrick to the Standard Registry of Biological Parts, anyone can access the design and create the bacteria. In a synthetic biology future, this would be as easy as playing with lego. I like to believe that as such, the organism has somehow been released into the world. More importantly, I like to believe that the work adds a much needed aesthetic and conceptual diversity to the toolbox that will soon be used to build artificial life. Beyond these legal restrictions, political, ethical and ideological considerations are in play too. It is the work's aim to approach this grey zone. And in that sense too, the pigeon proves a powerful messenger. Indeed, feral pigeons present themselves as the ideal platform and interface for urban biotechnologies. On the one hand, they are by many seen as venom or flying rats. On the other hand, one could argue they are actually already a product of biotechnology: Over generations, they have been designed and bread to come quicker, to look pretty, to deliver post, to spy, tumble or race. Perhaps pigeons as we know them, have always been an artificial life-form?

コーエン・ヴァン・バーレン

リビタル・コーエン（Revital Cohen）とテューア・ヴァン・バーレン（Tuur Van Balen）はロンドンを拠点に、独創的なオブジェ、写真、パフォーマンス、映像作品を制作しながら、生命学とテクノロジー間の緊張への探求を行っている。構成された自然や機械的な臓器などに発想を得て、ポスト・ヒューマンボディ、あつらえの代謝機能、人工動物や詩的な機械などのクリエイションを提示している。http://www.cohenvanbalen.com/
Revital Cohen and Tuur Van Balen run a London based experimental practice that produces fictional objects, photographs, performances and videos exploring the tensions between biology and technology. Inspired by designer species, composed wilderness and mechanical organs, they set out to create posthuman bodies, bespoke metabolisms, unnatural animals and poetic machines.

*Scientific collaboration – James Chappell / Photographs by Tuur Van Balen and Pieter Baert Supported by the Flemish Authorities / Thanks to Jan Boelen, Cate Edgar, Keith Plastow, Albert Stratton, Kasper Van Rompay & Joep Verburg

Prize Nominee Works &
Excellent Works

Poster

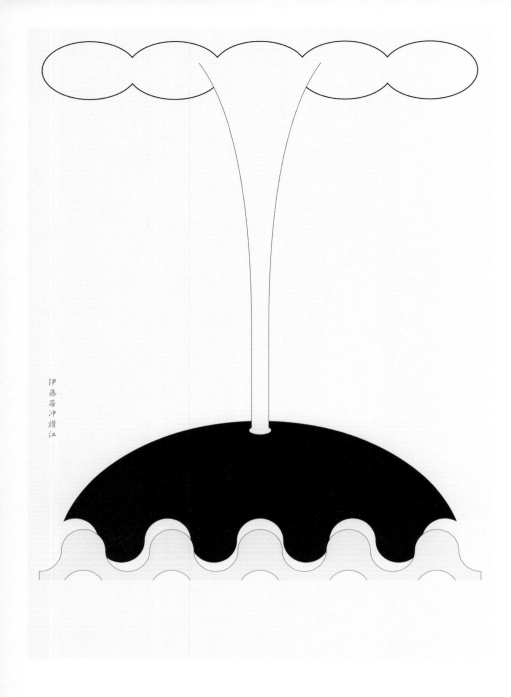

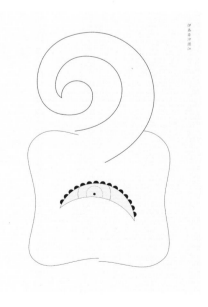

Prize Nominee Work

011 Poster
TD. AD. D. 服部一成 Kazunari Hattori
　　　CL. デザインアソシエーション NPO
　　　　　Design Association NPO
　　　PT. DFP 行書体

江戸時代の絵師、伊藤若冲をテーマにした展覧会
への出品作品。若冲の「象鯨図屏風」をモチーフに、
二点一組の縦位置のポスターを作った。似ても似
つかない淡白なものになってしまった。

This was displayed at an exhibition on the theme of Jakuchu Ito, a painter of the Edo Period. I created a pair of vertical posters, using Jakuchu's "Zo To Kujira Zu Byobu" as a motif, but my work became very plain and actually quite unlike the motif.

Long Good-bye!

Pappa TARAHUMARA
Final Festival

December 2011 – March 2012
http://pappa-tara.com/fes

"ロンググッドバイ" パパタラ ファイナルフェスティバル

作・演出・振付：小池博史

出演： 小川摩利子　松島 誠　白井さち子　関口満紀枝　あらた真生　池野拓哉　菊地理恵　橋本 礼　南波 冴　荒木亜矢子　石原夏実
縫原弘子　開 桂子　ヤン・ツィ・クック　小谷野哲郎　アセップ・ヘンドラジャッド

「三人姉妹」2011・12・20（火）～22（木）〈会場〉北沢タウンホール　　　「SHIP IN A VIEW」2012・1・27（金）～29（日）〈会場〉シアター1010
「島・island」2012・1・13（金）～15（日）〈会場〉森下スタジオ Cスタジオ　　　「パパ・タラフマラの白雪姫」2012・3・29（木）～31（土）〈会場〉北沢タウンホール

〈お問い合わせ・チケット取り扱い〉パパタラファイナルフェスティバル実行委員会 http://pappa-tara.com/fes/tickets tel：03-3385-2066

解散反対

Prize Nominee Work

012 Poster

TD. AD. 葛西 薫	Kaoru Kasai
D. 引地摩里子	Mariko Hikichi
C. 安藤 隆	Takashi Ando
CL. (株)サイ	Sai Inc.
PT. Clarendon	

30年の活動を休止して発展的解散となった舞踏集団「パパタラフマラ」。その名はただただ走る民族と言われるメキシコの「タラフマラ族」に由来する。そこで、どこまでも走り続けてほしいと願い、「走る」を画にした。

The "Pappa TARAHUMARA" dance group went on hiatus after 30 years, in order to forge new creative directions. The group was named after the Tarahumara tribe, known as a "running" tribe in Mexico. I expressed my wish for "continuation" in a design inspired by "running."

ギンザ・グラフィック・ギャラリー
第314回企画展

AGI展

Alliance Graphique Internationale 国際グラフィック連盟

2012年10月4日(木)−10月27日(土)
11:00−19:00(土曜日は18:00まで) 日曜・祝日休館 入場無料
〒104-0061 東京都中央区銀座7-7-2 DNP銀座ビル1F Tel. 03-3571-5206

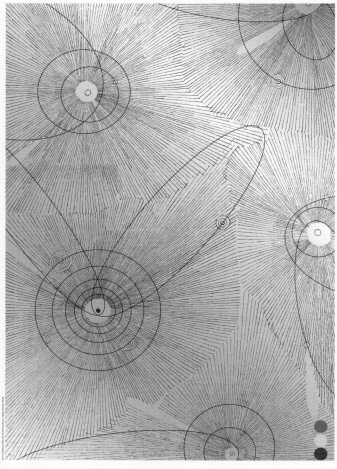

永井一正 Kazumasa NAGAI
五十嵐威暢 Takenobu IGARASHI
勝井三雄 Mitsuo KATSUI
中村誠 Makoto NAKAMURA
浅葉克己 Katsumi ASABA
佐藤晃一 Koichi SATO
松永真 Shin MATSUNAGA
サイトウマコト Makoto SAITO
松井桂三 Keizo MATSUI
佐藤卓 Taku SATOH
中島英樹 Hideki NAKAJIMA
新島実 Minoru NIIJIMA
三木健 Ken MIKI
U.G.サトー U.G. SATO
蛯名龍郎 Tatsuo EBINA
北川一成 Issey KITAGAWA
澤田泰廣 Yasuhiro SAWADA
杉崎真之助 Shinnoske SUGISAKI
長友啓典 Keisuke NAGATOMO
原研哉 Kenya HARA
松下計 Kei MATSUSHITA
葛西薫 Kaoru KASAI
立花文穂 Fumio TACHIBANA
佐藤可士和 Kashiwa SATO
永井一史 Kazufumi NAGAI
服部一成 Kazunari HATTORI
平野敬子 Keiko HIRANO

Gunter Rambow グンター・ランボー
Seymour Chwast シーモア・クワスト
Holger Matthies オルガー・マチス
Ivan Chermayeff アイヴァン・チャマイエフ
Jan Rajlich sen. ヤン・ライリッヒ
Pierre Bernard ピエール・ベルナール
Uwe Loesch ウーヴェ・レシュ
Niklaus Troxler ニクラウス・トロックスラー
Kit Hinrichs キット・ヒンリック
Lars Müller ラース・ミュラー
Paula Scher ポーラ・シェア
Ralph Schraivogel ラルフ・シュライフォーゲル
Kan Tai-Keung カン・タイクン
Kari Piippo カリ・ピッポ
Michel Bouvet ミシェル・ブーヴェ
Philippe Apeloig フィリップ・アベロワ
David Tartakover デイヴィッド・タルタコーバ
Stefan Sagmeister ステファン・サグマイスター
Vladimir Chaika ウラジーミル・チャイカ
Cyan シアン
Leonardo Sonnoli レオナルド・ソノリ
Wang Xu ワン・シュ
Freeman Lau フリーマン・ラウ
István Orosz イストヴァン・オロス
Stanley Wong スタンリー・ウォン
Tommy Li トミー・リー
Wang Min ワン・ミン
Jianping He ジャンピン・ヘ
Majid Abbasi マジド・アバッシ

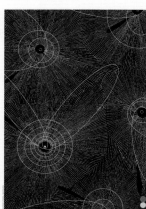

Prize Nominee Work

013 Poster
TD. AD. 浅葉克己 Katsumi Asaba
　　D. 金森彩 Aya Kanamori
　　CL. ギンザ・グラフィック・ギャラリー
　　　　 ginza graphic gallery
　　PT. 游明朝体 / 石井中太ゴシック

Prize Nominee Work

014 Poster
TD. Jeong In-gee
CL. Non-commercial work

Prize Nominee Work

015 Poster
TD. D. Cybu Richli
      Fabienne Burri
  CL. Posterfestival Lucerne
  PT. Custom-made for the project:
      C2F-Urban

このポスターは、展覧会「コマース・アート」のコーポレートデザインの一部で、コンセプトの一番の特徴はこのポスターのために創られたフォント「C2F-Poster」である。展覧会では、芸術性と実施の他者性ゆえに多くの中で際立った商業ポスターが展示された。このポスターはドイツ語と英語で読むことができる。

The poster is part of the corporate design for the exhibition "Commerce Art". A strong part of the concept was the font "C2F-Poster", which we specially created for this. The exhibition showed a selection of commercial productposters, what stand out from the crowd because of their artistic quality and the alterity of implementation. The Poster can be read on two sides; German and English.

016 Poster
TD. AD. D. 色部義昭 Yoshiaki Irobe
PR. 福島 治　Osamu Fukushima
I. 山口修平 Shuhei Yamaguchi
CL. クリエイションギャラリー G8
Creation Gallery G8

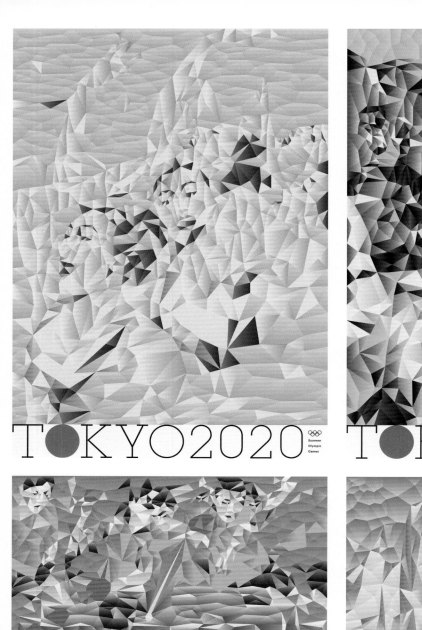

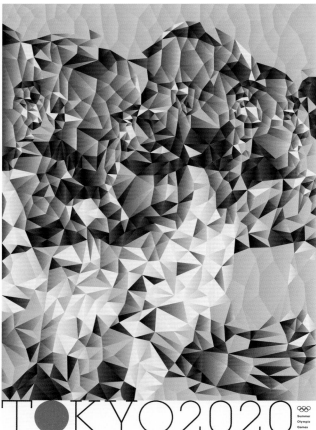

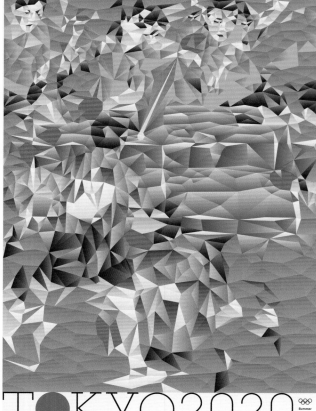

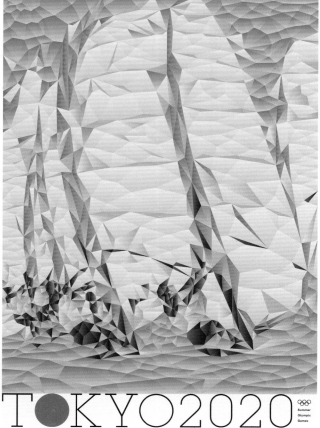

017

017 Poster
TD. AD. D. 尾﨑友則 Tomonori Ozaki
　　　CL. Non-commercial work
　　　PT. Lubalin Graph / Univers

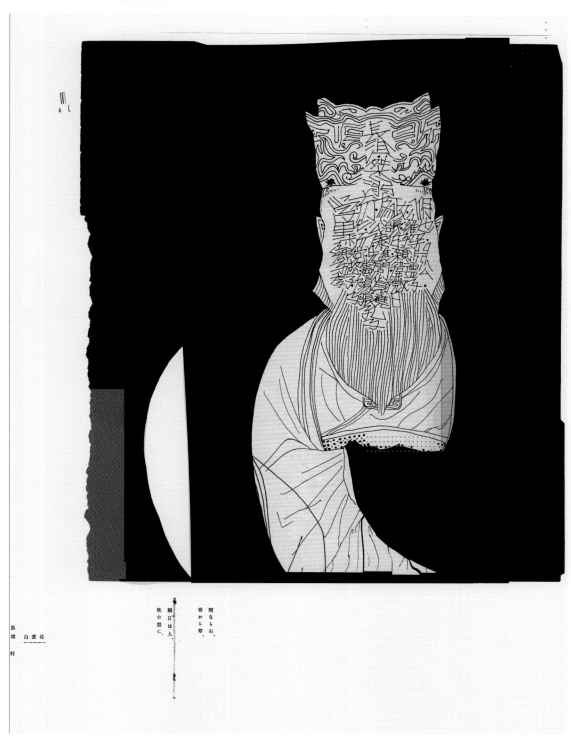

018 Poster
TD. 木村高典　Takanori Kimura
CL. Non-commercial work
PT. Custom-made for the project

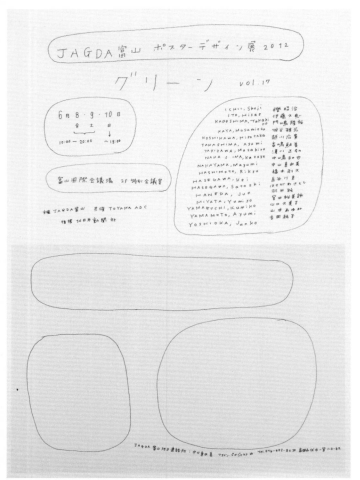

019

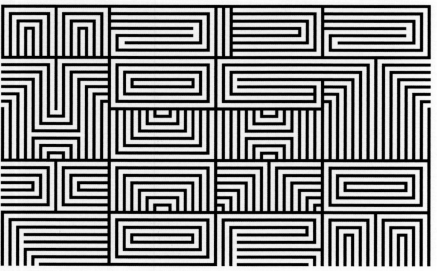

020

Coca-Cola lessons Shuntaro Tanikawa

021

019 Poster
TD. AD. D. 宮田裕美詠 Yumiyo Miyata
　　PD. 熊倉桂三　Katsumi Kumakura
　　　　高 智之　Tomoyuki Taka
　　CL. JAGDA 富山
　　　　JAGDA Toyama
　　PT. Handwriting characters

020 Poster
TD. AD. シラスノリユキ　Noriyuki Shirasu
　　　　D. 冨田浩行　Hiroyuki Tomita
W(Poem). 谷川俊太郎　Shuntaro Tanikawa
　　CL. スワログフィルム　Swallog Film
　　PT. Custom-made for the project

021 Poster
TD. MADA LAB. / John Warwicker
CL. MADA (Monash Art, Design & Architecture)
PT. Custom-made for the project

砂丘の実論。

鳥取は、先取りのまちになる。
エンジン01文化戦略会議
オープンカレッジin鳥取
2012年3月23日(金)・24日(土)・25日(日)
とりぎん文化会館梨花ホール、鳥取環境大学

砂丘の実論。
鳥取は、先取りのまちになる。
エンジン01文化戦略会議
オープンカレッジin鳥取

022 Poster
TD. AD. 浅葉克己   Katsumi Asaba
        D. 清水龍之介 Ryunosuke Shimizu
        C. 岡田直也   Naoya Okada
        P. 植田正治   Shoji Ueda
     CL. エンジン01 文化戦略会議 ENJIN01
     PT. 游明朝体 / Custom-made for the project

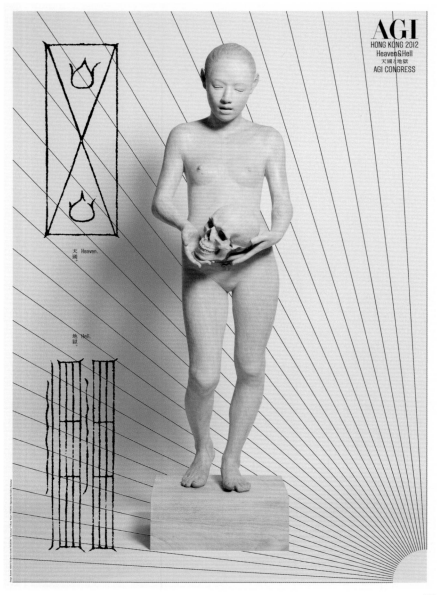

023

024

023 Poster
TD. AD. 浅葉克己　Katsumi Asaba
　　D. 石原千明　Chiaki Ishihara
　　A. 池島康輔　Kosuke Ikeshima
　　P. 米田 渉　Wataru Yoneda
　CL. AGI香港　AGI Hong Kong
　PT. Custom-made for the project

024 Poster
TD. AD. 佐野研二郎　Kenjiro Sano
　TD. D. 市東 基　　Motoi Shito
　　CL. デザインアソシエーションNPO
　　　　Design Association NPO
　　PT. Custom-made for the project

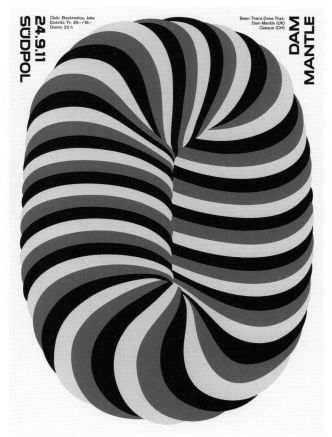

025

025 Poster
TD. Felix Pfäffli
CL. Südpol Luzern
PT. Lucarna / Ambauen Grotesk

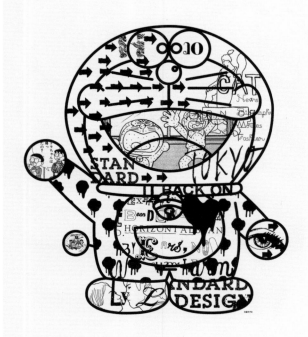 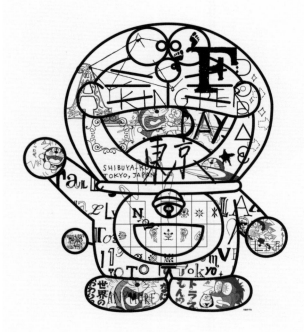

026

027

028

026 Poster
TD. 千原徹也 Tetsuya Chihara
CL. Non-commercial work
PT. Custom-made for the project

027 Poster
TD. Andreas Uebele
CL. Düsseldorf University of Applied Sciences,
Department of Design

028 Poster
TD. Felix Pfäffli + Mathis Pfäffli
CL. Hochschule Luzern
PT. AK11 / Typewriter Gothic

川内倫子展　照度　あめつち　影を見る

Kawauchi Rinko
Illuminance, Ametsuchi, Seeing Shadow

2012年5月12日(土)－7月16日(月・祝)

東京都写真美術館
恵比寿ガーデンプレイス内　www.syabi.com

川内倫子展　照度　あめつち　影を見る

Kawauchi Rinko
Illuminance, Ametsuchi, Seeing Shadow

2012年5月12日(土)－7月16日(月・祝)

東京都写真美術館
恵比寿ガーデンプレイス内　www.syabi.com

029

仲條正義展
忘れちゃってEASY
思い出してCRAZY

Masayoshi Nakajo
Forgetting makes things easy;
remembering drives you crazy.

会期／2012年6月23日(土)〜8月12日(日)
平日11時－19時　日・祝日11時－18時
毎週月曜休　*7月16日(月)は祝日ですが休館いたします
入場無料

資生堂ギャラリー
〒104-0061 東京都中央区銀座 8-8-3 東京銀座資生堂ビル地下1階
tel.03-3572-3901　fax.03-3572-3951　http://group.shiseido.co.jp/gallery
主催：資生堂

SHISEIDO 940 Anniversary

SHISEIDO GALLERY

030

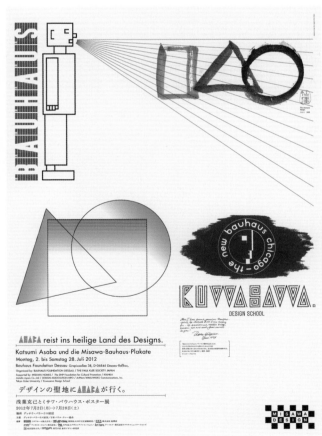

031

029 Poster
TD. AD. 葛西 薫　Kaoru Kasai
　　D. 増田 豊　Yutaka Masuda
　　P. 川内倫子　Rinko Kawauchi
　CL. (財)東京都写真美術館
　　　Tokyo Metropolitan Museum of Photography
　PT. 筑紫明朝

030 Poster
TD. AD. D. 仲條正義　Masayoshi Nakajo
　CL. (株)資生堂
　　　Shiseido Co., Ltd.
　PT. 秀英初号明朝

031 Poster
TD. AD. 浅葉克己　Katsumi Asaba
　　D. 石原千明　Chiaki Ishihara
　　C. 日暮伸三　Shinzo Higurashi
　CL. デッサウ・バウハウス財団　Stiftung Bauhaus Dessau
　　　日本パウル・クレー協会　Paul Klee Society Japan
　PT. Custom-made for the project

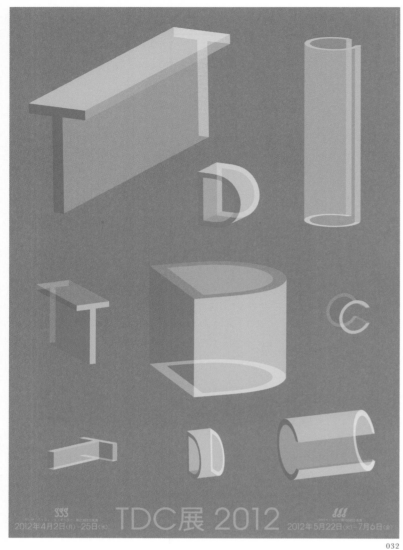

032

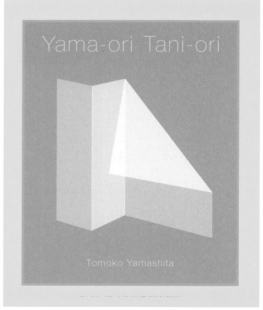

033

032 Poster
TD. AD. D. 山下ともこ Tomoko Yamashita
　　CL. 東京タイプディレクターズクラブ
　　　　Tokyo Type Directors Club
　　PT. Custom-made for the project

033 Poster
TD. AD. D. 山下ともこ Tomoko Yamashita
　　CL. モンターニュ社 Montagne-sha
　　PT. Helvetica Neue Light

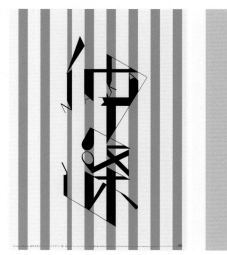

034

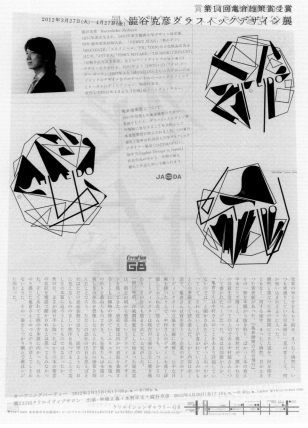

035

034 Poster
TD. 澁谷克彦 Katsuhiko Shibuya
CL. クリエイションギャラリー G8
　　Creation Gallery G8

035 Poster
TD. 澁谷克彦 Katsuhiko Shibuya
CL. クリエイションギャラリー G8
　　Creation Gallery G8

036

037

038

036 Poster
TD. 塚本 陽 Kiyoshi Tsukamoto
CL. Imagica TV
PT. UKNumberPlate

037 Poster
TD. 市東 基 Motoi Shito
CL. 丁貳肆捌
PT. Custom-made for the project

038 Poster
TD. AD. 浅葉克己 Katsumi Asaba
　　　　D. 石原千明 Chiaki Ishihara
　　　　C. 渡辺裕一 Yuichi Watanabe
CL. Open Yokohama 実行委員会
PT. 游明朝体 / Custom-made for the project

73

039

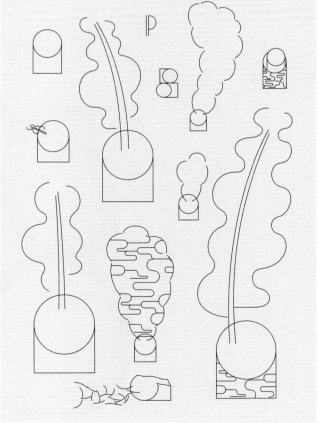

040

041

039 Poster
TD. AD. D. 宮田裕美詠 Yumiyo Miyata
　　　CD. 高橋修宏 Nobuhiro Takahashi
　　　PR. 邊井徹伸 Tesshin Nabei
　　　PD. 熊倉桂三 Katsumi Kumakura
　　　　　 高 智之 Tomoyuki Taka
　　　CL. 武者小路千家 富山官休会
　　　　　 Mushakouji Senke Toyama Kankyukai
　　　PT. Handwriting characters

040 Poster
TD. AD. D. 中村至男 Norio Nakamura
　　　CL. The Cave, between the books
　　　PT. DNP秀英体明朝

041 Poster
TD. AD. D. 樋口寛人 Hiroto Higuchi
　　　CL. Non-commercial work
　　　PT. Custom-made for the project

GALERIE
JOSEPH TANG
1, RUE CHARLES-
FRANÇOIS
DUPUIS
BÂTIMENT B /
2E ÉTAGE
75003 PARIS
FRANCE
T + 33 9 53 69
55 35
INFO@
GALERIEJOSEPHTANG
.COM
MA-SA 11-19H

08
MARS-19 AVRIL
2012
CHLOÉ QUENUM
INTERVALLE

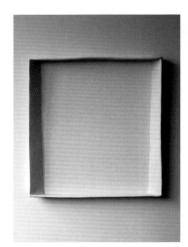

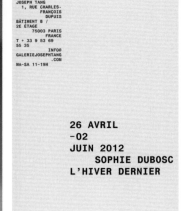

GALERIE
JOSEPH TANG
1, RUE CHARLES-
FRANÇOIS
DUPUIS
BÂTIMENT B /
2E ÉTAGE
75003 PARIS
FRANCE
T + 33 9 53 69
55 35
INFO@
GALERIEJOSEPHTANG
.COM
MA-SA 11-19H

26 AVRIL
-02
JUIN 2012
SOPHIE DUBOSC
L'HIVER DERNIER

042

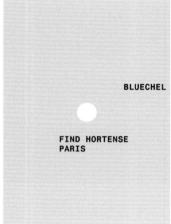

GALERIE
JOSEPH TANG
1, RUE CHARLES-
FRANÇOIS
DUPUIS
BÂTIMENT B /
2E ÉTAGE
75003 PARIS
FRANCE
T + 33 9 53 69
55 35
INFO@
GALERIEJOSEPHTANG
.COM
MA-SA 11-19H

BLUECHEL

FIND HORTENSE
PARIS

20 OCTOBRE - 15
DÉCEMBRE
2011
SEAN BLUECHEL
VERNISSAGE
18-23H

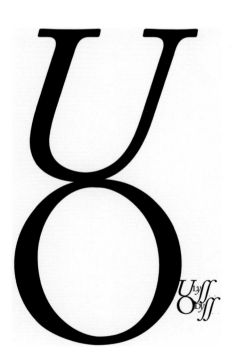

043

042 Poster
TD. Andre Baldinger & Toan Vu-Huu
CL. Galerie Joseph Tang
PT. Monospace 821 Bold

043 Poster
TD. CL. John Warwicker
CL. MADA
    (Monash Art, Design & Architecture)
PT. Custom-made for the project

オレの原子力

$$黒田征太郎 = \frac{原子力}{え}$$

オレの ジュウカッテ

$$黒田征太郎 = \frac{キママ}{え}$$

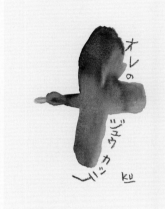

オレの ジュウカッテ

$$黒田征太郎 = \frac{キママ}{え}$$

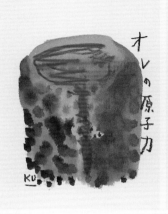

オレの原子力

$$黒田征太郎 = \frac{原子力}{え}$$

044

045

044 Poster
TD. AD. D. 青木克憲　Katsunori Aoki
I. CL. 黒田征太郎　Seitaro Kuroda
PT. ZEN オールド明朝

045 Poster
TD. AD. D. C. 丸山 建　Ken Maruyama
C. 丸山美香　Mika Maruyama
CD. 山本 敦　Atsushi Yamamoto
CL. デザイナーズネットワーク長岡
Designers' Network Nagaoka
PT. りょうゴシック PlusN R／Courier Std Medium／
Custom-made for the project

046

047

046 Poster
TD. AD. D. 田頭慎太郎　Shintaro Tagashira
　　CD. 村松秀俊　Hidetoshi Muramatsu
　　CL. AD ROOM
　　PT. Custom-made for the project

047 Poster
TD. AD. D. I. 本田千尋　Chihiro Honda
　　CL. Non-commercial work
　　PT. リュウミン

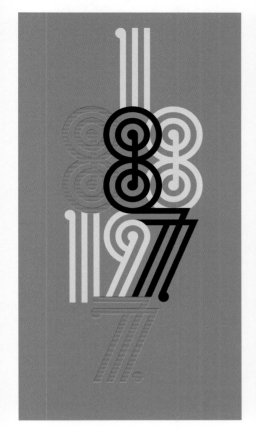
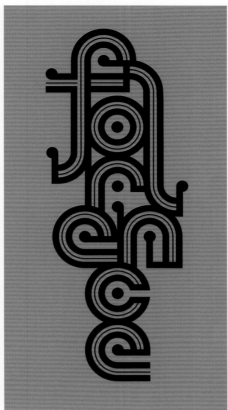
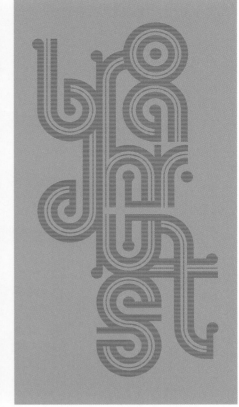

048

049

048 Poster
TD. Gene Bawden
CL. Monash University
PT. Custom-made for the project

049 Poster
TD. Brighten the Corners
     (Billy Kiosoglou/Frank Philippin)
CL. Hochschule Darmstadt
PT. Times New Roman

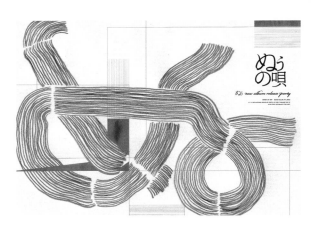

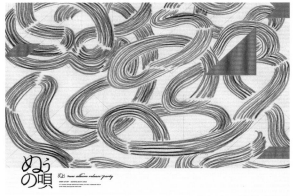

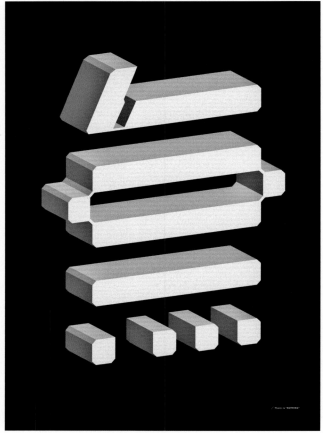

050

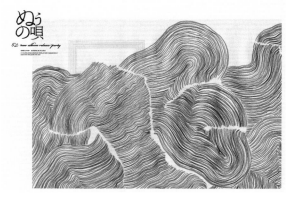

052

051

051 Poster
TD. AD. 浅葉克己 Katsumi Asaba
D. 石原千明 Chiaki Ishihara
P. 鈴木 薫 Kaoru Suzuki
CL. Non-commercial work
PT. Custom-made for the project

050 Poster
TD. 佐々木 俊 Shun Sasaki
CL. Non-commercial work
PT. Custom-made for the project

052 Poster
TD. AD. D. 小山秀一郎 Shuichirow Koyama
I. 中山信一 Shinichi Nakayama
CL. ぬぅ
PT. Custom-made for the project

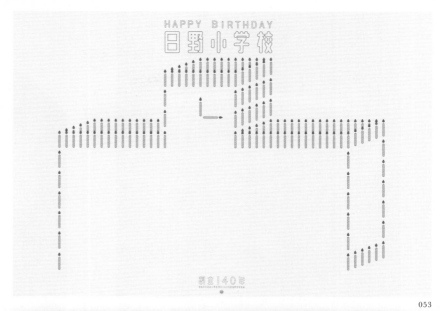

053

054

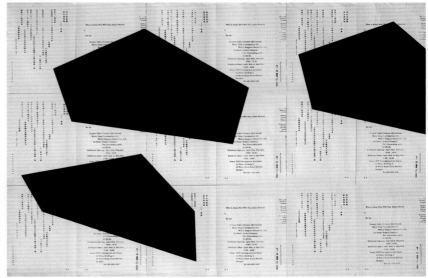

055

053 Poster
TD. AD. D. 松永美春　Miharu Matsunaga
CL. 日野小学校　Hino elementary school
PT. Custom-made for the project

054 Poster
TD. AD. D. 目時綾子　Ayako Metoki
CL. 足土嘉奈子　Kanako Azuchi
出村美奈　Mina Demura

055 Poster
TD. D. Fang Jianping
TD. Ding Fan
CL. Tang Contemporary Art
PT. Ming Ti / Kai Ti / Garamond

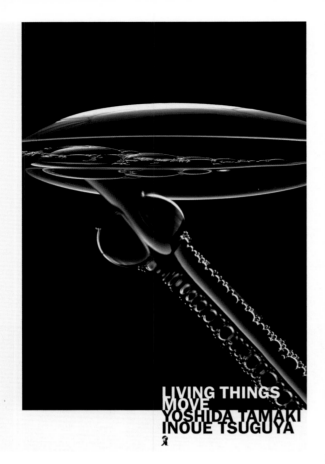

a

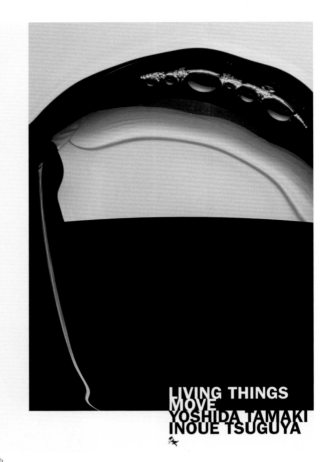

b

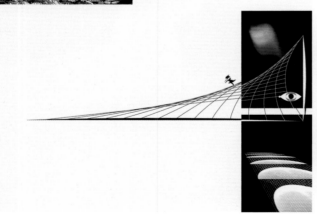

c

d

056

056 Poster
TD. AD. D. 井上嗣也　Tsuguya Inoue
　　　P. 新 良太　　　Ryota Atarashi（c/d）
　　　　吉田多麻希　Tamaki Yoshida（a/b/c/d）
　　CL. ギャラリー・スイフル　Gallery SUIFUL
　　PT. ITC Franklin Gothic Demi

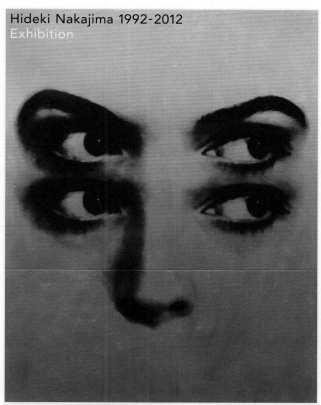

057

058

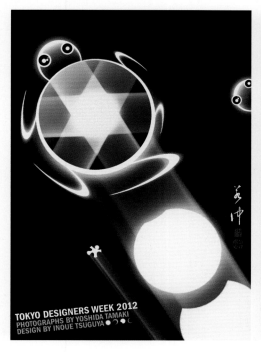

059

057 Poster
TD. AD. 中島英樹　Hideki Nakajima
CL.（株）大和プレス　Daiwa Press
PT. 中ゴシックBBB／Avenir

058 Poster
TD. AD. D. 滝本 圭　Kei Takimoto
CL. Non-commercial work
PT. DIN

059 Poster
TD. AD. D. I. 井上嗣也　Tsuguya Inoue
P. 吉田多麻希　Tamaki Yoshida
CL. デザインアソシエーションNPO
　　Design Association NPO
PT. ITC Franklin Gothic Demi Condensed

060

061

062

063

060 Poster
TD. AD. 長友啓典　Keisuke Nagatomo
　I. 黒田征太郎　Seitaro Kuroda
　D. 中村 健　Takeshi Nakamura
　CL. 椿組　Tsubakigumi
　PT. Hand Writing

061 Poster
TD. D. I. Do-Hyung Kim
　I. Vier5
　CL. Non-commercial work
　PT. Custom-made for the project

062 Poster
TD. AD. D. 丸山 建　Ken Maruyama
　CL. スキsyumiten　Suki syumiten
　PT. Custom-made for the project

063 Poster
TD. Jeong In-gee
　CL. Non-commercial work

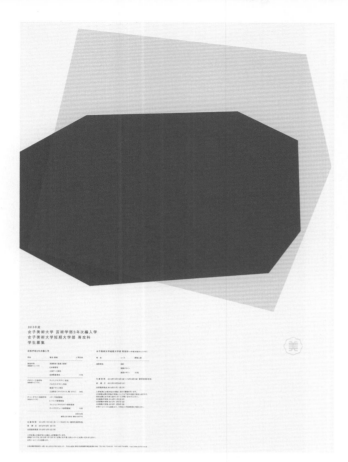

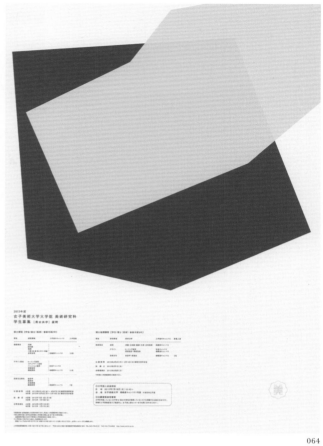

064

065

066

064 Poster
TD. AD. D. 林 規章 Noriaki Hayashi
    CL. 女子美術大学
        Joshibi University of Art and Design
    PT. 中ゴシック BBB

065 Poster
TD. AD. D. C. 広本理絵 Rie Hiromoto
    CL. Non-commercial work
    PT. ひねくれホント

066 Poster
TD. AD. D. I. 石黒 潤 Jun Ishiguro
    PT. Custom-made for the project

067

As the year 2   01   2   suggests, stay consistent
in your beginnings and
your endings.

Be   positive and let things   be.
Break   from old routines and give yourself a   break.
Cheer   for a stranger and be of good   cheer.
Fight   the good   fight.
Follow   your dreams and the rest will   follow.
Go   outdoors and learn to let   go.
Grow   in knowledge and let your heart   grow.
Have   a thankful heart and treasure what you have.
Listen   to your heart but give others a   listen.
Live   and let   live.
Speak   your mind and let the truth   speak.
Work   hard and make things   work.

It's not easy to remember
our goals and stay true
to them at the finish line,
but it's certainly worth
the effort.

Have a great year ahead.
--
pupilpeople

068

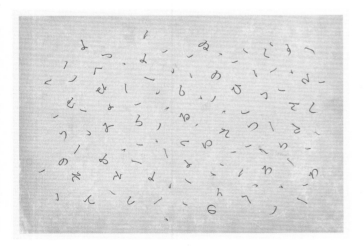

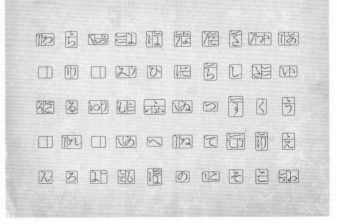

069

067 Poster
TD. 佐々木 俊 Shun Sasaki
CL. Non-commercial work
PT. Custom-made for the project

068 Poster
TD. Sean Kelvin Khoo
C. Arlene Rieneke
CL. Pupilpeople
PT. Akzidenz Grotesk

069 Poster
TD. 藤巻洋紀 Hiroki Fujimaki
CL. Non-commercial work
PT. リュウミン

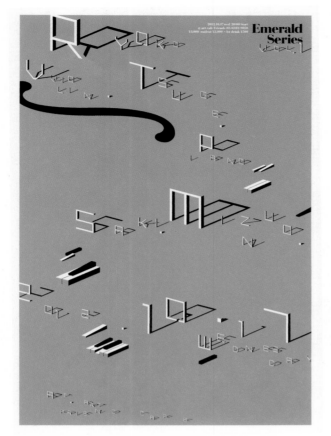

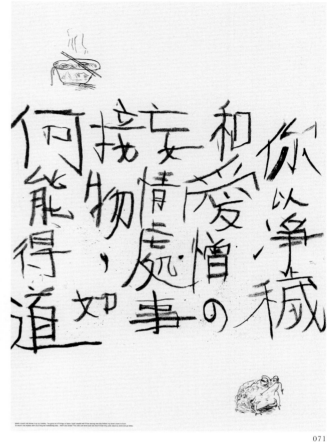

070

071

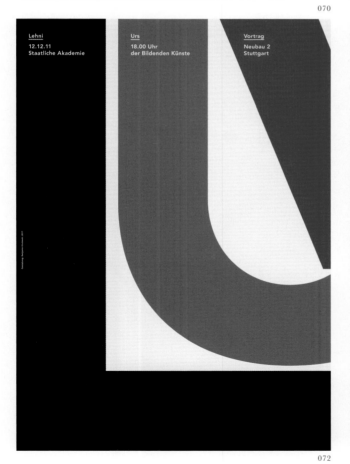

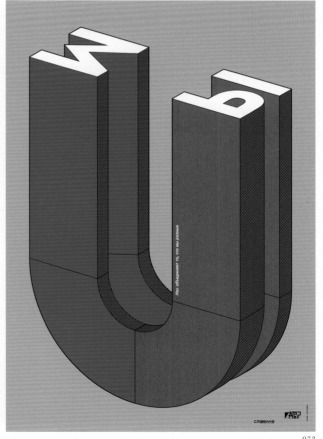

072

073

072 Poster
TD. Benjamin Kivikoski
CL. State Academy of Art and Design,
Stuttgart
PT. Custom-made for the project/
Avenir Next

073 Poster
TD. D. Ilya Bryabrin
CL. Strelka Festival
PT. Custom-made for the project/
Akzidenz-Grotesk

070 Poster
TD. AD. D. 田頭慎太郎 Shintaro Tagashira
CL. 服部展明   Nobuaki Hattori
PT. Bauer Bodoni

071 Poster
TD. D. I. Han Xiaoliang
CL. Non-commercial work
PT. Hand-painted

074

075

076

074 Poster
TD. AD. D. 平野篤史 Atsushi Hirano
　CL. LEWS 纏
　PT. Custom-made for the project

075 Poster
TD. AD. D. 平野篤史 Atsushi Hirano
　P. 本多康司 Koji Honda
　CL. LEWS 纏
　PT. Custom-made for the project

076 Poster
TD. 浦田高史 Koushi Urata
　CL. Non-commercial work

077

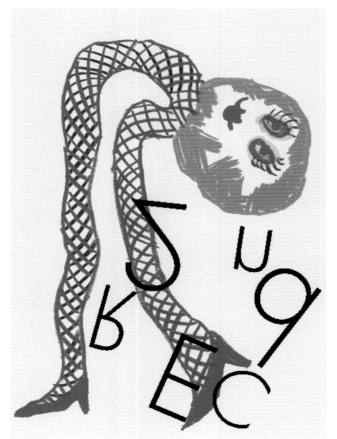

078

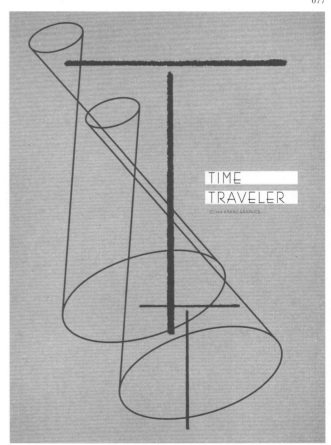

079

077 Poster
TD. AD. D. A. 稲田尊久　Takahisa Inada
　　　　A. 稲田はるな　Haruna Inada
Laser Cut 馬場将実　Masami Baba
　　　　P. 横田竹虎　Taketora Yokota
　　　　CL. Non-commercial work
　　　　PT. Custom-made for the project

078 Poster
TD. AD. 佐古田英一　Eiichi Sakota
D. A. 佐藤ゆかり　Yukari Sato
CL. Non-commercial work
PT. Futura Light

079 Poster
TD. AD. D. 天野裕一　Yuichi Amano
CL. Non-commercial work
PT. Custom-made for the project /
Bernie

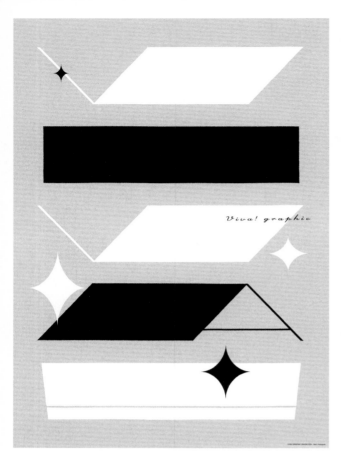

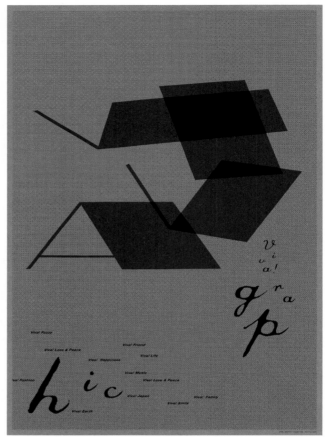

080

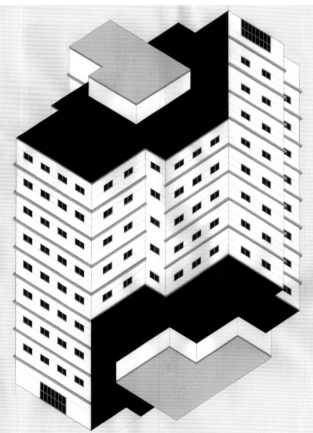

081

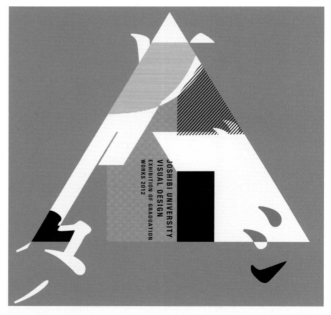

082

080　Poster
TD. AD. 森 和之　　Kazuyuki Mori
　　D. 村松弘友紀　Hiroyuki Muramatsu
　　CL. ビバ！グラフィック事務局
　　　　Viva! Graphic Secretariat
　　PT. Commercial Script

081　Poster
TD. AD. 河野 智　Satoshi Kohno
　　CL. Non-commercial work
　　PT. Custom-made for the project

082　Poster
TD. AD. 白村玲子　Reiko Hakumura
　　CL. 女子美術大学
　　　　Joshibi University of Art and Design
　　PT. 女子美游明朝体 /
　　　　Custom-made for the project

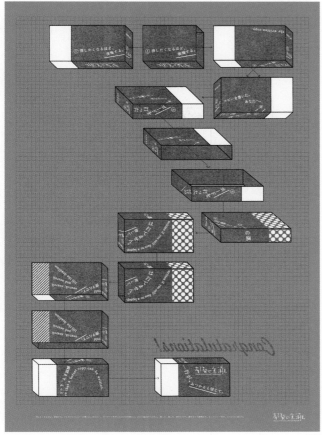

083

084

085

086

083 Poster
TD. AD. D. 平井秀和　Hidekazu Hirai
　　　C. 都築 徹　Toru Tsuzuki
　　　CL. 宣伝会議コピー講座 都築徹クラス
　　　　　Sendenkaigi Co., Ltd.
　　　PT. Jott Condenced Italic /
　　　　　ZEN オールド明朝 R

084 Poster
TD. AD. 後 智仁　Tomohito Ushiro
　　　D. 村田 渉　Wataru Murata
　　　　　盛澤 優　Yu Morisawa
　　　CL. Non-commercial work

085 Poster
TD. 間宮伊吹　Ibuki Mamiya
CL. IMSST
PT. Custom-made for the project

086 Poster
TD. AD. D. 矢後直規　Naonori Yago
CL. Tama-pro
PT. S明朝

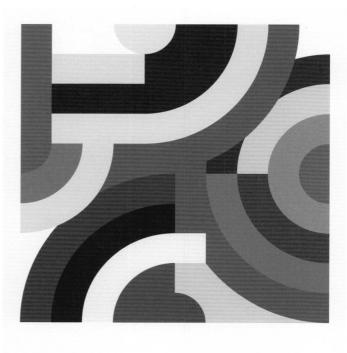

087

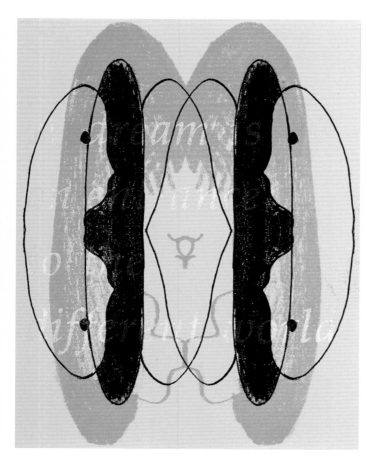

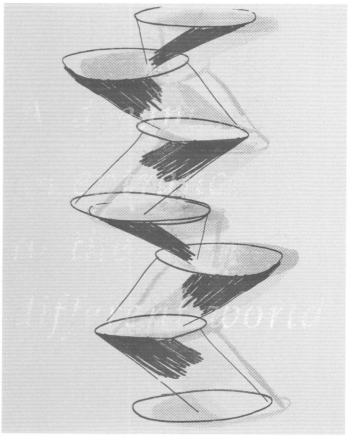

088

087 Poster
TD. CL. John Warwicker
　　CL. MADA
　　　　(Monash Art, Design & Architecture)
　　PT. MADA Light

088 Poster
TD. AD. 岩崎悦子　Etsuko Iwasaki
　　PD. 蝦名龍郎　Tatsuo Ebina
　　CL. (有)E.　E. Co., Ltd.
　　PT. Book Antiqus

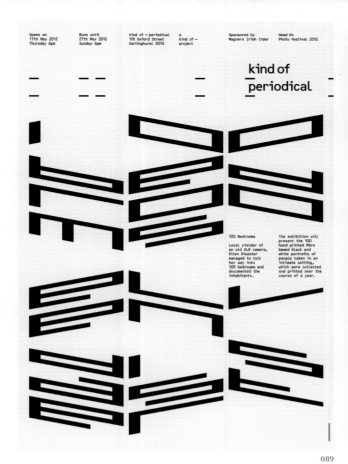

089

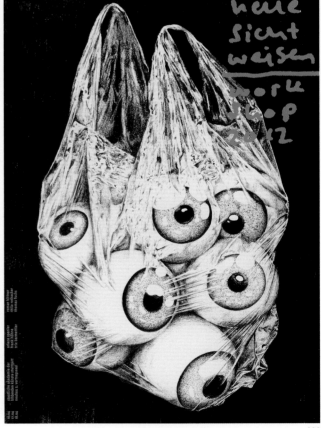

091

092

091 Poster
TD. Matthias Christ
    Philipp Schmidt
CL. State Academy of Art and Design, Stuttgart
PT. Custom-made for the project /
    Super Grotesk A

089 Poster
TD. Wing Lau
CL. Kind of gallery, Sydney

090 Poster
TD. Mark Boule
CL. ABK Stuttgart

092 Poster
TD. Mark Boule
CL. ABK Stuttgart

093

2012
HIROSHIMA
APPEALS

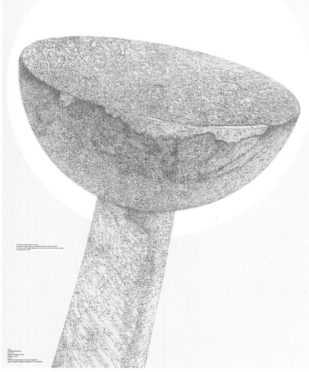

094

095

093 Poster
TD. AD. D. ST . 竹内佐織 Saori Takeuchi
　　 P . 島村朋子 Tomoko Shimamura
　HM. 梅澤優子 Yuko Umezawa
　　CL. Gold and Bouncy
　　PT. Custom-made for the project

094 Poster
TD. 奥村靫正 Yukimasa Okumura
CL. 日本グラフィックデザイナー協会 JAGDA
　(財) 広島国際文化財団
　Hiroshima International Cultural Foundation

095 Poster
TD. D. Ignatius Hernawan Tanzil
　　　 D. Agra Satria
　　CL. LeBoYe
　　PT. A-Z of the Archipelago /
　　　　Bulldog, Bonn

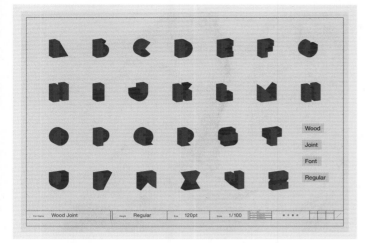

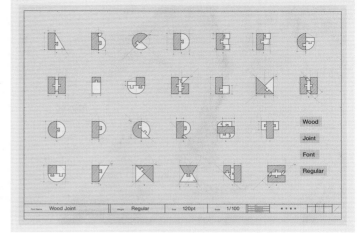

096

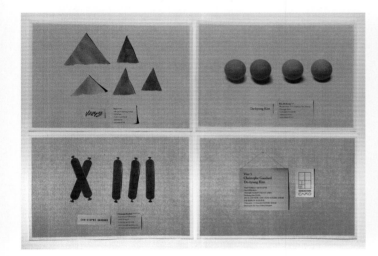

097

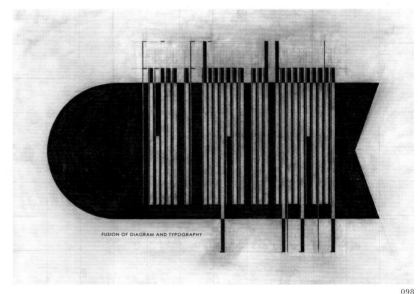

098

096 Poster
TD. AD. D. 松本幸二　Koji Matsumoto
　　CL. 上田英和建築計画事務所
　　　　Hidekazu Ueda Architects
　　PT. Custom-made for the project

097 Poster
TD. D. I. Do-hyung Kim
　　I. The Troxlers
　　CL. Doosung Paper
　　PT. Custom-made for the project／
　　　　Adobe Garamont Pro

098 Poster
TD. AD. D. 中山智裕　Tomohiro Nakayama
　　CL. Non-commercial work
　　PT. Century Gothic Regular

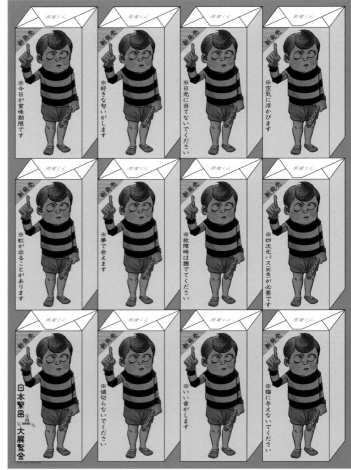

099 Poster
TD. AD. D. 土居裕彰　Hiroaki Doi
　　　D. P. 古田洋志　Hiroshi Furuta
　　　CL.「日常の変容展」運営委員会
　　　　　The Changes of Everyday exhibition-
　　　　　Steering Committee
　　　PT. リュウミン／Minion

100 Poster
TD. AD. D. 服部一成　Kazunari Hattori
　　　A. 水木プロダクション
　　　　　Mizuki Production
　　　CL. 日本繁昌大展覧会実行委員会
　　　PT. 教科書 ICA

101 Poster
TD. AD. D. 永樂雅也　Masaya Eiraku
　　　CL. Non-commercial work
　　　PT. Letter Gothic Std-Slanted

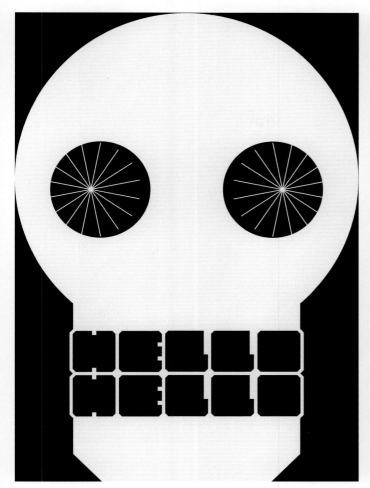

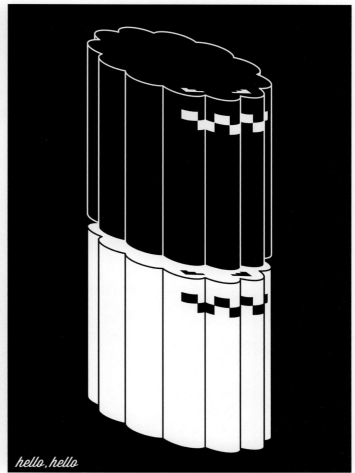

102

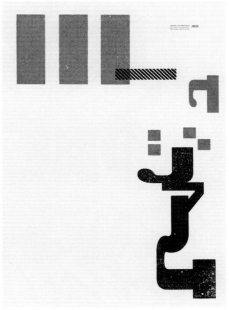

103

102 Poster
TD. 若杉智也 Tomoya Wakasugi
CL. Non-commercial work
PT. Custom-made for the project/
Wisdom Script

103 Poster
TD. AD. D. 林 規章 Noriaki Hayashi
CL. 女子美術大学
    Joshibi University of Art and Design
PT. Custom-made for the project

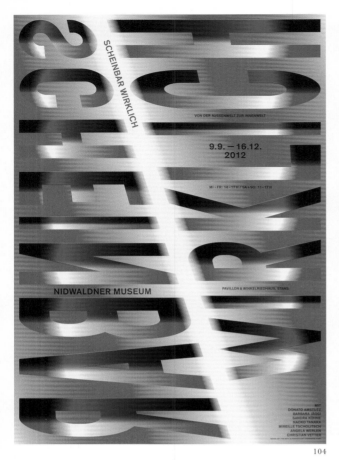

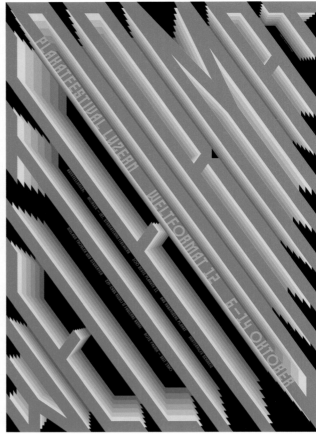

104

105

106

107

104 Poster
TD. D. Cybu Richli
    Fabienne Burri
CL. Museum of Canton Nidwalden
PT. Theinhart Medium

105 Poster
TD. D. Cybu Richli
    Fabienne Burri
CL. Weltformat Posterfestival Lucerne
PT. Custom-made for the project:
    C2F-Urban

106 Poster
TD. Jianping He
CL. ginza graphic gallery
PT. Custom-made for the project /
    Hiragino Kaku Gothic Pro /
    DIN

107 Poster
TD. AD. D. 原田祐馬　Yuma Harada
P. 増田好郎　Yoshiro Masuda
    太田拓実　Takumi Ota
CL. 静岡市美術館
    Shizuoka City Museum of Art
PT. こぶりなゴシック / DIN Next

108

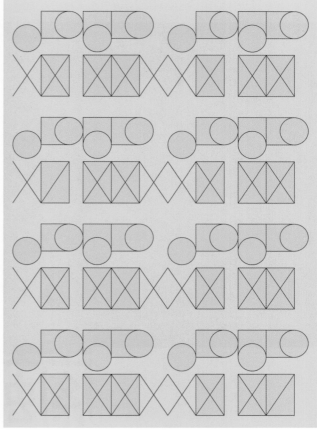

109

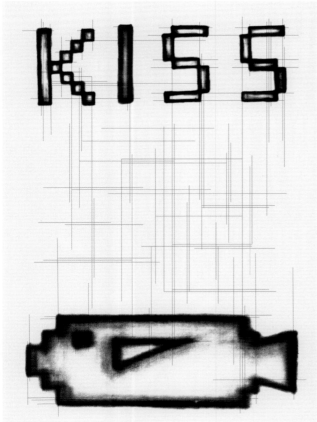

110

111

108 Poster
TD. D. I. Zhang Lin
　CL. Non-commercial work
　PT. Custom-made for the project

109 Poster
TD. AD. D. 岸 さゆみ　Sayumi Kishi
　CL. Non-commercial work
　PT. Custom-made for the project

110 Poster
TD. 菊井美沙希　Misaki Kikui
　CL. Non-commercial work

111 Poster
TD. AD. D. 北林 誠　Makoto Kitabayashi
　CL. Recto Verso Gallery
　PT. A-OTF A1明朝 Std Bold /
　　　Custom-made for the project /
　　　Helvetica Greek Upright

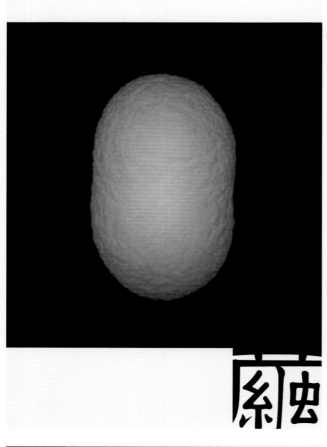
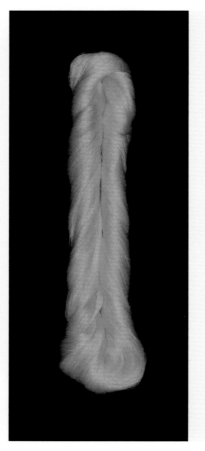

112

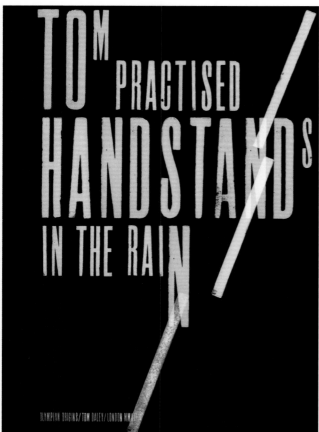

113

112 Poster
TD. AD. D. 林 規章　Noriaki Hayashi
P. 長沢慎一郎　Shinichiro Nagasawa
CL. 青山八木　Aoyama Yagi
PT. Custom-made for the project

113 Poster
TD. tomato / Jason Kedgley + Dylan Kendle
CL. FIT

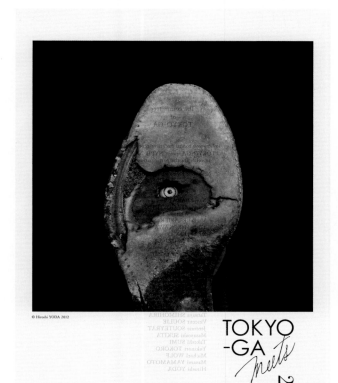

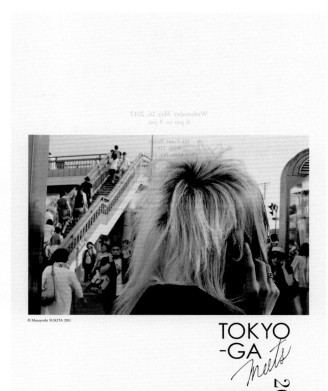

114

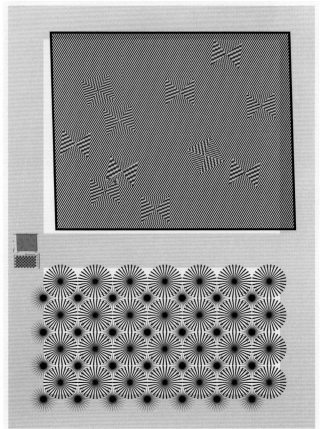

115

116

114 Poster
TD. AD. D. 内田真弓　Mayumi Uchida
CD. 柿木原政広　Masahiro Kakinokihara
P. 与田弘志　Hiroshi Yoda
鋤田正義　Masayoshi Sukita
CL. (株)クレー・インク　Klee Inc.
PT. Century Gothic / Bodoni BE

115 Poster
TD. 石見俊太郎　Shuntaro Iwami
CL. Non-commercial work
PT. Custom-made for the project

116 Poster
TD. 石見俊太郎　Shuntaro Iwami
CL. Non-commercial work
PT. Custom-made for the project

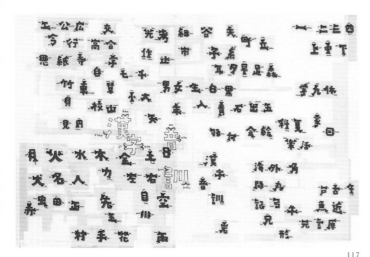

117

118

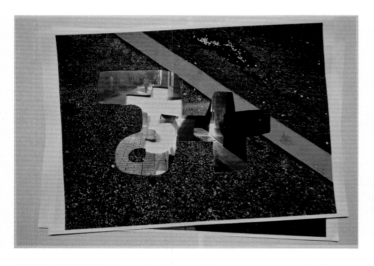

119

117 Poster
TD. AD. D. 根岸明寛 Akitomo Negishi
   CL. Non-commercial work
   PT. Hand writing

118 Poster
TD. Atelier mit Meerblick
   D. Mark Bohle
      Levin Stadler
   CL. Niklaus Troxler
   PT. Yeni Zaman

119 Poster
TD. AD. D. P. 根岸明寛 Akitomo Negishi
   CL. Non-commercial work
   PT. Hand writing

Editorial,
Book Design

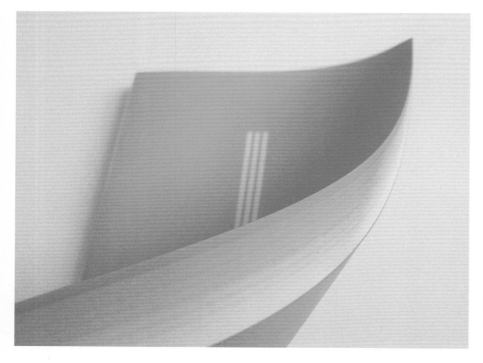

Prize Nominee Work

120 Note book
TD. Qing Zhao
    Yanrong Pan
CL. Hanqingtang design

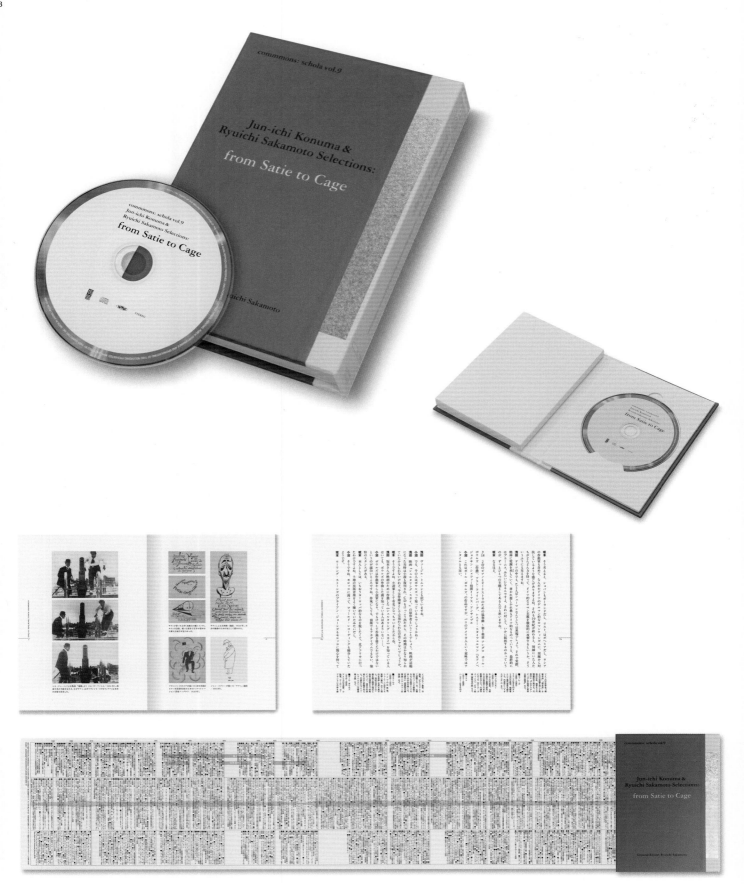

Prize Nominee Work

121 Book
TD. 中島英樹　Hideki Nakajima
CL. エイベックス・マーケティング（株）
　　Avex Marketing Inc.
PT. A1明朝 / Garamond

このCD、年表付きの本は、坂本龍一氏が総合監修をつとめ、全30巻の新しい音楽の百科辞典を目指し制作されています。年間、2冊が限界のため、揃うまで後10年かかる予定です。その時でも、その後でも古く感じさせないようなデザイン、タイポグラフィに注意しています。

This book, with a CD and a timeline, is produced as part of a new encyclopedia of music, to be composed of 30 volumes. Mr. Ryuichi Sakamoto serves as the editor-at-large. It will take another decade before completion because only two volumes can be produced annually at maximum. I pay attention to the design and typography such that they will not appear outdated when the encyclopedia is completed.

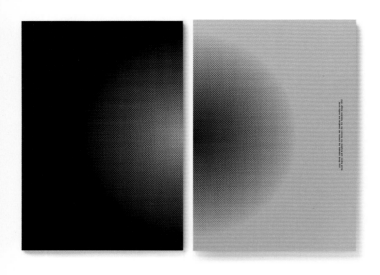

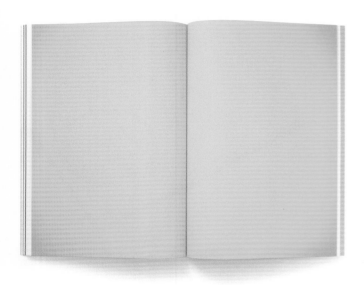
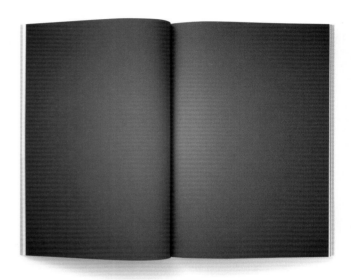

Prize Nominee Work

122 Book
TD. Brighten the Corners
　　(Billy Kiosoglou／Frank Philippin)
CL. Zumtobel Group
PT. Courier

光というテーマを受け、アニュアルレポートは、対照的だが相補的な２冊に分けた。一方は、クーリエ８ポイントのみを使用した、白黒の文字の詰まったタイプセット。もう一方は、純粋な色の文字のない１冊で、芸術家アニッシュ・カプーアの作品「Wounds and Absent Objects」の再解釈である。

Responding to the theme of light, the annual report was separated into two contrasting, but complementary volumes — a black & white, text-heavy volume typeset exclusively in Courier 8pt and a "silent" volume of pure colour, a reinterpretation of "Wounds and Absent Objects" by artist Anish Kapoor.

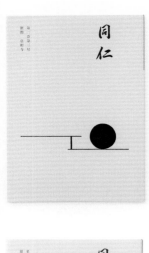

Prize Nominee Work

123 Magazine
TD. AD. D. 菊地敦己　Atsuki Kikuchi
CL. 銀閣慈照寺　Ginkaku-ji Temple
PT. 游明朝体

銀閣 慈照寺が発行する小誌『同仁』。茶花香をはじめ、宗教、哲学、美学、歴史、建築などの各分野の専門家が寄稿している。ノドの中央に穴をあけ糸で縛った製本が特徴。表紙絵は慈照寺の名所の一部を図案化したもの。

This magazine, Dojin, is issued by Jishoji Temple (Ginkakuji). Experts in the fields of chakako, religion, philosophy, art, history, and architecture, etc., contribute to it. The magazine is characterized by the way it is bound. A string passes through the holes at the Center of the inner margin. The cover painting was designed in the likeness of a famous part of the temple.

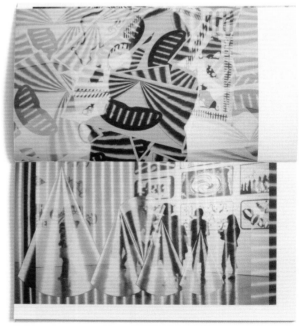

124 Book
TD. AD. D. I. 渡邉良重　Yoshie Watanabe
　　D. 岩永和也　Kazuya Iwanaga
　　CL.（株）リトル・モア
　　　　Little More Co., Ltd.

125 Catalogue
TD. AD. D. 仲條正義　Masayoshi Nakajo
　　CL.（株）資生堂　Shiseido Co., Ltd.
　　PT. 秀英初号明朝

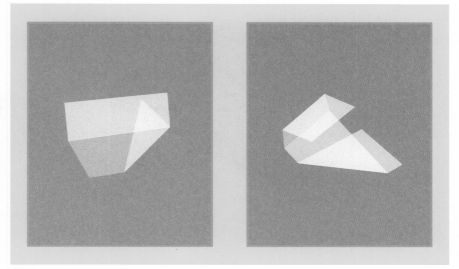

126

127

126 Art book
TD. AD. D. 山下ともこ　Tomoko Yamashita
CL. モンターニュ社 Montagne-sha
PT. Helvetiva Neue Light

127 Book
TD. AD. D. 菊地敦己　Atsuki Kikuchi
CL. BOOKPEAK
PT. 游明朝体 /
Custom-made for the project

128

129

130

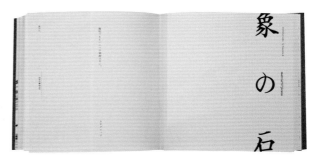

131

128 Book
TD. D. Wang Zhi Hong
 CL. Apexpress
 PT. Morisawa Ryumin Light /
　Berthold Akzidenz Grotesk

129 Book
TD.D. Wang Zhi Hong
 CL. Apexpress
 PT. Georgia /
　Morisawa Ryumin Regular

130 Annual book
TD. AD. 中島英樹　Hideki Nakajima
 D. 田中幸洋　Yukihiro Tanaka
 CL. 東京タイプディレクターズクラブ
　Tokyo Type Directors Club
 PT. A1明朝 / ゴシックMB101 /
　Garamond / Helvetica

131 Book
TD. AD. D. E. 山田和寛　Kazuhiro Yamada
 PRI-CO. 佐藤雅洋　Masahiro Sato
 CL. Nipponia
 PT. 弘道軒清朝体 / Tribute /
　築地活文舎五号仮名

132

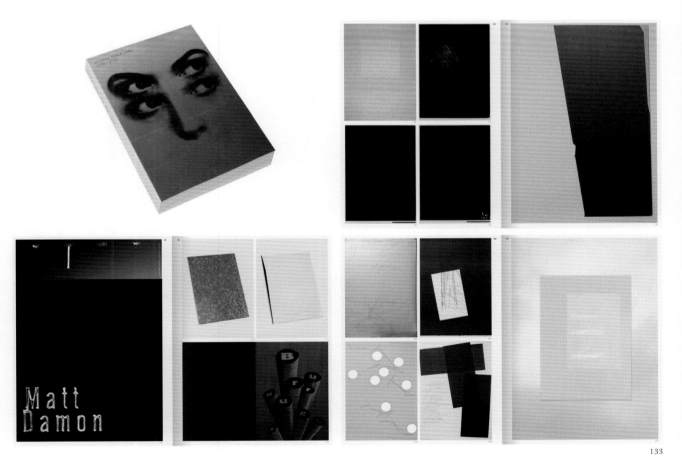

133

132 Book
TD. AD. 中島英樹　Hideki Nakajima
　　D. 三牧広宣　Hironobu Mimaki
　　CL. （株）大和プレス　Daiwa Press
　　PT. 中ゴシックBBB / Avenir

133 Book
TD. AD. 中島英樹　Hideki Nakajima
　　CL. （株）大和プレス　Daiwa Press
　　　　（株）二見書房
　　　　Futami Shobo Publishing Co., Ltd.
　　PT. 中ゴシックBBB / Avenir

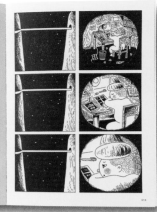

134

135

136

134 Book
TD. AD. D. 林 規章　　Noriaki Hayashi
　　　　D. 平野雅彦　Masahiko Hirano
　　　　CD. 吉田知哉　Tomoya Yoshida
　　　　TL. 佐賀一朗　Ichiro Saga
　　　　CL. (株)ビー・エヌ・エヌ新社　BNN, Inc.
　　　　PT. Custom-made for the project

135 Book
TD. Guang Yu
CL. SC, Badger & Press

136 Photo book
TD. AD. D. 青木克憲　　Katsunori Aoki
　　　　A. 安居智博　Tomohiro Yasui
　　　　P. 青山たかかず　Takakazu Aoyama
　　　　CL. バタフライ・ストローク・株式會社
　　　　　Butterfly・Stroke Inc.
　　　　ヤスイ工房　Yasui Factory

137

138

139

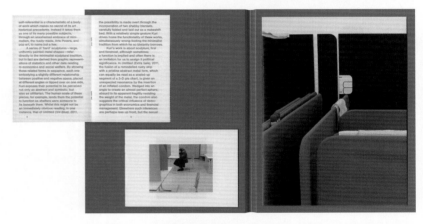

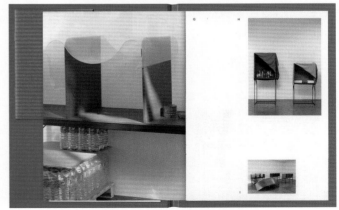

140

137 Book
TD. AD. D. 服部一成 Kazunari Hattori
CL. (有) 四月社
　Shigatsusha Inc.
PT. TBちび丸ゴシック

138 Magazine
TD. AD. D. 服部一成 Kazunari Hattori
CL. (株) リトル・モア
　Little More Co., Ltd.
PT. 太ゴ B101

139 Annual book
TD. AD. D. 仲條正義 Masayoshi Nakajo
CL. 東京タイプディレクターズクラブ
　Tokyo Type Directors Club
PT. Custom-made for the project /
　DIN Schrift

140 Art book
TD. OK-RM, London
P. Marius W. Hansen
CL. South London Gallery
PT. Helvetica BQ Roman

141

142

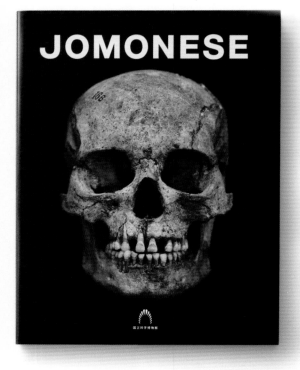

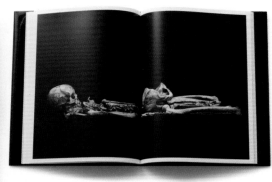

143

141 Art book
TD. AD. D. 中村至男　Norio Nakamura
　　　CL. （株）福音館書店
　　　　　Fukuinkan Shoten Publishers, Inc.
　　　PT. DNP秀英体丸ゴシック

142 Photo book
TD. AD. 葛西 薫　Kaoru Kasai
　　　D. 増田 豊　Yutaka Masuda
　　　P. 上田義彦　Yoshihiko Ueda
　　CL. （株）ワニブックス
　　　　Wani Books Co., Ltd.
　　PT. MODERNIQUE

143 Photo book
TD. AD. 佐藤 卓　Taku Satoh
　　　D. 野間真吾　Shingo Noma
　　　P. 上田義彦　Yoshihiko Ueda
　　CL. 国立科学博物館
　　　　National Museum of Nature and Science
　　PT. Custom-made for the project/
　　　　Century Old Style Std / Helvetica Neue

13

144

145

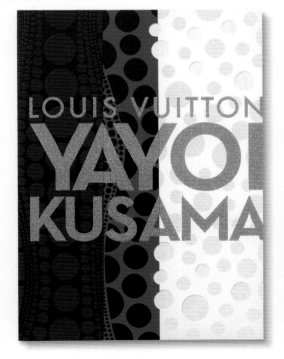

146

144 Book
TD. AD. 原田祐馬　Yuma Harada
　　D. 山副佳祐　Keisuke Yamazoe
　　P. 増田好郎　Yoshiro Masuda
　　E. 多田智美　Tomomi Tada
　　　坂本美幸　Miyuki Sakamoto
　　　永江 大　Dai Nagae
　CL. 総合資格学院　Sogo Shikaku Co., Ltd.
　PT. 中ゴシック / 秀英丸ゴシック / tlas Grotesk

145 Book
TD. AD. D. 菊地敦己　Atsuki Kikuchi
　CL. （株）デコ　Deco
　PT. 游明朝体 / Perpetua

146 Art book
　TD. Theseus Chan
　　D. MAA (Lead Designer) / Geraldine Chua /
　　　Farah Siman / Ernest Ho
PRI. CON. also DOMINIE
PRO-CO. Ashu Nakanishiya
　CL. Louis Vuitton Japan
　PT. Modified Neutra

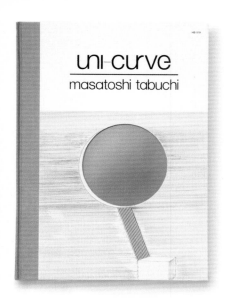

147

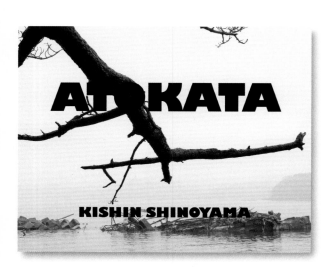

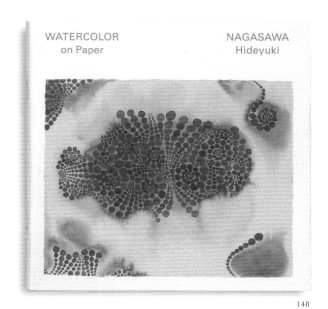

148

149

147 Art book
TD. AD. D. 松田洋和　Hirokazu Matsuda
　　I. 田渕正敏　Masatoshi Tabuchi
CL. Hekichi
PT. Helvetica Neue /
　　Custom-made for the project

148 Book
TD. AD. D. 鈴木壮一　Soichi Suzuki
A. CL. 長沢秀之　NAGASAWA Hideyuki
PD. 熊倉桂三　Katsumi Kumakura
PM. 板倉利樹　Toshiki Itakura
PT. Univers

149 Photo book
TD. 奥村靫正　Yukimasa Okumura
CL.（株）日経BP社
　　Nikkei Business Publications, Inc.

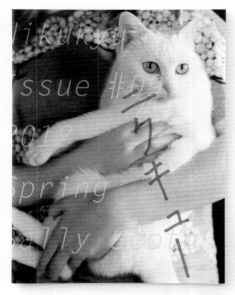

150

Entrance

151

Bring a new consciousness to being through coming into contact with various energies

152

150 Catalogue
TD. AD. D. 菊地敦己　Atsuki Kikuchi
CL. (株)ニューヨーカー　Newyorker Ltd.
PT. Custom-made for the project /
　游明朝体 / Letter Gothic

151 Catalogue
TD. AD. 岩崎悦子　Etsuko Iwasaki
　D. 斉藤友秀　Tomohide Saito
PD. 蝦名龍郎　Tatsuo Ebina
CL. (有)E.　E. Co., Ltd.
PT. Book Antiqus

152 Book
TD. Theseus Chan
　D. Farah Siman (Lead Designer) /
　MAA / Geraldine Chua / Ernest Ho
　E. Mutsuko Ota / Shogo Hagiwara
PRI. CON. also DOMINIE
PRO-CO. Ashu Nakanishiya
CL. JTQ Inc.
PT. Customized Fette Egyptienne

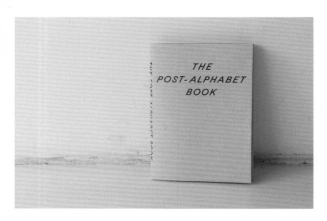 

153

154

155

156

154 Art book
TD. AD. D. 白澤真生　Masao Shirasawa
CD. A. 荒木由香里　Yukari Araki
P. 尾崎芳弘　Yoshihiro Ozaki
CL. MYY BOOKS
PT. 筑紫明朝 / Orator

156 Art book
TD. Fraser Muggeridge studio
D. Stephen Barrett
Fraser Muggeridge
CL. Focal Point Gallery
PT. Times / Helios

153 Book
TD. AD. D. 軍司匡寛　Tadahiro Gunji
CL. Non-commercial work
PT. Costomized LL Circular

155 Book
TD. 宮川　宏　Hiroshi Miyakawa
CL. Piece to Peace

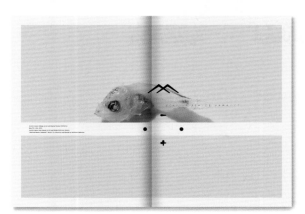
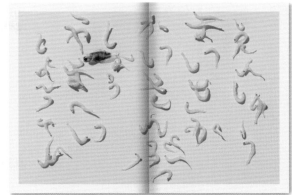

157

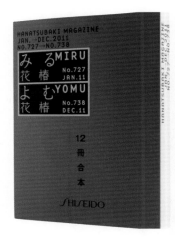

158

159

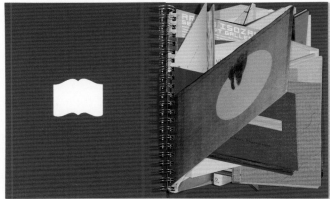

160

157 Art book
TD. AD. D. 杢谷吉也　Yoshinari Mokutani
　　　P. 堀口眞澄　Masumi Horiguchi
　　　CL. 女子美術大学短期大学部
　　　　　Joshibi University of Art and Design
　　　PT. Custom-made for the project

158 Book
TD. AD. D. 仲條正義　Masayoshi Nakajo
　　　CD. 上岡典彦　Norihiko Ueoka
　　　CL. （株）資生堂　Shiseido Co., Ltd.

159 Book
TD. Qing Zhao
　　Weiwei Zhou
CL. Jie Yu

160 Book
TD. AD. D. 永井裕明　Hiroaki Nagai
　　　D. 藤井 圭　Kei Fujii
　　　本間 亮　Ryo Honma
　　　P. 金子親一　Shinichi Kaneko
　　　CO. 堀川玲菜　Rena Horikawa
　　　CL. N.G.Inc.
　　　PT. 宋朝体

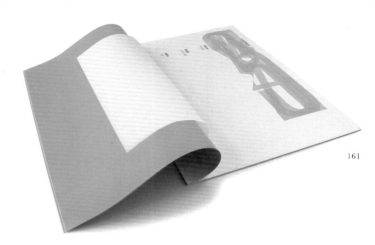

161

162

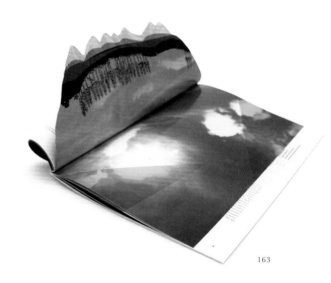

163

164

162 Book
TD. He Jun
CL. Guancxi Normal University Press
PT. M Song / M Fang Song /
Linotype Centennial

161 Book
TD. Lin, Chi Tai
CL. Self-initiated

163 Book
TD. Nicolas Haeberli
Seán Kennedy
CL. economiesuisse
PT. DIN

164 Book
TD. AD. D. 菊地敦己　Atsuki Kikuchi
CL. BOOKPEAK
PT. 游築見出し明朝体 /
New Century Schoolbook /
Custom-made for the project

165

166

167

168

165 Photo book
TD. AD. 中島英樹　Hideki Nakajima
　　D. 古谷哲朗　Tetsuro Furutani
CL. Izu Photo Museum
PT. 見出しゴシックMB31／
　　Helvetica

166 Photo book
TD. AD. D. 服部一成　Kazunari Hattori
　　A. 中平卓馬　Takuma Nakahira
CL. オシリス　Osiris Co., Ltd.
PT. Berthold Akzidenz Grotesk／
　　太ゴB101

167 Book
TD. AD. D. 服部一成　Kazunari Hattori
CL. （株）リトル・モア
　　Little More Co., Ltd.
PT. イワタ明朝体オールド／
　　Futura Light Condensed

168 Book
TD. 佐藤亜沙美　Asami Sato
CL. 日経BP社
　　Nikkei Business Publications, Inc.
PT. 毎日新聞明朝／筑紫明朝／
　　Bodoni Old Face

169

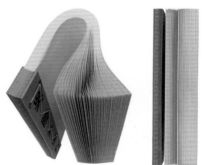

170

A G I
ALLIANCE GRAPHIQUE
INTERNATIONALE
JAPAN
2012

171

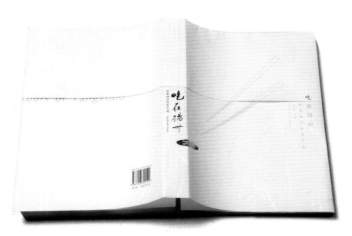

172

170 Book
TD. AD. D. Kuokwai Cheong
D. Lai Houiok
CL. Art Teacher Communication
Association of Macao
PT. Std / DFHei / Helvetica Neue

169 Book
TD. Qing Zhao
CL. Hanqingtang design

171 Book
TD. AD. D. 服部一成　Kazunari Hattori
CL. ギンザ・グラフィック・ギャラリー
ginza graphic gallery
PT. MSゴシック

172 Book
TD. Qing Zhao
Shuying Sun
CL. Phoenix science press

173

174

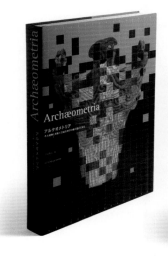

175

176

173 Book
TD. AD. D. 平野篤史　Atsushi Hirano
CL. (株) LEWS纏
PT. Custom-made for the project

174 Book
TD. 佐藤亜沙美　Asami Sato
CL. (株) 平凡社
　　Heibonsha Limited, Publishers
PT. 筑紫A丸ゴシック / 筑紫明朝 /
　　游ゴシック体 / 毎日新聞明朝 /
　　游築初号ゴシック

175 Book
TD. AD. D. 中野豪雄　Takeo Nakano
D. 鈴木直子　Naoko Suzuki
CL. 東京大学総合研究博物館
　　The University Museum,
　　the University of Tokyo
PT. 本明朝 / Rotis

176 Book
TD. AD. D. 樋口寛人　Hiroto Higuchi
PD. 築山万里子　Mariko Tsukiyama
CL. トンネル　Tunnel
PT. Caslon

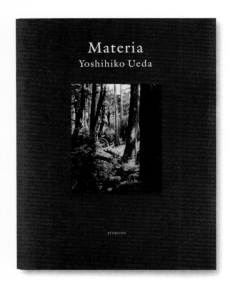

177

178

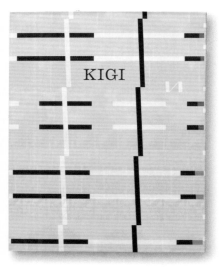

179

177 Photo book
TD. AD. 中島英樹　Hideki Nakajima
　　 D. 古谷哲朗　Tetsuro Furutani
CL. （株）求龍堂
　　Kyuryudo Art Publishing Co., Ltd.
PT. きざはし金陵 / Galliard

178 Photo book
TD. AD. 葛西 薫　Kaoru Kasai
　　 P. 川内倫子　Rinko Kawauchi
CL. （株）青幻舎　Seigensha., Ltd.
PT. Perpetua / 筑紫明朝

179 Book
TD. AD. D. 植原亮輔　Ryosuke Uehara
　　　　 渡邉良重　Yoshie Watanabe
　　 D. 二瓶 渡　Wataru Nihei
　　　　 汐田瀬里菜　Serina Shiota
CL. （株）リトル・モア
　　Little More Co., Ltd.

180

181

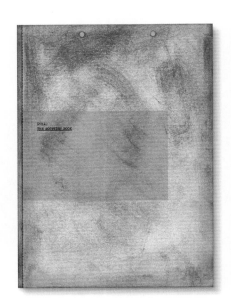

182

181 Program
TD. Neeser & Müller
D. I. Thomas Neeser
    Thomas Müller
    Dominique Raemy
P. Kathrin Schulthess
CL. Festival Rümlingen, Neue Musik,
    Theater, Installationen
PT. Custom-made for the project, Line, Norit

182 Book
TD. Theseus Chan
D. Geraldine Chua
E. Alison Harley
CON-DI. Hywel Davies
PRI. CON. also DOMINIE
PRO-CO. Oona Brown
CL. The School of Textiles and Design-
    Heriot Watt University

180 Book
TD. D. Pedro Inoue
CL. Gestalten
PT. Priori Serif / Shango

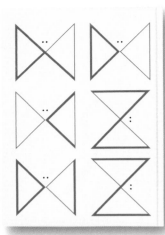

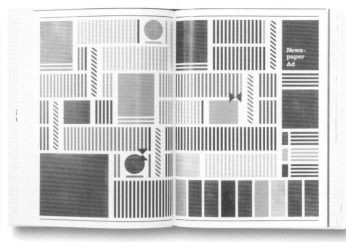

183

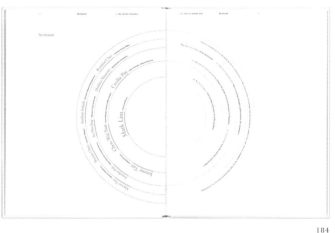

185

184

186

183 Annual book
TD. AD. 佐野研二郎　Kenjiro Sano
D. 石黒篤史　Atsushi Ishiguro
塚本 陽　Kiyoshi Tsukamoto
P. 森本美絵　Mie Morimoto
CL. 東京アートディレクターズクラブ
Tokyo Art Directors Club
PT. Clarendon

184 Annual report
TD. D. Lee Weicong
CD. Larry Peh
CL. General Insurance -
Association of Singapore
PT. Conqueror AW Didot /
Signerica / Granjon

185 Book
TD. AD. 葛西 薫　Kaoru Kasai
D. 引地摩里子　Mariko Hikichi
CL. (株) 河出書房新社
Kawade Shobo Shinsha, Publishers
PT. Custom-made for the project

186 Magazine
TD. Sonya Dyakova
CL. frieze

187

188

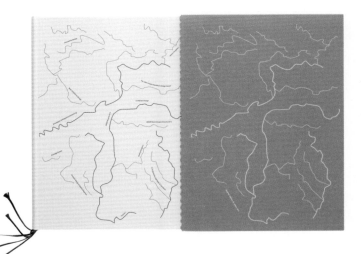
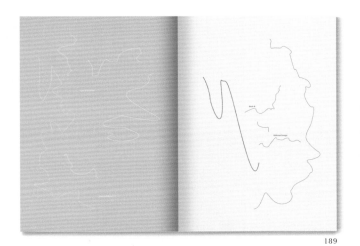

189

190

187 Magazine
TD. Leslie David
P. Ami Sioux
　　Estelle Hanania
CL. NIKE
PT. Futura

188 Book
TD. AD. 葛西 薫　Kaoru Kasai
　　D. 増田 豊　Yutaka Masuda
　　I. 大橋 歩　Ayumi Ohashi
CL. (株)マガジンハウス
　　Magazine House, Ltd.
PT. Custom-made for the project

189 Annual book
TD. AD. D. 丸橋 桂　Katsura Marubashi
CL. 日本グラフィックデザイナー協会
　　JAGDA
PT. akkurat

190 Editorial
TD. AD. 大原大次郎　Daijiro Ohara
P. ホンマタカシ　Takashi Homma
CL. (株)リトル・モア
　　Little More Co., Ltd.

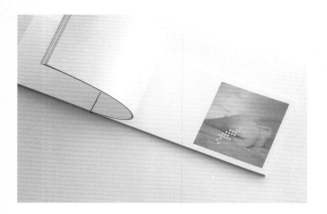

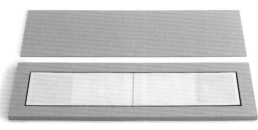

191

192

193

1000%
の建築

1000%
の建築

1000% の建築

谷尻 誠

すぐわかる?!
毎日を感動にかえる発想法

194

191 Photo book
TD. AD. D. 池上直樹　Naoki Ikegami
　　　P. 岩本竜典　Tatsunori Iwamoto
　　　CL. 岩本竜典写真事務所
　　　　　Tatsunori Iwamoto Photo Studio
　　　PT. 丸明オールド

192 Book
TD. Juanjo Justicia
CL. Maira Soares

193 Note book
TD. D. Franziska Morlok
　　　Till Beckmann
　　　Jenny Hasselbach
CL. Revolver Publishing
PT. Schulbuch

194 Book
TD. AD. D. 竹田麻衣子　Maiko Takeda
　　　CD. 谷尻 誠　Makoto Tanijiri
　　　PR. 武井実子　Jitsuko Takei
　　　I. 須山奈津希　Natsuki Suyama
　　　E. 大須賀 順　Jun Osuka
　　　C. 武井カルロス正樹　Masaki Carlos Takei
　　　CL. (株)エクスナレッジ　X-Knowledge Co., Ltd.
　　　PT. 游ゴシック体/活版活字組合せ/Custom-made for the project

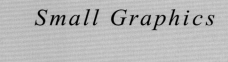

Small Graphics

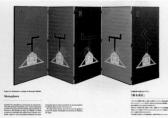

Prize Nominee Work

195 Art pieces
TD. AD. 浅葉克己　Katsumi Asaba
　　D. 石原千明　Chiaki Ishihara
CL. SAP
PT. 游明朝体 / Custom-made for the project

ギンザ・グラフィック・ギャラリー
第314回企画展

Alliance Graphique Internationale 国際グラフィック連盟

2012年10月4日（木）–10月27日（土）

永井一正
五十嵐威暢
勝井三雄
中村 誠
浅葉克己
佐藤晃一
松永 真
サイトウマコト
松井桂三
佐藤 卓
中島英樹
新島 実
三木 健
U.G.サトー
蛯名龍郎
北川一成
澤田泰廣
杉崎真之助
長友啓典
原 研哉
松下 計
葛西 薫
立花文穂
佐藤可士和
永井一史
服部一成
平野敬子
Gunter Rambow
Seymour Chwast
Holger Matthies
Ivan Chermayeff
Jan Rajlich sen.
Pierre Bernard
Uwe Loesch
Niklaus Troxler
Kit Hinrichs
Lars Müller
Paula Scher
Ralph Schraivogel
Kan Tai-Keung
Kari Piippo
Michel Bouvet
Philippe Apeloig
David Tartakover
Stefan Sagmeister
Vladimir Chaïka
Cyan
Leonardo Sonnoli
Wang Xu
Freeman Lau
István Orosz
Stanley Wong
Tommy Li
Wang Min
Jianping He
Majid Abbasi

ggg

ギンザ・グラフィック・ギャラリー
第314回企画展

Alliance Graphique Internationale 国際グラフィック連盟

2012年10月4日（木）–10月27日（土）
11:00–19:00（土曜日は18:00まで）日曜・祝日休館 入場無料
〒104-0061 東京都中央区銀座7-7-2 DNP銀座ビル1F Tel. 03-3571-5206

永井一正 Kazumasa NAGAI
五十嵐威暢 Takenobu IGARASHI
勝井三雄 Mitsuo KATSUI
中村 誠 Makoto NAKAMURA
浅葉克己 Katsumi ASABA
佐藤晃一 Koichi SATO
松永 真 Shin MATSUNAGA
サイトウマコト Makoto SAITO
松井桂三 Keizo MATSUI
佐藤 卓 Taku SATOH
中島英樹 Hideki NAKAJIMA
新島 実 Minoru NIISHMA
三木 健 Ken MIKI
U.G.サトー U.G. SATO
蛯名龍郎 Tatsuo EBINA
北川一成 Issey KITAGAWA
澤田泰廣 Yasuhiro SAWADA
杉崎真之助 Shinsuke SUGISAKI
長友啓典 Kenya HARA
松下 計 Kei MATSUSHITA
葛西 薫 Kaoru KASAI
立花文穂 Fumio TACHIBANA
佐藤可士和 Kashiwa SATO
永井一史 Kazufumi NAGAI
服部一成 Kazunari HATTORI
平野敬子 Keiko HIRANO
Gunter Rambow グンター・ランボー
Seymour Chwast シーモア・クワスト
Holger Matthies オルガー・マチス
Ivan Chermayeff アイヴァン・チャマイエフ
Jan Rajlich sen. ヤン・ライリッヒ
Pierre Bernard ピエール・ベルナール
Uwe Loesch ウヴェ・レシュ
Niklaus Troxler ニクラウス・トロックスラー
Kit Hinrichs キット・ヒンリッチ
Lars Müller ラース・ミュラー
Paula Scher ポーラ・シェア
Ralph Schraivogel ラルフ・シュライフォーゲル
Kan Tai-Keung カン・タイケン
Kari Piippo カリ・ピッポ
Michel Bouvet ミシェル・ブーヴェ
Philippe Apeloig フィリップ・アペロワ
David Tartakover デイヴィッド・タルタコーバ
Stefan Sagmeister ステファン・サグマイスター
Vladimir Chaïka ウラジーミル・チャイカ
Cyan シアン
Leonardo Sonnoli レオナルド・ソノリ
Wong Xu ワン・シュ
Freeman Lau フリーマン・ラウ
István Orosz イストヴァン・オロス
Stanley Wong スタンリー・ウォン
Tommy Li トミー・リー
Wang Min ワン・ミン
Jianping He ジャンピン・ヘ
Majid Abbasi マジッド・アッバシ

ggg

ギンザ・グラフィック・ギャラリー
第314回企画展

Alliance Graphique Internationale 国際グラフィック連盟

2012年10月4日（木）–10月27日（土）

AGI
国際グラフィック連盟（Alliance Graphique
Internationale）の略称。1952年にフランスの
パリで創立されたグラフィックデザイナーの団体。
現在では世界35カ国、398名（日本27名）がメン
バー。創立当初から毎年開催地を変えデザイ
ン総会を開催してきた。会期中には展覧会やセ
ミナーなど様々な交流が行われる。日本では1988
年（東京）と2006年（東京・京都）に総会を開催。
今年は9月に香港で開催される。

オープニングパーティ
日時 10月4日（木）17:30–19:00
会場 ギンザ・グラフィック・ギャラリー

トークショー
会期中にAGI会員によるギャラリートークを開催します。
詳細は決まりしだいギャラリーHPにてお知らせします。

ギンザ・グラフィック・ギャラリー
〒104-0061
中央区銀座7-7-2 DNP銀座ビル
Tel. 03-3571-5206
Fax. 03-3289-1389
開館 11:00–19:00（土曜日は18:00まで）
休館 日曜・祝日／地下鉄銀座駅下車徒歩5分
www.dnp.co.jp/foundation

ggg

Prize Nominee Work

196 DM/Flyer

TD. AD. 浅葉克己　Katsumi Asaba
　　　D. 金森 彩　　Aya Kanamori
　　　CL. ギンザ・グラフィック・ギャラリー
　　　　　ginza graphic gallery
　　　PT. 游明朝体／石井中太ゴシック

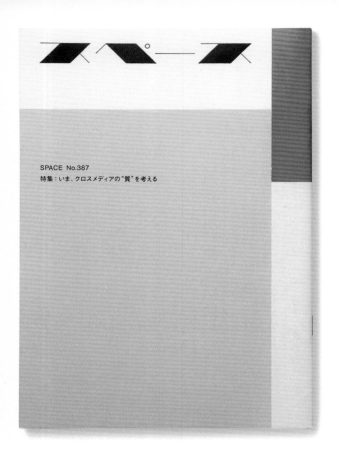

SPACE No.387
特集：いま、クロスメディアの"質"を考える

SPACE No.388
特集：一倉宏×葛西薫 特別対談「広告の今、広告の未来」

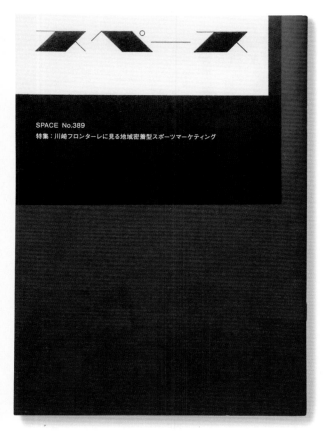

SPACE No.389
特集：川崎フロンターレに見る地域密着型スポーツマーケティング

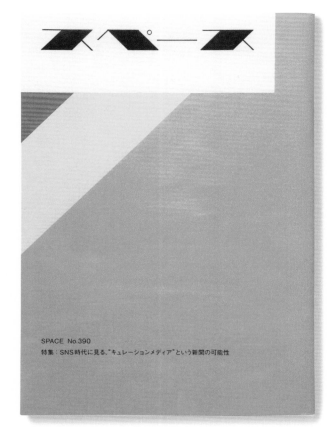

SPACE No.390
特集：SNS時代に見る、"キュレーションメディア"という新聞の可能性

Prize Nominee Work

197 PR magazine
TD. AD. 葛西 薫　Kaoru Kasai
　　　D. 増田 豊　Yutaka Masuda
　　 CL. （株）毎日新聞社
　　　　 The Mainichinews Papers
　　 PT. Custom-made for the project

毎日新聞社の広報誌。方眼紙の上に水平線と45度のラインだけでレタリングしているうちにこんなロゴタイプができた。このレトロな形に触発されて、背景の色面もロゴも手描きに。その時間、デザインの勉強をしているようで楽しい。

Lettering on graph paper using only horizontal and 45-degree lines resulted in this logotype for Mainichi Newspapers' PR magazine. This retrospective shape led me to handwrite both the colored background and the logo. I enjoyed this process, which was much like learning design.

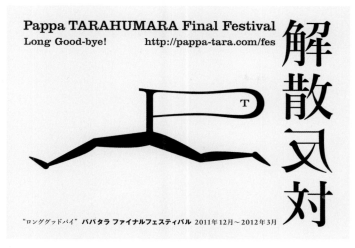

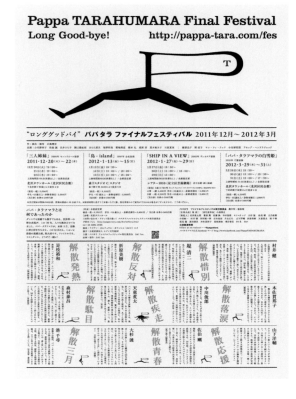

Prize Nominee Work

198 DM／Invitation／T-shirt

TD. AD. 葛西 薫　　Kaoru Kasai
　　D. 引地摩里子　Mariko Hikichi
　　C. 安藤 隆　　Takashi Ando
CL. (株)サイ　　Sai Inc.
PT. Clarendon

「パパタラフマラ」の解散にあたり、ラスト1年間、賑やかにさまざまな記念イベントを行なった。その波瀾の30年を振り返り、未来的過去なのか過去的未来なのか、この舞踏集団らしい "人騒がせな" デザインをと思った。

The dissolution of the "Pappa TARAHUMARA" dance group was accompanied by a variety of commemorative events over the last year. Looking back at their eventful 30 years, I tried to create an "impactful" design suitable for this group, expressing a futuristic past or a past-like future.

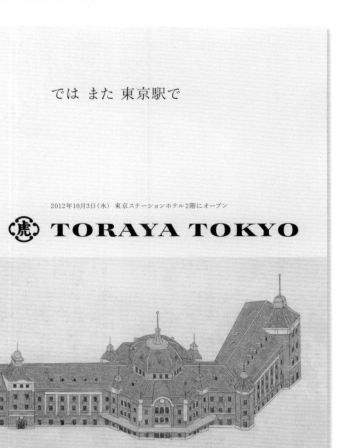

では また 東京駅で

2012年10月3日（水）東京ステーションホテル2階にオープン

TORAYA TOKYO

Prize Nominee Work

199 Invitation
TD. AD. D. 中本陽子　Yoko Nakamoto
CD. AD. 葛西 薫　Kaoru Kasai
　　　I. Philippe Weisbecker
　　　C. 小宮由美子　Yumiko Komiya
　　PR. 坂東美和子　Miwako Bando
　　　　常木宏之　Hiroyuki Tsuneki
　　CL. Toraya Tokyo
　　PT. RcP本明朝－M新小がな

復元された東京駅丸の内駅舎に TORAYA TOKYO がオープンし、その告知のツールです。簡素な作りを念頭におきつつ、素材やレイアウトに細心しました。制作時に駅舎は建設途中でしたので、模型を手作りし、独自のアングルを探りました。

This is an advertising tool for TORAYA TOKYO, which opened in the restored Tokyo Station Marunouchi Building. With a simple structure in mind, I paid utmost attention to the material and layout. The building was still under construction when I created this, so I made a model and explored a unique angle.

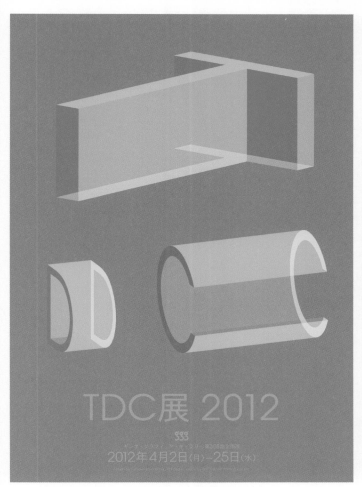

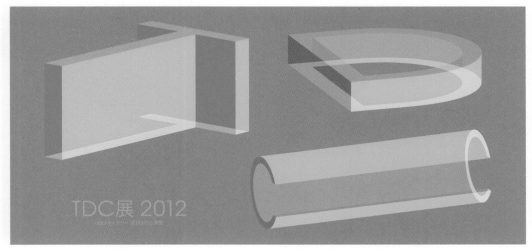

Prize Nominee Work

200 DM / Flyer
TD. AD. D. 山下ともこ Tomoko Yamashita
CL. 東京タイプディレクターズクラブ
Tokyo Type Directors Club
PT. Custom-made for the project

TDC展の告知のチラシ・招待状・ハガキ等のデザイン。アルファベットの頭文字を自由に立体的にしてみた。軽やかでありつつ、ごろんと置いてある感じを出してみたかった。プロセスインクのイエローとブラックをもちいた2色刷り。背景は白でもなく、黒でもなく、中間のグレーを選んだ。

I tried to freely use initials for three-dimensional designs in the advertisement flyer, invitation card, and post card, etc., of the TDC Exhibition. I wanted to give a light feeling of "just being left there." This is printed in two-process ink colors (yellow and black) with the background in gray between white and black.

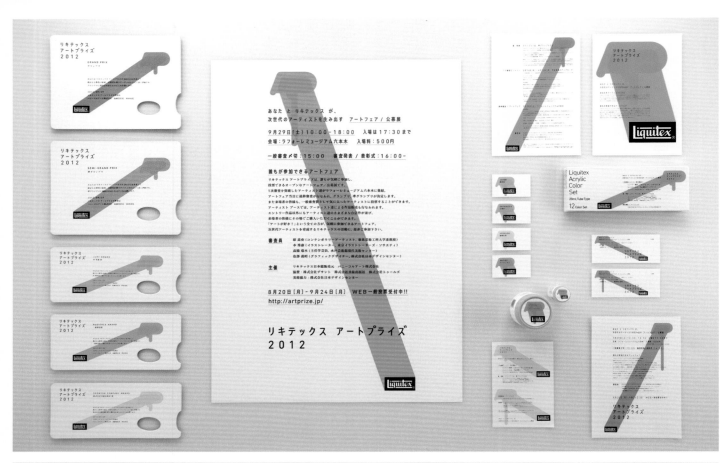

Prize Nominee Work

201 Diploma / Application requirements
TD. AD. D. 色部義昭　Yoshiaki Irobe
CL. バニーコルアート
bonny Col Art Co., Ltd.
PT. Custom-made for the project /
DIN Next Rounded / S明朝体

絵の具メーカー主催の公募展『Liquitex Art Prize』のためのグラフィックス。メディアごとに色と形に変化を与えながら、アクリル絵の具ののびやかな質感が受け手の脳裏に瑞々しく記憶されるよう心がけた。ペーパーパレット型の賞状は商品の抜き型を流用。コストを抑えながらリアリティを追求した。

These are graphics for "Liquitex Art Prize," an exhibition sponsored by a paint manufacturer. I changed colors and shapes for each media and tried to ensure that the smooth texture of acrylic paint will vividly remain in viewers' minds. I used a product punch for the paper palette-shaped award certificate to pursue this reality while reducing cost.

Prize Nominee Work

202 Calendar
TD. AD. D. 仲條正義　Masayoshi Nakajo
CD. 尾形久兵衛　Kyubei Ogata
CL. （株）資生堂　Shiseido Co., Ltd.
PT. Custom-made for the project

昔は大きなカレンダーは壁の穴かくしなど役に
たったようだが、無用の長物で、カレンダー展
にも応募が少なくなったと思われる。永年手が
けているので私としては愛着がある。カレンダ
ー展では毎年小さな賞しかいただいていないが、
TDCで評価されて嬉しい。

Large calendars were once useful for covering holes in walls, but they can no longer be used for that purpose—there seems to be only a few entries in calendar exhibitions nowadays. I have long been engaged in calendar production and have an attachment to that. I have won modest awards at annual calendar exhibitions, and I am happy to be recognized by the Tokyo TDC.

Prize Nominee Work

203 DM
TD. AD. CD. 植原亮輔　Ryosuke Uehara
D. 汐田瀬里菜　Serina Shiota
CL. シアタープロダクツ
Theatre Products
PT. Bodoni/
Custom-made for the project

2006年から続いているDMの仕事。DMとはいえ、毎回「ファッションの戦場に掲げる旗」のようなつもりで制作させてもらっています。主に女性をターゲットにしているブランドですが、少しだけベクトルを反対方向に振ることで、イメージを固定しないで分散。「わかりやす過ぎない感じ」もまた重要だと考えています。

I have been continuously involved in this direct-mail production since 2006. Although it is a mere direct mail, I always intend to "post a flag in the fashion battlefield." The primary target of the brand is females, but I try to disperse the image shown, instead of fixing it, by directing the vector slightly to the opposite side. I felt that something being "not too easy to understand" is also important.

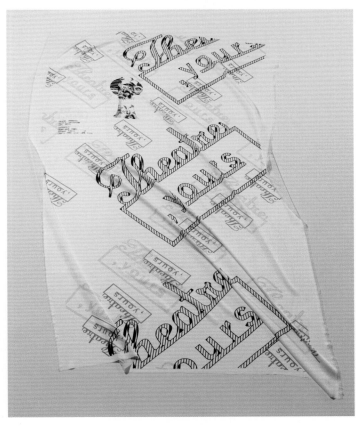

Prize Nominee Work

204 Textile
TD. AD. CD. 植原亮輔　Ryosuke Uehara
D. 汐田瀬里菜　Serina Shiota
CL. シアタープロダクツ
Theatre Products

「自分でつくる洋服」をテーマにしたコレクションの商品としてテキスタイル（柄とカタチ）をデザインさせてもらいました。また、この洋服は、僕がデザインした壺のカタチ（洋服の展開図＝パターン）をシアタープロダクツの武内さんが、その壺のフォルムを変えずに洋服として成立するように設計したものです。

I designed this textile (pattern and shape) as part of a collection on the theme of "handmade dresses." Mr. Takeuchi of THEATER PRODUCTS designed this dress, based on the shape of a vase that I designed (i.e., through a part breakdown of the dress; more specifically, the sewing pattern), maintaining the original vase shape.

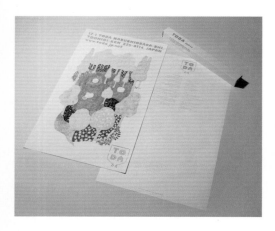

Prize Nominee Work

205 DM / Poster / Ticket

TD. AD. 植原亮輔　Ryosuke Uehara
　　CD. 豊嶋秀樹　Hideki Toyoshima
　　 D. 仲子なつ美　Natsumi Nakako
　　 C. 加藤麻司　Asaji Kato
　　 P. 後藤武浩　Takehiro Goto
　　CL. 森をひらくこと T.O.D.A.
　　PT. Custom-made for the project

人と共生する美しい森を復活させたいと、所有者である戸田さんは閉ざされた那須の森を開き、文化が生まれていく3つの建物をつくることを決めた。学校のような場所にという意向からあるルールや秩序をデザインに感じさせたいと思い、新しくできる道や建築物をイメージしたオリジナルフォントを制作した。

Ms. Toda, a forest owner, opened up her dark, unkempt forested area in Nasu, wishing to restore it into a beautiful forest coexisting with humans. She decided to build three buildings from which "cultures" would emerge. She intended to make the place something like a school, so I created an original font with a design reflecting a rule or a certain idea of discipline based on the image of the new area (roads and buildings).

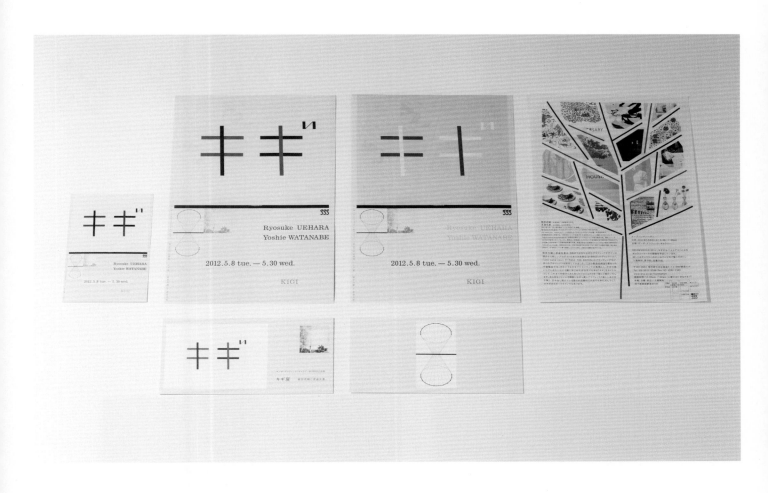

206 Flyer／DM
TD. AD. D. 植原亮輔　Ryosuke Uehara
　　　　渡邉良重　Yoshie Watanabe
　　CL. ギンザ・グラフィック・ギャラリー
　　　　ginza graphic gallery
　　PT. ionic

2012年5月にgggギャラリーで開催されたキギのデザインの展覧会のためにつくったポスターやチラシです。キギという文字が記号のような見え方をする面白さがあるので、また、その意味に我々の考え方が凝縮されているので、できるだけシンプルにその名前を伝えたいと思い、デザインしました。

This is a poster and flyer made for the KIGI Design Exhibition, held at the ginza graphic gallery (ggg) in May 2012. In our design, we tried to convey the name as simply as possible because the letters of "KIGI" look like a symbol in an interesting way; and our concept is condensed in the meaning.

207

208

208 CD jacket
TD. AD. 中島英樹　Hideki Nakajima
D. 田中幸洋　Yukihiro Tanaka
CL. commmons
　　エイベックス・マーケティング（株）
　　Avex Marketing Inc.
PT. News Gothic Medium

207 Small graphics
TD. P. Henricus Linggawidjaja
D. P. Edo
CL. Individw2
PT. Akkurat

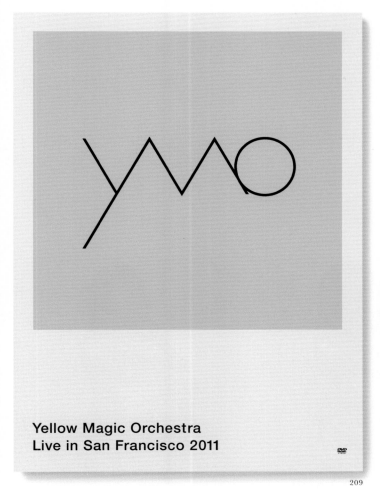

Yellow Magic Orchestra
Live in San Francisco 2011

209

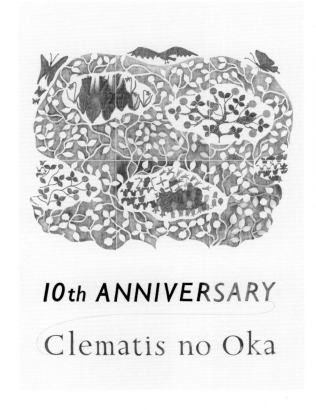

10th ANNIVERSARY

Clematis no Oka

210

209 DVD jacket
TD. AD. 中島英樹　Hideki Nakajima
　　 D. 三牧広宜　Hironobu Mimaki
　 CL. commmons
　　　　エイベックス・マーケティング（株）
　　　　Avex Marketing Inc.
　 PT. Helvetica /
　　　　Custom-made for the project

210 Note book / Poster
TD. AD. D. I. 渡邉良重　Yoshie Watanabe
　　 D. 岩永和也　Kazuya Iwanaga
　 CL. SGインベストメント（株）

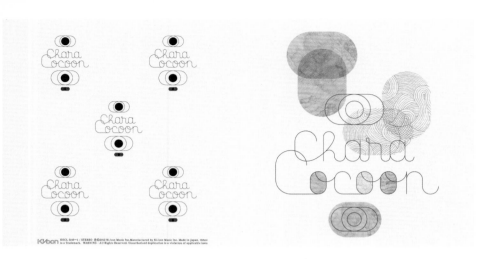

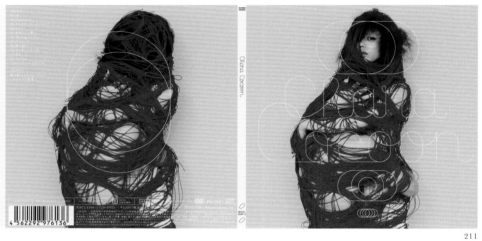

211

  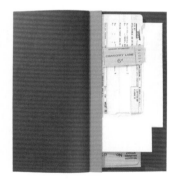 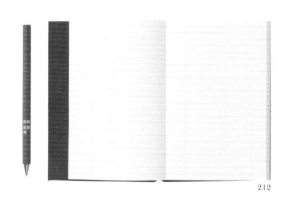

212

213

211 CD jacket
TD. AD. D. 長嶋りかこ　Rikako Nagashima
D. 矢後直規　Naonori Yago
P. 戎 康友　Yasutomo Ebisu
HM. 加茂克也　Katsuya Kamo
ST. タケダトシオ　Toshio Takeda
CL. キューンレコード（株）
　　Ki/oon Records Ind.
PT. Custom-made for the project

212 Business stationery
TD. D. 前原翔一　Shoichi Maehara
　　福澤卓馬　Takuma Fukuzawa
　　杉山耕太　Kota Sugiyama
CD. 宮田 識　Satoru Miyata
AD. 天宅 正　Masashi Tentaku
PR. 後藤 工　Takumi Goto
CL. D-BROS
PT. Custom-made for the project

213 Promotion tool
TD. AD. D. 髙谷 廉　Ren Takaya
CL. カタニ産業（株）
　　Katani Sangyo Co., Ltd.
PT. Original Typeface

214

215

216

214 Small graphics
TD. AD. C. 佐藤大介　Daisuke Sato
　　D. 田口貴士　Takashi Taguchi
　　CL. Non-commercial work
　　PT. A-OTFゴシックMB101Pro

215 Small graphics
TD. AD. D. 栗林和夫　Kazuo Kuribayashi
　　CL. （有）明るい部屋
　　　　Akaruiheya Inc.
　　PT. Custom-made for the project

216 School prospectus
TD. AD. 浅葉克己　Katsumi Asaba
　　D. 石原千明　Chiaki Ishihara
　　CL. 桑沢デザイン研究所
　　　　Kuwasawa Design School
　　PT. Custom-made for the project

217

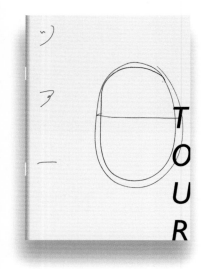

218

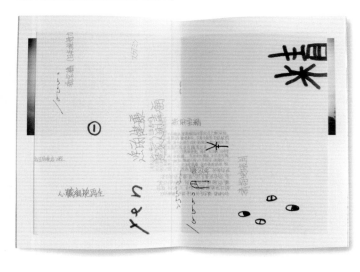

219

217 Graphic paper
TD. AD. D. I. 渡邉良重　Yoshie Watanabe
　　CL. ギンザ・グラフィック・ギャラリー
　　　　ginza graphic gallery

218 Applique
TD. AD. 植原亮輔　Ryosuke Uehara
TD. AD. I. 渡邉良重　Yoshie Watanabe
　　D. 岩永和也　Kazuya Iwanaga
　　CL. ウンナナクール　une nana cool
　　PT. Custom-made for the project

219 Small graphics
TD. D. P. Pu-Hui Chang
　　CL. Non-commercial work
　　PT. Gill Sans MT Italic /
　　　　Custom-made for the project

220

A3

A4

221

222

220 Flyer
TD. AD. D. 加瀬 透　Toru Kase
P. 江崎 愛　Ai Ezaki
後藤洋平　Yohey Goto
CL. お米は生きている
Okome Wa Ikiteiru
PT. Custom-made for the project

221 Tote bag
TD. AD. 秋山具義　Gugi Akiyama
D. 池田美咲　Misaki Ikeda
CL. Non-commercial work
PT. Helvetica Bold

222 DM
TD. AD. D. 髙谷 廉　Ren Takaya
CL. 伊藤 允　Mitsuru Ito
PT. Universe 67 Bold Condenced

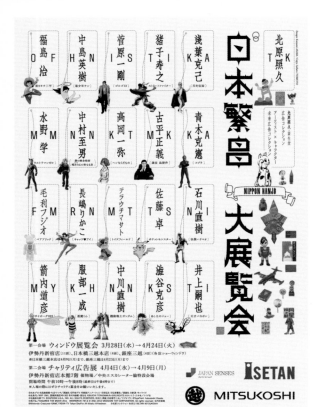

14

223

224

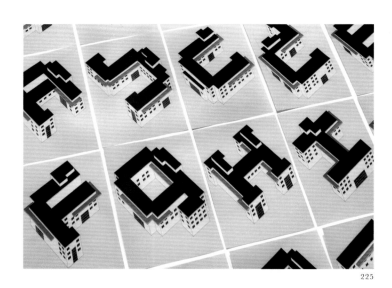

225

223 Flyer / DM
TD. AD. 浅葉克己　Katsumi Asaba
　　 D. 清水龍之介　Ryunosuke Shimizu
　　 I. 赤木 仁　Zin Akagi
　　 C. 東本三郎　Saburo Tomoto
　　 CL. 日本繁昌大展覧会実行委員会
　　 PT. Custom-made for the project

224 DM
TD. AD. 高田 唯　Yui Takada
　　 D. 市川智美　Tomomi Ichikawa
　　 CL. nap gallery
　　 PT. 新聞特太明朝体 /
　　　　 ヒラギノ明朝

225 Small graphics
TD. AD. 河野 智　Satoshi Kohno
　　 CD. 山本ヒロキ　Hiroki Yamamoto
　　 CL. Non-commercial work
　　 PT. Custom-made for the project

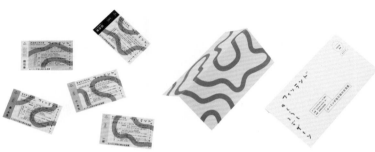

226

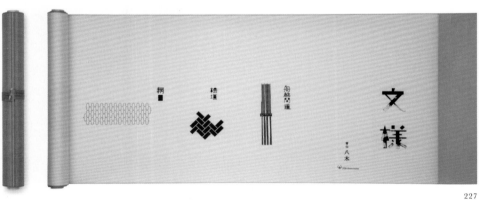

227

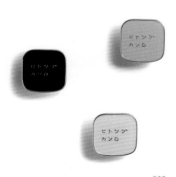

228

226 Flyer / DM / Ticket
TD. D. Tilmann S. Wendelstein
TD. I. Miki Kadokura
　CL. 青森県立美術館
　　　 Aomori Museum of Art
　PT. Custom-made for the project /
　　　 游ゴシック

227 Small graphics
TD. AD. D. 林 規章　　Noriaki Hayashi
　　CL. 青山八木　Aoyama Yagi
　　PT. Custom-made for the project

228 Shop card / Pins
TD. AD. 関本明子　　Akiko Sekimoto
　　D. 岩永和也　　　Kazuya Iwanaga
　　PR. 川又俊明　　　Toshiaki Kawamata
　　　　細田幸子　　　Sachiko Hosoda
　　　　中岡美奈子　　Minako Nakaoka
　　　　藤村るり子　　Ruriko Fujimura
　　CL. カンロ（株）Kanro Co.,Ltd.
　　PT. Custom-made for the project

229

230

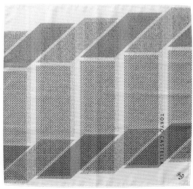

231

229 Small graphics
TD. AD. 植原亮輔　Ryosuke Uehara
　　D. 汐田瀬里菜　Serina Shiota
　　CL. ギンザ・グラフィック・ギャラリー
　　　　ginza graphic gallery
　　PT. Helvetica

230 Calendar
TD. He Jun
CL. Madam Zhu's kitchen
　　YOUAREHEREDESIGN
PT. Custom-made for the project

231 Cloth wrapper
TD. AD. D. 上西祐理　Yuri Uenishi
　　CD. 小郷拓良　Takeru Kogo
　　CL. 上野風月堂　Ueno Fugetsudo
　　PT. Times New Roman /
　　　　Custom-made for the project

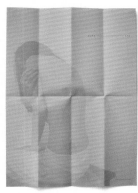

232

233

234

232 Small graphics
TD. Henricus Linggawidjaja
 D. Andri Mondong
    Michelle Praminta
 P. Nicoline Patricia
    Cartographia
    Clarissa Kwok
CL. Fontana Hotel
PT. Bauer Bodoni/Gotham/Times New Roman

233 Tote bag
TD. AD. D. 齋藤 浩　Hiroshi Saito
 CL. Non-commercial work
 PT. リッタイポ (Original Font)

234 Brochure
TD. AD. D. 大塚南海子　Namiko Otsuka
 CL. 東京都現代美術館
    Museum of Contemporary Art Tokyo
 PT. Avant Garde Gothic/Clarendon/Peignot

235

236

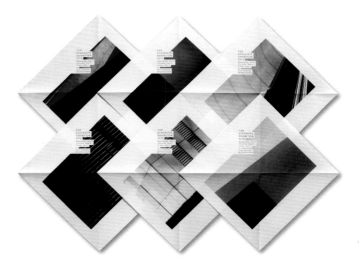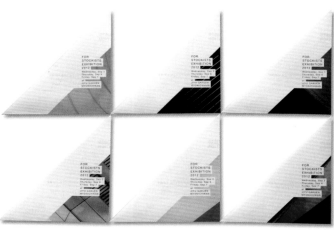

237

235 Small graphics
TD. AD. 服部一成　Kazunari Hattori
　　D. 田部井美奈　Mina Tabei
　　C. 国井美果　Mika Kunii
　　P. 梶山アマゾン　Amazon Kajiyama
　PR. 川島蓉子　Yoko Kawashima
　CL. 経済産業省　Ministry of Economy, Trade and Industry
　　　伊藤忠ファッションシステム（株）
　　　Itochu Fashion System Co., Ltd.
　PT. Poplar Std Black／新丸ゴ／Century Gothic

236 DM
TD. AD. D. 村松里紗　Lisa Muramatsu
　　　　　正光亜実　Ami Masamitsu
　CL. Non-commercial work
　PT. Didot

237 Small graphics
TD. AD. D. 高田唯　Yui Takada
　　AD. 江藤公昭　Kimiaki Eto
　　P. 加藤純平　Jyunpei Kato
　CL. FOR STOCKISTS-
　　　EXHIBITION 実行委員会
　PT. Helvetica Neue Roman

150

238

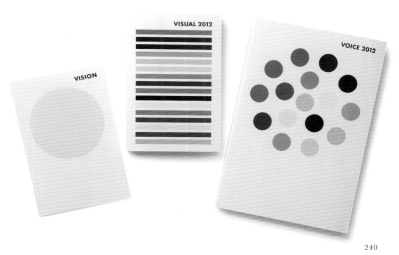

239

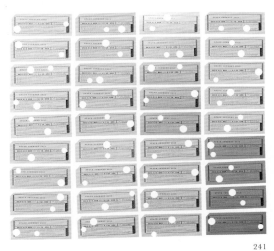

240

241

238 Invitation
TD. AD. D. 内田真弓　Mayumi Uchida
　　CD. 柿木原政広　Masahiro Kakinokihara
　　P. 与田弘志　Hiroshi Yoda
　　　鋤田正義　Masayoshi Sukita
　　CL. (株)クレー・インク　Klee Inc.
　　PT. Century Gothic / Bodoni BE

239 DM
TD. AD. 原 健三　Kenzo Hara
　　CL. HYPHEN
　　PT. Avant Garde

240 Small graphics
TD. AD. 葛西 薫　Kaoru Kasai
　　D. 増田 豊　Yutaka Masuda
　　CD. 山本康一郎　Koichiro Yamamoto
　　E. 西田善太　Zenta Nishida
　　　伊藤総研　Soken Ito
　　　星野 徹　Toru Hoshino
　　CL. (株)ユナイテッドアローズ
　　　United Arrows Ltd.
　　PT. Futura

241 DM
TD. AD. D. 竹内佐織　Saori Takeuchi
　　C. 牧田智之　Tomoyuki Makita
　　　牧田敬子　Keiko Makita
　　CL. Doubleloop
　　PT. 游明朝 /
　　　Custom-made for the project

242

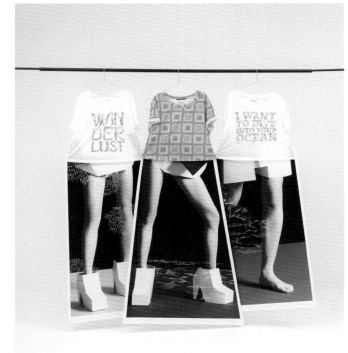

243

MUSIC TODAY LAFORET

15:00

Shuta Hasunuma PRESENTS

19:00

2012年3月20日（祝・火）

蓮沼執太フィル

phew × 高橋悠治

（オルタイチ）

Oorutaichi loves The Acustico Paz Nova Band

佐々木敦

ミュージックトゥデイラフォーレ

LAFORET
MUSEUM

244

245

244 Flyer
TD. AD. D. 菊地敦己　Atsuki Kikuchi
CL. 蓮沼執太　Shuta Hasunuma
PT. A-OTF見出ゴ／
　　A-OTF見出ミン／
　　Century Schoolbook

243 Small graphics
TD. AD. D. ST. 竹内佐織　Saori Takeuchi
D. 中谷亜美　Ami Nakaya
P. 島村朋子　Tomoko Shimamura
HM. 梅澤優子　Yuko Umezawa
CL. Gas As Interface
PT. Custom-made for the project

242 DM
TD. D. 福岡南央子　Naoko Fukuoka
CL. 色ちゃん　irochan
PT. こぶりなゴシック／
　　アンチック／
　　Custom-made for the project

245 Flyer / DM
TD. AD. D. 宮田裕美詠　Yumiyo Miyata
PD. 熊倉桂三　Katsumi Kumakura
　　高 智之　Tomoyuki Taka
CL. JAGDA富山
　　JAGDA Toyama
PT. Handwriting characters／
　　中ゴシックBBB

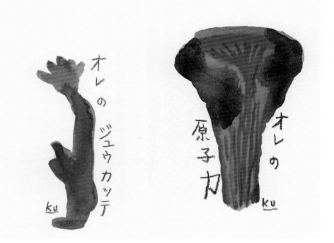
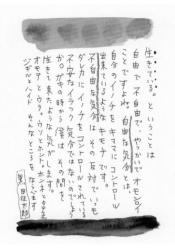

246

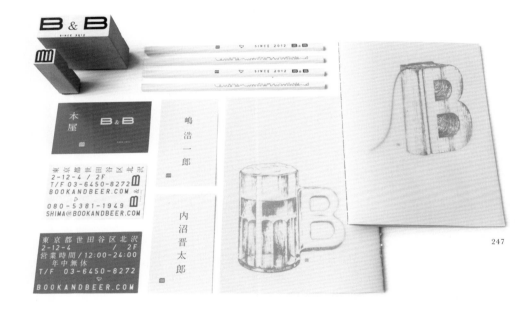

247

248

249

249 Novelty
TD. AD. D. 池上直樹　Naoki Ikegami
　　　　CL. 北陸ウェブ（株）
　　　　　　Hokuriku Web Co., Ltd.
　　　　　　（株）紐屋　Himoya Co., Ltd.
　　　　PT. DIN Pro Medium/
　　　　　　Custom-made for the project

246 DM
TD. AD. D. 青木克憲　Katsunori Aoki
　　　I.CL. 黒田征太郎　Seitaro Kuroda
　　　PT. ZENオールド明朝

247 Small graphics / Stationery
TD. AD. 小杉幸一　Koichi Kosugi
　　　D. 小暮菜月　Natsuki Kogure
　　　CL. B & B　Book & Beer

248 Small graphics
TD. AD. D. 菊地和広　Kazuhiro Kikuchi
　　　CL. モリタ（株）Morita Co., Ltd.
　　　PT. Custom-made for the project

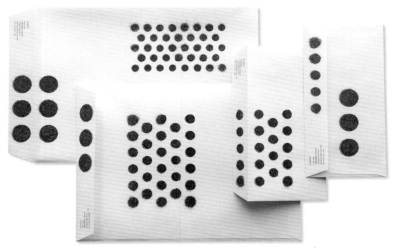

250

251

252

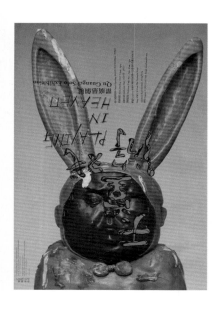

253

250 Envelope
TD. AD. D. 寺島賢幸　Masayuki Terashima
CL. sunaie
PT. Custom-made for the project

251 Shop card
TD. I. Tilmann S.Wendelstein
CL. Happy Shop, Berlin
PT. 游ゴシック

252 DM
TD. AD. 小杉幸一　Koichi Kosugi
CL. TYO プロダクションズ
TYO Productions
PT. Matricla

253 Small graphics
TD. I. Gu Lei
CL. Aura Gallery
PT. Garamond/
Custom-made for the project

Type Design

15

Tablet Gothic

68

sturdy, straightforward clean appearance

El surcoreano Hahn Bin que debutará en el Carnegie Hall en octubre olvidó su violín de medio

KRAFTVOLL

Wiedergefunden: Das Zündappauto

35

SUPER

%

Rozhněvaná Generace:

Jací jsou dnešní dvacátníci

LA CIGÜEÑA TOCABA EL SAXOFÓN DETRÁS DEL PALENQUE SEXY MÖNCHE VERGÄREN FADES QUELLWASSER ZU SÜSSEM BIER VÖLLIG WEISSES PONY MIT ZÖPFEN JAGT QUER ÜBER

Graphic designers of any nationality and background know very well that the art of composing titles correctly is not easy, Especially when it comes to periodical publi-

42 fonts

Tablet Gothic – character set & styles

'"#&*,-.:;?!¿¡@@ABCDEFGHIJKLMNOPQRSTUVWX YZabcdefghijklmnopqrstuvwxyz[]{}<>/|\~--0123 456789$€¢£¥ƒ§©®™ªº«»‹›""''•¶--‐--ÀÁÂ ÀÂÆÇÉÉÊÈÍÍÎÌÐÑÓÓÔÒÕØÚÚÛÙŸßàáâãäåæ çèéêëìíîïðñòóôõøùúûüýÿ đĐ̧ĚĒĖĘȨ̄ĒĘĞĠĢ̧Ğ̌Ģ̇Ģ̧Ħ̌Ħ̌Ň̌ĺ̌Ĭ̌Ī̌Į̌Į̌Į̌ĨÌȷĴĶ ĹĽĿŁĻĿ̌Ňŋ̌Ňňň̌Ň̌ŊÒŌÓ̌Ő̌Œ̌ŔŘ̌Ŗ̌Ŗ̌Ś̌Š̌Š̌ş̌Ŝ̌ş ŠŞ̌Ť̌Ŧ̌Ŧ̌Ť̌Ţ̌ŪÚ̌Ů̌Ū̌Û̌Ů̌Ų̌Ų̌Ŵ̌Ŵ̌Ŵ̌Ŵ̌Ŵ̌Ŷ̌Ý̌Ŷ̌Ž̌ ż̌Ž̌Ż̌Ž̌ť̌ĺ̌fb fh fi fj fk fl ff ffb ffh ffi ffj ffk ffl tt 012 3456789 0123456789 0123456789 ¼ ½ ¾ ½ ⅓ ⅔ 0123456789 $€£¢¥ƒ,.%‰-=≈≤≥<>¬+±÷×∂ΩΔ∏ΣΔΩμnμ√∞∫◊.

abcnrs
TABLET GOTHIC WIDE BOLD

abcnrs
TABLET GOTHIC NORMAL BOLD

abcnrs
TABLET GOTHIC NARROW BOLD

abcnrs
TABLET GOTHIC SEMICONDENSED BOLD

abcnrs
TABLET GOTHIC CONDENSED BOLD

abcnrs
TABLET GOTHIC COMPRESSED BOLD

Tablet Gothic Wide Thin · Tablet Gothic Wide Light · Tablet Gothic Wide Regular · Tablet Gothic Wide Semibold · Tablet Gothic Wide Bold · Tablet Gothic Wide Extrabold · Tablet Gothic Wide Heavy

Tablet Gothic Thin · Tablet Gothic Light · Tablet Gothic Regular · Tablet Gothic Semibold · Tablet Gothic Bold · Tablet Gothic Extrabold · Tablet Gothic Heavy

Tablet Gothic Narrow Thin · Tablet Gothic Narrow Light · Tablet Gothic Narrow Regular · Tablet Gothic Narrow Semibold · Tablet Gothic Narrow Bold · Tablet Gothic Narrow Extrabold · Tablet Gothic Narrow Heavy

Tablet Gothic SemiCondensed Thin · Tablet Gothic SemiCondensed Light · Tablet Gothic SemiCondensed Regular · Tablet Gothic SemiCondensed Semibold · Tablet Gothic SemiCondensed Bold · Tablet Gothic SemiCondensed Extrabold · Tablet Gothic SemiCondensed Heavy

Tablet Gothic Condensed Thin · Tablet Gothic Condensed Light · Tablet Gothic Condensed Regular · Tablet Gothic Condensed Semibold · Tablet Gothic Condensed Bold · Tablet Gothic Condensed Extrabold · Tablet Gothic Condensed Heavy

Tablet Gothic Compressed Thin · Tablet Gothic Compressed Light · Tablet Gothic Compressed Regular · Tablet Gothic Compressed Semibold · Tablet Gothic Compressed Bold · Tablet Gothic Compressed Extrabold · Tablet Gothic Compressed Heavy

Title for news: Tablet Gothic, back and to the future

Graphic designers of any nationality and background know very well that the art of composing titles correctly is not easy, Especially when it comes to periodical publications where there is a need for both flexibility and graphic coherence. Tablet Gothic was originally engineered as a titling type family, meant to help designers working on publications that require vertical as hard copies and a variety of digital platforms at the same time. As such, it is a grotesque sans serif that looks to the future of publishing with a clear understanding of its history, and reminiscences that go back to nineteenth century Britain and Germany.

Tablet Gothic delivers the sturdy, straightforward and clean appearance expected from a grotesque, but it allows itself a good measure of personality to make it stand out on the page. Its 42 styles –six series of condensation and seven weights in each series– guarantee that, whatever the publication format is, there's a Tablet Gothic font that will do the job and perform well both technically and aesthetically. Furthermore, the rounder styles, Tablet Gothic Wide, Normal and Narrow achieved amazing results in very small sizes, producing a beautiful texture and highly readable text blocks.

Tablet Gothic fonts can be purchased individually, by series or as a complete bundle (best value: just €12 per font).

Tablet Gothic – OpenType features

ALL CAPS		
¿para texto?		¿PARA TEXTO?
1708 a-b [ende]		1708 A-B [ENDE]
LIGATURES		
attractive, affiliate		attractive, affiliate
TABULAR FIGURES & CLASSIC ZERO		
0123456789\$€¥		0123456789\$€¥ƒ
SLASHED ZERO		
0		0
NUMERATOR / DENOMINATOR		
0123456789/0123456789		0123456789/0123456789
ARBITRARY FRACTIONS		
1/2 3/4 1/6 5/7 21/98		1/2 3/4 1/6 5/7 21/98
SUPERIOR / INFERIOR		
H2O ab8 y35		H2O x5y y35
TURN DOUBLE-STOREY TERM		
fincan		fincan
DISCRETIONARY LIGATURES		
mutum,esc. MULTUM.ESC		mutum,esc. MULTUM.ESC

Veronika Burian and José Scaglione met at the University of Reading whilst completing their MA in Type Design, launching the independent type foundry TypeTogether (TT for short) in 2006. TT developed out of the desire to publish high quality typefaces and work on new type projects together (hence the name). The foundry provides common grounds for intense cooperation with other type designers, creating an interesting and diverse platform. TypeTogether's main interest is finding innovative and stylish solutions to old problems for the professional market of text typefaces, with a focus on editorial use. This is where the greatest challenges are faced: creating typefaces that perform well in continuous reading, that also have a high degree of personality. The aesthetical and functional efficiency of TT's fonts is accompanied by excellence in technical performance.

(columns repeat in various weights: Tablet Gothic Wide Roman Regular, Tablet Gothic Narrow Regular, Tablet Gothic Condensed Regular, Tablet Gothic SemiCondensed Regular)

Národní divadlo začalo s vydáváním cd v roce 2002, po nástupu novního ředitele **Daniela Dvořáka**, který do funkce šéfa opery přivzal svého dřívějšího kolegu ze Státní opery Prahu **Jiřího Nekvasila**. První vydáno operou byl Mozartův Don Giovanni, vyšly i tři nahrávky Zprávy pro akademii Jana Klusáka, Smolíkovu Nagano a další. Zatím poslední je komplet s nahrávkou mimořádného provedení Prstenu Nibelungova od Richarda Wagnera, které vzbudilo velkou pozornost na scéně před 2 lety. To slouží jako dokumentace, propagace opery Národního

Speech and writing are the means by which human society communicates. Writing is a graphic record of speech. Such is the terse definition of the concepts to which this book is related. But what a wealth of ideas, shapes and potentialities stand behind these sober words defining the meaning of a simple term—writing. When looking into the shapes and details of the design of typefaces as well as their structural properties in order to use them, influences which led to different modifica-

> "Even if they get captured again, they have had a longer life"

10 %

Huis van het boek

Die große Illusion verpackt

Today's matter

Aljaškou na kole

DINTON, THAME AND PRINCES RISBOROUGH

Magnificent Mike is captain marvel as Dinton move top

BY DAMIEN LUCAS
damien.lucas@press.co.uk
01296 619774 @BHSportsEditor

Dinton moved joint top of the league with a dominant winning draw at rivals Thame.

On a surprisingly clear but cool day at Thame CC, Thame won the toss and invited Dinton to bat on what looked like a damp wicket.

Dinton openers Rob King and Lee Marland soon found conditions difficult, with the Thame opening bowlers finding some extravagant seam movement.

The mixture of accurate seam bowling and some hanging Patel (3-54)

liff rebuilt the innings ably supported by Shakil Ahmed (18) and the rest of the lower order as his side finished on a respectable 186 all out.

Thame's reply began badly as Dinton's opening bowlers, Nheem Amin and Faisal Ali started very well.

With a mixture of pace and bounce and quick accurate swing Thame were reduced to 19-3.

A particular highlight Nheem Amin bowling Thame's talented overseas batsmen first ball with a beautiful in-swinger firmly putting Dinton in the driving seat.

With Thame looking to regroup and build on a drying pitch, Dinton introduced experienced twins Alister Gibbins

an impressive victory, Dinton brought back quicks Nheem Amin and Faisal Ali, who bowled well and got very close to bringing home the win.

Dinton's unbeaten run and promotion push continues as they move joint top while Thame drop to second bottom.

Elsewhere, Princes Risborough Seconds rallied to secure a draw against Harefield Fourths.

Risborough won the toss and inserted Harefield on a wet wicket. But opener Collet hit 87 and was supported later on by Ogden (72a) as Harefield made 246-7.

From their 52 overs, Graeme and FF 11 overs and

48 Tablet Gothic   3 Juni 2012

01. PŘEDNÁŠKY
Na těchto *hodinových přednáškách* svou tvorbu představují přední čeští i zahraniční typografové.

02. WEBFONTS
What great great news. I'm a Mac user and I always hated viewing webfonts on PCs with

03. KATALOG
Our font catalog shows our fonts being used at many sizes and in different european languages.

04. IMMOBILIEN
Berliner Altbau wird 2012 saniert Vorderhaus, Seitenflügel. Im Quergebäude befindet sich ein tolles

Moaides 6 %

Prize Nominee Work

254 Type design
TD. Veronika Burian
    Jose Scaglione
CL. TypeTogether

タブレットゴシックは、アナログメディアとデジタルメディアの両方での出版向けに、包括的な汎用タイプファミリーとして作られた。19世紀の英国とドイツに歴史的な起源を持つ特徴を若干備えた、がっしりとしてグロテスクなsansである。

Tablet Gothic was engineered as a comprehensive versatile type family, meant for publications in both analog and digital media. It is a sturdy grotesque sans with a pinch of personality that is historically rooted in 19th century Britain and Germany.

McLovely & Money
Shucklack
Renegades of Funk
Alien Nation
The Year of the Boomerang
Snakecharmer
981 Pounds
Mic Check One, Two
Anti-Myth Rhythm Rock Shocker
Land of hypocrisy
Kilimandjaro

Prize Nominee Work

255 Type design
TD. Octavio Pardo
CL. Non-commercial work

Sutturahは、新しいタイポグラフィ質感の模索として誕生した。私の目にはこのフォントがデザインの過程で受けた大きな影響のひとつ（グランジグループであるレイジ・アゲインスト・ザ・マシーンの音楽）を完璧に反映しているように見えるが、このフォントが甘く優しい言葉にぴったりだと思っている人々もいる。

Sutturah was born as an exploration of new typographic textures. It's funny because some people sees it as an ideal font for candies and yummy words although I see it as a perfect reflect of one of the main influences during the design process: the music of the grunge group "Rage Against the Machine."

Prize Nominee Work

256 Type design
TD. CL. PT. Liu Yong qing

Fuga Kai Arial は、手書き文字の過剰な角張りを避け、一定の精神性を持たせるために、書道の筆運びの法則と、フォントストラクチャに関する個人的理解に従っている。この実験は、タイプフェイスを最初の試みの文化的な雰囲気へと回帰させるためのものである。

Fuga Kai Arial is according to the the calligraphic brushstrokes law and personal understanding of the font structure, to avoid the excessive square of written characters, and let it have a certain spirituality, this experiment is to make Typeface return to the cultural atmosphere of the first attempt.

PRESENTING

VIER REGULAR

A CUSTOM TYPEFACE BY WHY NOT ASSOCIATES

ZONDAG

DE KRUITFABRIEK, 17.50

ABCDEFGHIJKLMNOPQRSTUVWXYZ
1234567890
&.,/-(){}:;?!‹›€£$@ÃÅÄÞßŒ‰™

Prize Nominee Work

257 Type design
TD. Why Not Associates
CL. Woestijnvis & SBS Belgium
PT. Vier Regular

ベルギーの新しいテレビチャンネルVier向けの、スクリーン上とスクリーン外でのアイデンティティ。このプロジェクトでは、サブチャンネル用のロゴ、チャンネル・アイデントの方向性に関わるコラボレーションに加え、オリジナルのタイプフェイス「Vier Regular」を制作した。

On and off screen identity for a new Belgian television channel Vier. This included creating a bespoke typeface, Vier Regular, as well as logos for its sub channels and collaboration on the direction of the channels idents.

Green Tea with Lime and Lemongrass

Dampfnudeln

Roasted Aubergine with Chilli Yoghurt

Eisbein auf Sauerkraut

Vanilla Crème Brûlée

FIGS AND YOUNG PECORINO WITH HONEY

Speckgrießknödelsuppe

FLEISCHKÄSE

Fruit Scone with Cornish Clotted Cream and Strawberry Preserve

SPÄTBURGUNDER

JAF Bernino Sans – Light
JAF Bernino Sans – Light Italic
JAF Bernino Sans – Regular
JAF Bernino Sans – Regular Italic
JAF Bernino Sans – Semibold
JAF Bernino Sans – Semibold Italic
JAF Bernino Sans – Bold
JAF Bernino Sans – Bold Italic
JAF Bernino Sans – Extrabold
JAF Bernino Sans – Extrabold Italic

JAF Bernina Sans – Light
JAF Bernina Sans – Light Italic
JAF Bernina Sans – Regular
JAF Bernina Sans – Regular Italic
JAF Bernina Sans – Semibold
JAF Bernina Sans – Semibold Italic
JAF Bernina Sans – Bold
JAF Bernina Sans – Bold Italic
JAF Bernina Sans – Extrabold
JAF Bernina Sans – Extrabold Italic

JAF Bernino Sans – Narrow Light
JAF Bernino Sans – Narrow Regular
JAF Bernino Sans – Narrow Semibold
JAF Bernino Sans – Narrow Bold
JAF Bernino Sans – Narrow Extrabold

JAF Bernina Sans – Narrow Light
JAF Bernina Sans – Narrow Regular
JAF Bernina Sans – Narrow Semibold
JAF Bernina Sans – Narrow Bold
JAF Bernina Sans – Narrow Extrabold

JAF Bernino Sans – Condensed Light
JAF Bernino Sans – Condensed Regular
JAF Bernino Sans – Condensed Semibold
JAF Bernino Sans – Condensed Bold
JAF Bernino Sans – Condensed Extrabold

JAF Bernina Sans – Condensed Light
JAF Bernina Sans – Condensed Regular
JAF Bernina Sans – Condensed Semibold
JAF Bernina Sans – Condensed Bold
JAF Bernina Sans – Condensed Extrabold

JAF Bernino Sans – Compressed Light
JAF Bernino Sans – Compressed Regular
JAF Bernino Sans – Compressed Semibold
JAF Bernino Sans – Compressed Bold
JAF Bernino Sans – Compressed Extrabold

JAF Bernina Sans – Compressed Light
JAF Bernina Sans – Compressed Regular
JAF Bernina Sans – Compressed Semibold
JAF Bernina Sans – Compressed Bold
JAF Bernina Sans – Compressed Extrabold

Glyph set

LOWERCASE & ACCENTED LOWERCASE

a a b c d e f g g h i i j j k k l m n o p q r s t u v w x y z
ß ı æ œ ð þ à á â ã ä å ā ă à á â ã ä å ā ă ą ć ç č
d̄ ð è é ê ë ē ĕ ė ę ě ĝ ğ ġ ģ ĝ ğ ġ ĝ ñ í ì î ï ĩ ī ĭ j̃ ĵ
k̦ ĺ ļ ł l̇ ŀ ń ñ ñ ò ó ô õ ö ø ō ŏ ő ø ŕ ŗ ś ş š ş ß ţ ţ ŧ ũ ú û ü
ũ ū ŭ ů ų ű ŵ ẁ ẃ ẅ ỳ ý ŷ ÿ ỹ ý ÿ ź ž ż

UPPERCASE & ACCENTED UPPERCASE

A B C D E F G H I J K L M N O P Q R S T U V W X Y Z
Æ Œ Ð Þ Ə À Á Â Ã Ä Å Ā Ă Ą Ć Ç Č Ĉ Ð É È Ê Ë
É Ê Ê Ę Ĝ Ğ Ġ Ģ Ğ Ĥ Í Ì Î Ï Ĩ Ī Ĭ J̃ K̦ Ĺ Ļ Ł L̇ Ŀ Ń Ñ Ñ
Ó Ò Ô Õ Ö Ø Ō Ŏ Ő Ø Ŕ Ŗ Ś Ş Š Ş Ţ Ţ Ŧ Ú Ù Û Ü Ũ Ū Ŭ Ů
Ų Ũ Ŵ Ẁ Ẃ Ẅ Ý Ŷ Ÿ Ź Ž Ż

REDUCED SIZE UPPERCASE

A B C D E F G H I J K L M N O P Q R S T U V W X Y Z
Æ Œ Ð Þ Ə À Á Â Ã Ä Å Ā Ă Ą Ć Ç Č Ĉ Ð É È Ê Ë Ē
É Ê Ê Ę Ĝ Ğ Ġ Ģ Ğ Ĥ Í Ì Î Ï Ĩ Ī Ĭ J̃ K̦ Ĺ Ļ Ł L̇ Ŀ Ń Ñ Ñ
Ó Ò Ô Õ Ö Ø Ō Ŏ Ő Ø Ŕ Ŗ Ś Ş Š Ş Ţ Ţ Ŧ Ú Ù Û Ü Ũ Ū Ŭ Ů
Ų Ũ Ŵ Ẁ Ẃ Ẅ Ý Ŷ Ÿ Ź Ž Ż

CASE-SENSITIVE FORMS

( ) [ ] { } ! ! ? ? i i ¿ ¿ © & = ≠ < > + − × ÷ ~ - – — : « » ( )

SMALL CAPS

A B C D E F G H I J K K L M N O P Q R S T U V W X Y Z Æ Œ Ð
Ə Þ À Á Â Ã Ä Å Ā Ă Ą Ć Ç Č Ĉ Ð É È Ê Ë Ē É Ê Ê Ę Ĝ Ğ
Ğ Ĝ Ģ Ĥ Í Ì Î Ï Ĩ Ī Ĭ J̃ K̦ Ĺ Ļ Ł L̇ Ŀ Ń Ñ Ñ Ó Ò Ô Õ Ö Ø Ō Ŏ
Ø Ŕ Ŗ Ś Ş Š Ş Ţ Ţ Ŧ Ú Ù Û Ü Ũ Ū Ŭ Ů Ų Ũ Ŵ Ẁ Ẃ Ẅ Ý Ŷ Ÿ
Ź Ž Ż 1 2 3 4 5 6 8 7 9 0 $ $ ¢ ¢ € € ¥ ₹ ₺ # ( ) [ ] { } ! ! ? ?
i i ¿ ¿ £ ¥ © † ‡ % ‰

NUMBERS, FRACTIONS, SUPERIORS & INFERIORS

1234568790 $$¢¢€€¥₹₺#%‰
1234568790 $$¢¢€€¥₹₺#
1234568790 $$¢¢€€¥₹₺#%‰
1234568790 $$¢¢€€¥₹₺#

H₀₁₂₃₄₅₆₇₈₉₀+−.,()   Hₐbcdefghijklmnopqrstuvwxyz
H⁰¹²³⁴⁵⁶⁷⁸⁹⁰+−.,()   Hᵃbcdefghijklmnopqrstuvwxyz

PUNCTUATION & MATHEMATICAL SIGNS

¶ № § @ © . . : : ; ; ? ? ! ! ¿ ¿ i i „ " " ' ' ( ) [ ] { } · · · − - —
( ) « » . = ≠ = ~ < > ≤ ≥ ± + − × ÷ = ∞ ∂ → ↑ ← ↗
↘ ↙ ↖ _ ^ ∆ π ∫ √ & ¦ | / \ · · · … … ª º ™ ® ° † ‡ % ‰

258

259

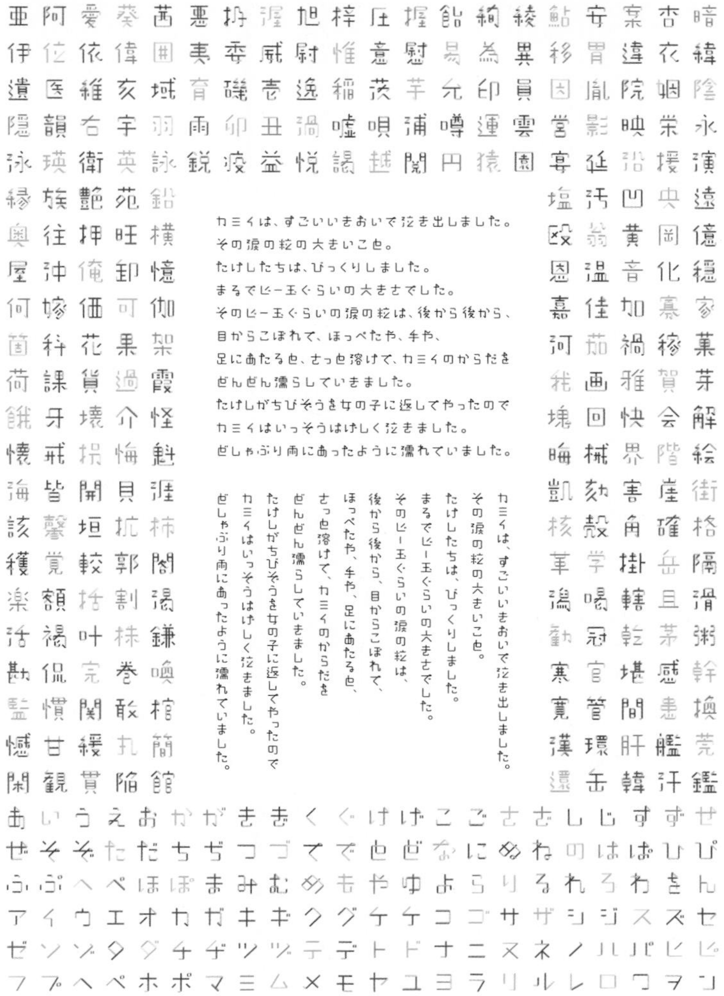

亜　阿　愛　葵　茜　悪　挨　渥　旭　梓　圧　握　飴　絢　綾　鮎　安　案　杏　暗　韓
伊　佗　依　偉　囲　夷　委　威　尉　惟　意　慰　易　為　異　移　胃　違　院　咽　栄
遺　医　維　亥　城　育　礎　壱　逸　稲　茨　允　印　員　因　胤　影　映　延　漢
隠　韻　右　宇　羽　雨　卯　丑　渦　嘘　唄　浦　噂　運　雲　園　猿　園　享　塩　澳
泳　瑛　衛　英　詠　鋭　疫　益　悦　謁　越　閲　円　段　翕　渚　億　穏

カミくは、すごいいきおいで泣き出しました。
その涙の粒の大きいこと。
たけしたちは、びっくりしました。
まるでビー玉ぐらいの大きさでした。
そのビー玉ぐらいの涙の粒は、後から後から、
目からこぼれて、ほっぺたや、手や、
足に当たる色、さっと溶けて、カミくのからだを
ぜんぜん濡らしていませんでした。
たけしがちびそうきな女の子に返してやったので
ぜしゃぶり雨に当ったように濡れていました。

260 Type design
TD. AD. 豊島 晶　Aki Toyoshima
CL. FONT1000

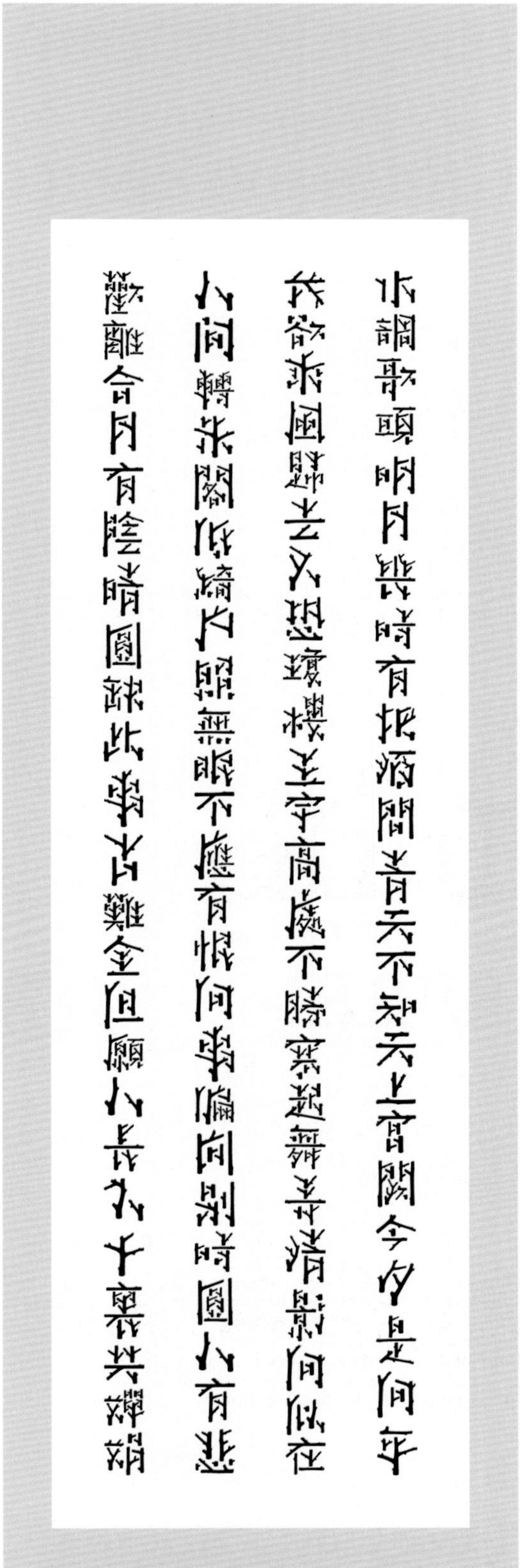

261 Type design
TD. Deng Lihua
CL. Graduation design

16

Karambolage im Visier

Béchamelsoße als Amuse-Gueule beim Poissonnier

Grotesque Zivilcourage

Nach dem Ratatouille ein Mousse au Chocolat?

Eskapade Regular
ABCDEFGHIJKLMNOPQRSTUVWXYZabcdefghijklmnopq
rstuvwxyz0123456789$€£¥ƒ0123456789ÀÁÂÃÄÅÆÆ
ÇÈÉÊËÌÍÎÏĐÑÒÓÔÕÖØÙÚÛÜÝÞßàáâãäåæçèéêëìíîïïîð
óòôõöøùúûüÿþÿÅàÂàÁàÇČĆĊČĈĊďĎďÐĐÉÈÊĚĘÊĘĔĜĞĠĜ
ĝĜĝĞĤĦhĦĥĨĪĬİıĭĳİ ĴĳĴĶķĸĹĻĽĿŁŃÑŋŅÑŇŋŊŐÒÓÔÕ
ÖŒŒœŔŖŘŕŔŚŠŜŞŠŞŞŠŢŤŦŢŤŢŬŪŬŮŰŮŲŴŵŴŴ
ŴŴŵŶŷŸÝŹŻŽŻŽŽžż
½⅓¼⅔⅛¾½⅜⅝⅞ 0123456789 0123456789‰% ''"""„
«»°#&*,-_—·…:;?!¡¿@[]{}()\/|§©®™№†‡¶
◊∂∆Πμπ ^¬√∞∫≈≠≤≥<=>◊+−±×÷

Eskapade Italic
ABCDEFGHIJKLMNOPQRSTUVWXYZabcdefghijklmnopq
tuvwxyz0123456789$€£¥ƒ0123456789ÀÁÂÃÄÅÆÆÇÈÉÊ
ÏÍÎÏĐÑÒÓÔÕÖØÙÚÛÜÝÞßàáâãäåæçèéêëìíîïîîîîî ðóòôõöøÿ
ùúûüÿþÿÅàÂàÁàÇČĆĊČĈĊďĎďÐĐÉÈÊĚĘÊĘĔĜĞĠĜĝĜĝĞĤĦh
ĥĨĪ Ĭİ ıĭĳİ ĴĳĴĶķ ĹĻĽĿŁŁ ŃÑŋŅ ÑŇŋŊŐÒÓÔÕÖŒŒœŔŖŘŕŔ
ŚŠŜŞŠŞŞŠŢŤŦŢŤŢŬŪŬŮŰŮŲŴŵŴŴŴŴŵŶŷŸÝŹŻŽŻŽŽž
Th ƒƒ fi fl fk ƒ b fh ft ff fi ffi ffl ſt st ſp ſt čt ck ſ
½⅓¼⅔⅛¾½⅜⅝⅞0123456789 0123456789‰% ''"""„, «»◊
#&*,-_—·…:;?!¡¿@[]{}()\/|§©®™№†‡¶
◊∂∆Πμπ ^¬√∞∫≈≠≤≥<=>◊+−±×÷

Eskapade Fraktur Regular
A B C D E F G H I J K L M N O P Q R S T U V W X Y Z
A B C D E F G H I J K L M N O P Q R S T U V W X Y Z
abcdefghijklmnopqrstuvwxyz0123456789$€£¥ƒ0123456789
ÀÁÂÃÄÅÆÆÇÈÉÊËÌÍÎÏĐÒÓÔÕÖØÙÚÛÜÝÞßàáâãäåæçèéêë
ìíîïîîîîîðóòôõöøøùúûüÿþÿÅàÂàÁàÇČĆĊČĈĊďĎďÐĐÉÈÊĚĘÊĘĔ
ĜĞĠĜĝĜĝĞĤĦhĦĥĨĪĬİıĭĳİ ĴĳĴĶķĸĹĻĽĿŁŃÑŋŅÑŇŋŊŐÒÓÔÕÖŒŒœŔŖŘŕŔ
ŚŠŜŞŠŞŞŠŢŤŦŢŤŢŬŪŬŮŰŮŲŴŵŴŴŴŴŵŶŷŸÝŹŻŽŻŽŽžż
ff fi fk fb fh ft fj ffi ffl fft ch ck tt ſ ½⅓¼⅔⅛¾½⅜⅝⅞
0123456789 ‰%'',.«»◊#&*,-_—·…:;?!¡¿@[]{}()\/|§©®™

Eskapade Fraktur Italic
A B C D E F G H I J K L M N O P Q R S T U V W X Y Z
A B C D E F G H I J K L M N O P Q R S T U V W X Y Z
abcdefghijklmnopqrstuvwxyz0123456789$€£¥ƒ0123456789
ÀÁÂÃÄÅÆÆÇÈÉÊËÌÍÎÏĐÒÓÔÕÖØÙÚÛÜÝÞßàáâãäåæçèéêë
ðñòóôõöøøùúûüÿÿÅàÂàÁàÇČĆĊČĈĊďĎďÐĐÉÈÊĚĘÊĘĔĜĞĠĜĝĜĝĞ
ĤĦhĦĥĨĪĬİıĭĳİ ĴĳĴĶķ ĹĻĽĿŁŃÑŋŅÑŇŋŊŐÒÓÔÕÖŒŒœŔŖŘŕŔ
ŚŠŜŞŠŞŞŠŢŤŦŢŤŢŬŪŬŮŰŮŲŴŵŴŴŴŴŵŶŷŸÝŹŻŽŻŽŽžż
ff fi fk fb fh ft fj ffi ffl fft ch ck tt ſ ½⅓¼⅔⅛¾½⅜⅝⅞
0123456789 ‰%'',.«»◊#&*,-_—·…:;?!¡¿@[]{}()\/|§©®™
ª°†‡¶◊∂∆Πμπ ^¬√∞∫≈≠≤≥<=>◊+−±×÷

262

Font name: Dali

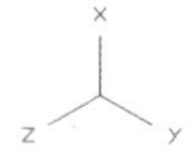

160pt / 36pt

ARAKI

WAS BORN IN TOKYO, STUDIED
PHOTOGRAPHY DURING HIS COLLEGE
YEARS AND THEN WENT TO WORK AT
THE ADVERTISING AGENCY DENTSU,
WHERE HE MET HIS FUTURE WIFE,
THE ESSAYIST YOKO ARAKI. AFTER
THEY WERE MARRIED, ARAKI
PUBLISHED A BOOK OF PICTURES
OF HIS WIFE TAKEN DURING THEIR
HONEYMOON TITLED SENTIMENTAL
JOURNEY.

Araki was born in Tokyo, studied
photography during his college
years and then went to work at the
advertising agency Dentsu, where
he met his future wife, the essayist
Yoko Araki. After they were married,
Araki published a book of pictures

110pt

Butterfly effect*
Question? Answer!
On & Off

Araki was born in Tokyo, studied photography during his college years and then went to work at the advertising agency Dentsu, where he met his future wife,
the essayist Yoko Araki. After they were married, Araki published a book of pictures of his wife taken during their honeymoon titled Sentimental Journey.

{ 1 2 3 4 5 # 6 7 8 9 0 }

Character set

Basic unit

48pt

It tells of a girl named
Alice who falls down a
rabbit hole into a fantasy
world populated by
peculiar, anthropomorphic
creatures.

12pt

Alice's Adventures in Wonderland is an 1865 novel written by English author Charles Lutwidge Dodgson under the pseudonym Lewis Carroll. It tells of a girl named Alice who falls down a rabbit hole into a fantasy world populated by peculiar, anthropomorphic creatures. The tale plays with logic, giving the story lasting popularity with adults as well as children. It is considered to be one of the best examples of the literary nonsense genre, and its narrative course and structure, characters and imagery have been enormously influential in both popular culture and literature, especially in the fantasy genre.

ALICE'S ADVENTURES IN WONDERLAND IS AN 1865 NOVEL WRITTEN BY ENGLISH AUTHOR CHARLES LUTWIDGE DODGSON UNDER THE PSEUDONYM LEWIS CARROLL. IT TELLS OF A GIRL NAMED ALICE WHO FALLS DOWN A RABBIT HOLE INTO A FANTASY WORLD POPULATED BY PECULIAR, ANTHROPOMORPHIC CHARACTERS. THE TALE PLAYS WITH LOGIC, GIVING THE STORY LASTING POPULARITY WITH ADULTS AS WELL AS CHILDREN, IT IS CONSIDERED TO BE ONE OF THE BEST EXAMPLES OF THE LITERARY DODGSON GENRE, AND ITS NARRATIVE COURSE AND STRUCTURE, CHARACTERS AND IMAGERY HAVE BEEN ENORMOUSLY INFLUENTIAL IN BOTH POPULAR CULTURE AND LITERATURE, ESPECIALLY IN

24pt

Alice's Adventures in
Wonderland is an 1865
novel written by English
author Charles Lutwidge
Dodgson under the
pseudonym Lewis Carroll.
It tells of a girl named
Alice who falls down a
rabbit hole into a fantasy
world populated by

ALICE'S ADVENTURES
IN WONDERLAND IS AN
1865 NOVEL WRITTEN BY
ENGLISH AUTHOR CHARLES
LUTWIDGE DODGSON UNDER
THE PSEUDONYM LEWIS
CARROLL. IT TELLS
OF A GIRL NAMED ALICE
WHO FALLS DOWN A
RABBIT HOLE INTO

263

(Alphabet specimen A–Z with dimension measurements, and jewellery alphabet photograph)

264

Mark & Logotype,
Corporate Stationery,
Branding

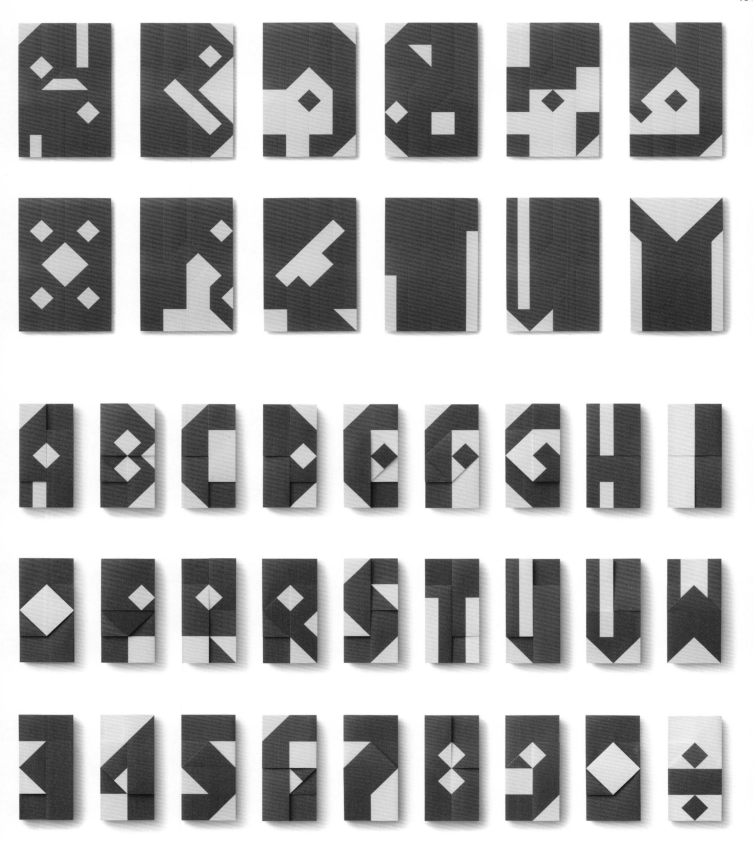

Prize Nominee Work

265 Event VI
TD. CD. AD. 小松洋一　Yoichi Komatsu
　　TD. AD. 瀬尾 大　Masaru Seo
　　TD. AD. 塚本哲也　Tetsuya Tsukamoto
　　　　TD. 折形デザイン研究所
　　　　　Origata Design Institute.

CD. 倉成英俊　Hidetoshi Kuranari
CL. IMF／世界銀行／財務省
　　IMF and the World Bank／Ministry of Finance
PT. 折形デザインフォント (Original Font)

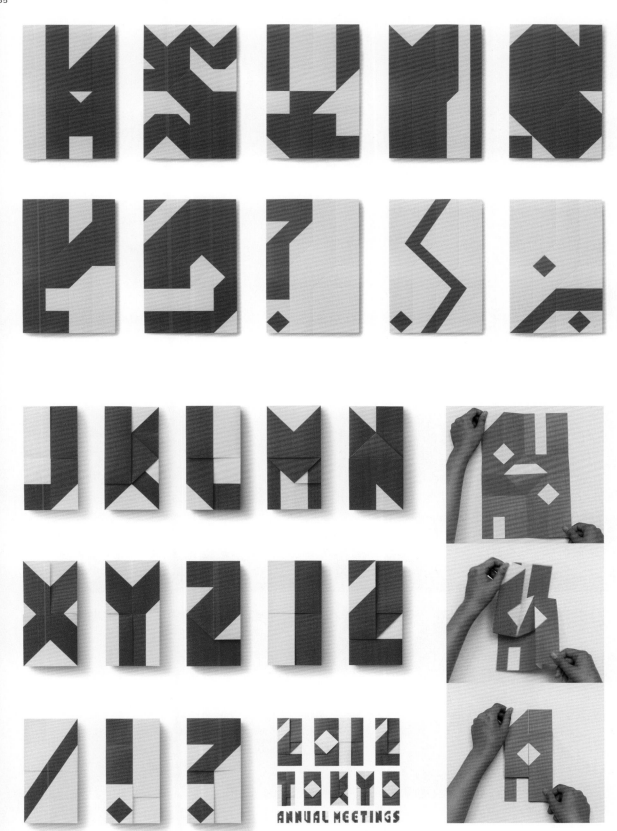

世界188カ国から1万人が参加したIMF世銀東京総会。そのフォントシステムを、日本古来の紙を折る作法「折り形」をリデザインして構築。紙を折ることで「対立するものを融和へ導く」精神を込めた。参加188カ国がひとつになることを願い、総会をひとつの精神で包み込んだ。

A total of 10,000 people from 188 countries around the world attended the IMF-World Bank Tokyo Meeting. Thus, for this meeting, I designed a font system incorporating the idea of *origata*, a traditional Japanese paper-folding method. Folding paper expresses the spirit of "leading conflicts to reconciliation." In this way, I wished for the unification of the 188 countries and aimed to express the meeting's spirit of unification.

ALICE IN WONDERLAND
ZATERDAG
20.30

TWO AND A HALF MEN
22.00

HUIZENJACHT
22.40

HELP, MIJN MAN IS EEN KLUSSER
23.00

VERMIST
21.55

CRIMINAL MINDS
22.55

PLAN B
23.55

Prize Nominee Work

266 Mark & Logotype / Branding
TD. Why Not Associates
CL. Woestijnvis & SBS Belgium
P T. Vier Regular

ベルギーの新しいテレビチャンネルVier向けの、スクリーン上とスクリーン外でのアイデンティティ。このプロジェクトでは、サブチャンネル用のロゴ、チャンネル・アイデントの方向性に関わるコラボレーションに加え、オリジナルのタイプフェイス「Vier Regular」を制作した。

On and off screen identity for a new Belgian television channel Vier. This included creating a bespoke typeface, Vier Regular, as well as logos for its sub channels and collaboration on the direction of the channels idents.

TORAYA TOKYO

 **TORAYA TOKYO**

Prize Nominee Work

267 Mark & Logo
TD. AD. CD. 葛西 薫　Kaoru Kasai
　　　　D. 徳田祐子　Yuko Tokuda
　　　CL. (株)虎屋
　　　　　Toraya Confectionery Co., Ltd.
　　　PT. Custom-made for the project

復元された東京駅の、南口２階回廊沿いにオープンした虎屋の甘味どころ。東京駅は日本の玄関、そして和菓子は今やWAGASHIと呼ばれる世界のスイーツであり、この店をTORAYA TOKYOと名付け、鍵虎と呼ぶ漢字のマークと組み合せた。

Toraya opened a sweets shop along the corridor on the second floor of the restored south side of Tokyo Station. The station is the gateway of Japan, and Japanese confectionery is now known to the world as *wagashi*. I combined the name of TORAYA TOKYO with Toraya's "kantora" Kanji ideogram.

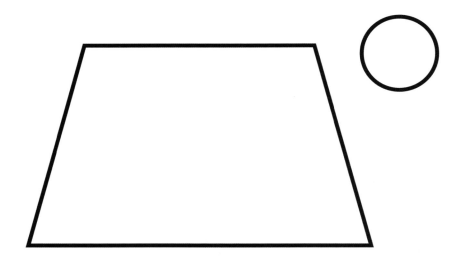

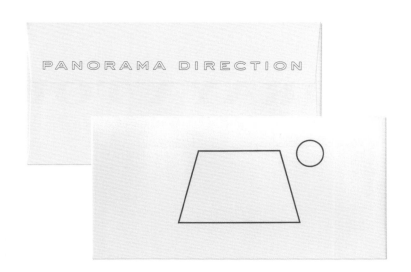

Prize Nominee Work

268 Mark & Logo / Corporate stationery
TD. AD. D. 松本健一　Kenichi Matsumoto
　　CL. Panorama Direction
　　PT. Sackers Gothic

コピーライター事務所の屋号のマークとロゴタイプ。パノラマという名前から、最初に山のかたちの名刺を考えつき、そのシルエットをそのまま使用し、太陽をつけて、パノラマの「パ」に、見えなくもないマークができた。

This is a trade name symbol and logotype idea for a copywriter's office. First, I thought of a mountain-shaped business card, inspired by the name utilizing, "Panorama," and used its silhouette with the sun, resulting in a mark that can look like "パ" (the Japanese monosyllable for the "pa" sound) for "Panorama."

Prize Nominee Work

269 Mark & Logo
TD. 市東 基　Motoi Shito
CL. Ｔ貳肆捌
PT. Custom-made for the project

Ｔ貳肆捌のタイポグラフィは年月と展望を表現している。シンプルな書体を重ねることで、平面の中に年輪のような密度のある造形を完成させた。と、もっともらしく綴っているが実際は自分でもどんなものになるか分からず、ただただ作り続けたのです。

The typographies of T, 2, 4, and 8 express dates and possibilities. I completed a dense format style akin to growth rings on a tree, on a flat surface, by layering a simple font. To be honest, however, I didn't know what it would turn out like. I just kept creating.

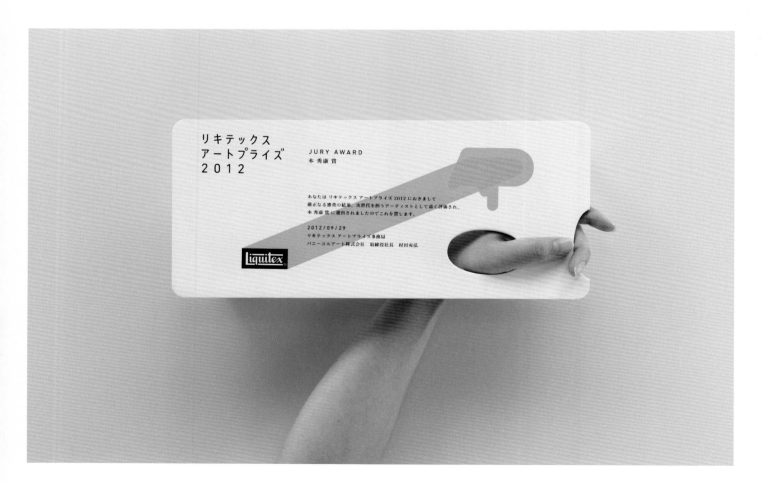

Prize Nominee Work

270 Mark & Logo
TD. AD. D. 色部義昭　Yoshiaki Irobe
　　CL. バニーコルアート㈱
　　　　 bonnyColArt Co., Ltd.
　　PT. Custom-made for the project /
　　　　 DIN Next Rounded / S明朝体

これは絵の具メーカー主催の公募展『Liquitex Art Prize』のためのロゴマークである。絵の具に見立てたArt Prizeの頭文字「AP」の上に筆に見立てたLiquitexのロゴをずらし重ねることで、キャンバスにさっとのせた瞬間の最も鮮やかな色が表現されるように設計した。

These are logos for the "Liquitex Art Prize," an exhibition sponsored by a paint manufacturer. By shifting the "Liquitex" logo and expressing a brush on "AP" (the initials for "Art Prize"), evoking images of paint, I tried to express the most vivid color of paint at the moment when it strikes canvas.

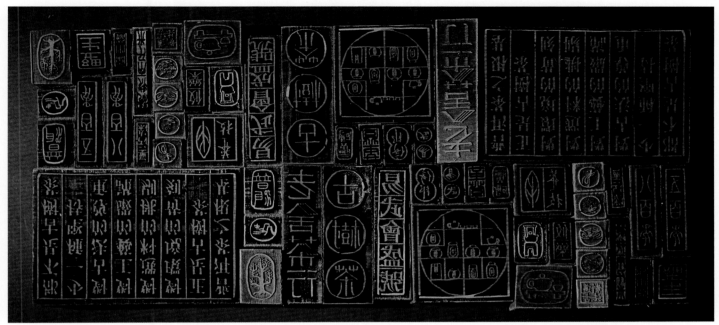

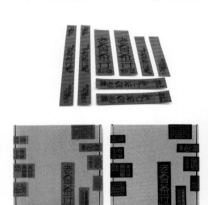

271

272

272 Mark & Logo
TD. AD. 三浦 遊　Yu Miura
　　CD. 澁谷克彦　Katsuhiko Shibuya
　　　　高橋 歩　Ayumu Takahashi
　　D. 渡部宏介　Kosuke Watabe
　　PR. 齋藤圭祐　Keisuke Saito
　　CL. (株)資生堂　Shiseido Co., Ltd.
　　PT. Shiseido Font

271 Branding
TD. D. I. Shaobin Lin
　　CL. Lao she Tea
　　PT. Custom-made for the project /
　　　　Multiple fonts

273

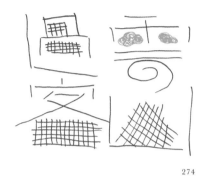

274

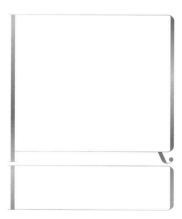

275

276

273 Logotype
TD. AD. 葛西 薫　Kaoru Kasai
　　D. 増田 豊　Yutaka Masuda
　　CL. （株）毎日新聞社
　　　　The Mainichinews Papers
　　PT. Custom-made for the project

274 Logotype
TD. D. I. Hong Hun Hun
　　CL. Getting by Cloudy Mount resort

275 Corporate design
TD. Olaf Jäger
　　D. Regina Jäger
　　CL. Dr. Florian Fries
　　PT. Thesis The Mix
　　　　(Lucas de Groot)

276 Mark & Logo
TD. AD. D. 野村勝久　Katsuhisa Nomura
　　CL. 山口県立美術館
　　　　Yamaguchi Prefectural Art Museum
　　PT. Custom-made for the project

CITIES AND NATURE WITH GHOSTS
YUDAI OSAWA

277

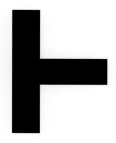

トンネル

Tunnel

278

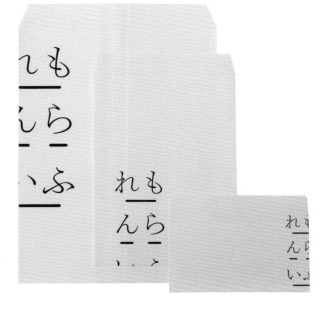

279

278 Mark & Logo
TD. AD. D. 鈴木信輔　Shinsuke Suzuki
　　　　樋口寛人　Hiroto Higuchi
　　P. 西澤智和　Tomokazu Nishizawa
　　CL. トンネル　Tunnel
　　PT. Custom-made for the project/
　　　　Akzidenz Grotesk

277 Mark & Logo
TD. AD. D. 大澤悠大　Yudai Osawa
　　CL. Non-commercial work
　　PT. Giraffe/
　　　　Custom-made for the project

279 Mark & Logo/Corporate stationery
TD. 千原徹也　Tetsuya Chihara
CL. Non-commercial work
PT. イワタ明朝オールド

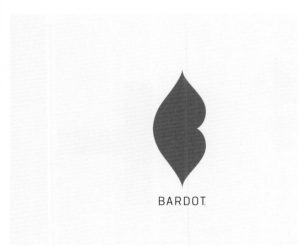

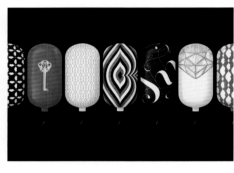

280

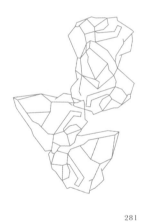

281

282

280 Branding
TD. Landor Associates
 (Tosh Hall / Lia Gordon / Jessica Minn)
CL. Advanced Ice Cream Technologies

281 Mark & Logo
TD. AD. D. 矢後直規　Naonori Yago
 CL.（株）イノウエ
  Inoue Co., Ltd.
 PT. Surrounding

282 Mark & Logo
TD. AD. D. 竹内佐織　Saori Takeuchi
 CL. Gas As Interface Co., Ltd.
 PT. Custom-made for the project

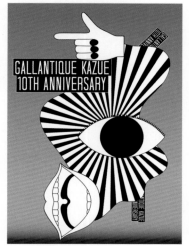

283

284

283 Logotype/CD
TD. AD. D. 長嶋りこ　Rikako Nagashima
　　　　D. 矢後直規　Naonori Yago
　　　　P. 藤田一浩　Kazuhiro Fujita
　　　CL. ギャランティーク和恵
　　　　　Gallantique Kazue
　　　PT. Custom-made for the project

284 Mark & Logo
TD. Zhang Dali
CL. Bantian Creative Cultural Industrial Park

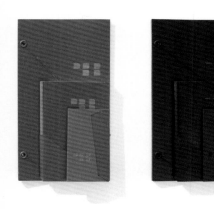

285

286

287

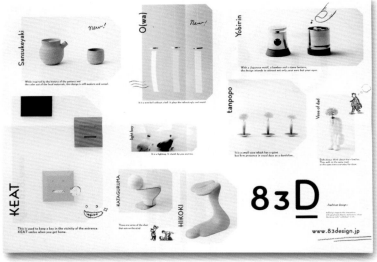

288

285 Mark & Logo
TD. D. 前原翔一　Shoichi Maehara
　　　福澤卓馬　Takuma Fukuzawa
　　　杉山耕太　Kota Sugiyama
CD. 宮田 識　Satoru Miyata
AD. 天宅 正　Masashi Tentaku
PR. 後藤 工　Takumi Goto
CL. D-BROS
PT. Custom-made for the project

286 Event identity
TD. Corina Neuenschwander
　　Noah Venezia
　　Manuel Zenner
　　Ine Meganck
CL. Werkplaats Typografie
PT. Helvetica Textbook /
　　Letter Gothic

287 Branding
TD. OK-RM, London
CL. Strelka institute
PT. Fugue by Radim Peško

288 Mark & Logo / Corporate stationery
TD. AD. D. 堤 裕紀　Yuki Tsutsumi
CL. 83design
PT. ConcertoRndSGOT Std

KIGI
キギ

植原亮輔
art director / creative director
KIGI co.,ltd.
Hillside terrace F-203,
18-8, Sarugakucho,
Shibuya-ku, Tokyo 150-0033,
Japan
Tel 03.3770.0664
iPhone 080.3312.5566
Fax 03.6416.4851
URL www.ki-gi.com
ue@ki-gi.com
ryosuke UEHARA

渡邉良重
art director / designer
KIGI co.,ltd.
Hillside terrace F-203,
18-8, Sarugakucho,
Shibuya-ku, Tokyo 150-0033,
Japan
Tel 03.3770.0664
iPhone 090.3104.6357
Fax 03.6416.4851
URL www.ki-gi.com
yoshie@ki-gi.com
yoshie WATANABE

289

290

STAIA
ROOM
HOME
PARTY

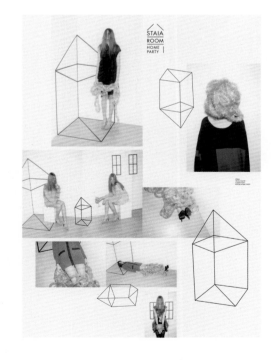

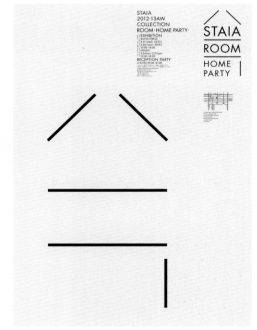

291

289 CI
TD. AD. D. 植原亮輔　Ryosuke Uehara
　CL. (株) キギ　KIGI Co., Ltd.
　PT. Custom-made for the project／
　　　ionic

290 Logotype
TD. AD. D. 平野篤史　Atsushi Hirano
　CL. (株) LEWS 纏
　PT. Custom-made for the project

291 Mark & Logo／DM
TD. AD. D. 長嶋りかこ　Rikako Nagashima
　P. 藤田一浩　Kazuhiro Fujita
　HM. 石川ひろこ　Hiroko Ishikawa
　CL. STAIA
　PT. Futura

292

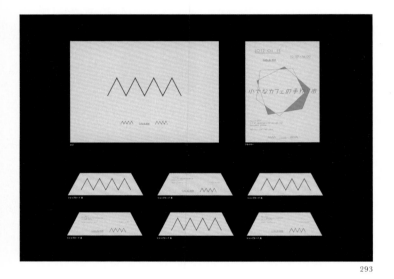

293

294

295

292 VI
TD. Domenic Lippa
D. Lucy Groom
CL. Emily Johnson
PT. T Star PRO

293 Mark & Logo/Shop card/Flyer
TD. AD. D. 常橋惠美　Emi Tsunehashi
CL. cafe de MM
PT. Apropa SSK/
　　Custom-made for the project

294 Invitation
TD. AD. D. 大原健一郎　Kenichiro Ohara
CL. (有)キャタピラープロデュイ
　　Caterpillar Produit Co., Ltd.
PT. Akzidenz Grotesk/Mason

295 CI
TD. Atelier mit Meerblick
CL. 175 Grad
PT. Gravur Condensed

MARK SHOX
SEBASTIAN MOSH
T BROWN

296

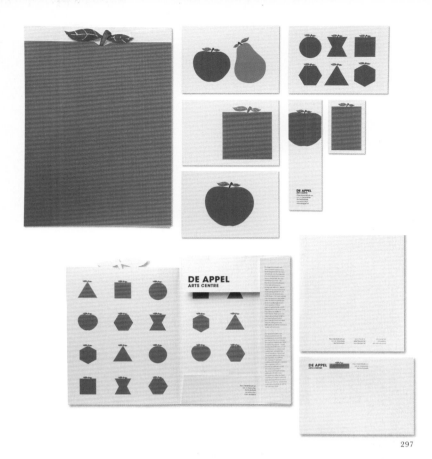

297

RONFOR SMILE

RONFOR SMILE

1. スポーツイベントの企画、コンサルティング
2. スポーツを通じた社会貢献活動に関する企画運営
3. 市民スポーツの振興に関する事業一般

RONFOR SMILE

代表取締役社長
森村ゆき

YUKI MORIMURA

Runforsmile株式会社
〒145-0072 東京都大田区田園調布本町34-16-403
tel 090-3133-5615 mail runforsmile@gmail.com
web http://www.runforsmile.com/
blog http://ameblo.jp/runforsmile/ twitter runforsmile

298

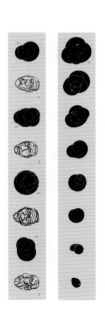 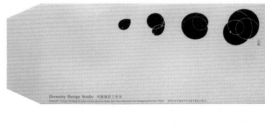     

299

296 Mark & Logo
TD. 市東 基 Motoi Shito
CL. G&C Productions
PT. Helvetica

297 Mark & Logo / Corporate stationery
TD. Thonik
CL. De Appel arts centre
PT. Avantgarde

298 Logotype
TD. 怡土希帆 Kiho Ito
CL. run for smile
PT. Custom-made for the project

299 Mark & Logo / Corporate stationery
TD. Chen Shaofeng
CL. Non-commercial work
PT. Custom-made for the project /
basemic times

en
HAUTE JOAILLERIE

300

GALERIE
JOSEPH TANG
1, RUE CHARLES-
FRANÇOIS
DUPUIS
BÂTIMENT B /
2E ÉTAGE
75003 PARIS
FRANCE
T + 33 9 53 69
55 35 M + 33
6 70 22 04 79
INFO@
GALERIEJOSEPHTANG
.COM

artteas

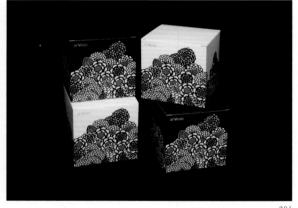

301

302

303

300 Mark & Logo / Corporate stationery
TD. Chris Lee
    Cara Ang
 D. May Chiang
CL. En Haute Joaillerie
PT. Baskerville

301 CI
TD. North
 D. Antony Hart
CL. Artteas
PT. Customised Novarese

302 VI
TD. Andre Baldinger
    Toan Vu-Huu
CL. Galerie Joseph Tang
PT. Monospace 821 Bold

303 Mark & Logo / Stationery
TD. Driv Loo
PR. Chris Wong
CL. Team Tech Production
PT. Albertus / Klavika

TERUHIRO YANAGIHARA／

304

305

THE PHOTOGRAPHERS' GALLERY

ROYAL
FISHING
KINDERHILFE

306

307

304 CI
TD. 三木 健 Ken Miki
CL. Isolation Unit
　　Teruhiro Yanagihara
PT. Helvetica Neue 67 Medium Condensed/
　　Helvetica Neue 57 Condensed/
　　ヒラギノ角ゴ ProN W6

305 CI
TD. Stephen Gilmore
　　Louis Mikolay
CL. Dalton Maag
PT. Aktiv Grotesk

306 VI
TD. North
　D. Antony Hart
CL. The Photographers' Gallery
PT. Customised Akzideuz Grotesk

307 CI
TD. Friederike Gaigl
CL. Royal Fishing Kinderhilfe e.V.

309

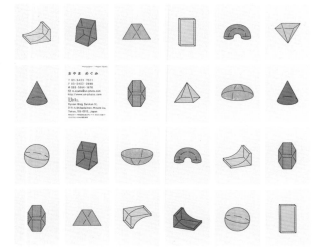

308

311

312

310

308 Mark & Logo / Name card
TD. AD. D. 前原翔一　Shoichi Maehara
　　PD. 北川武司　Takeshi Kitagawa
　　CL. UN
　　PT. Custom-made for the project

309/310 Mark & Logo / Name card
TD. D. 干場邦一　Kunikazu Hoshiba
　　CD. 岸 勇希　Yuuki Kishi
　　CL. (株)参十七度　37℃Co., Ltd.
　　PT. Custom-made for the project /
　　小塚ゴシックPro-R

311 Mark & Logo / Branding
TD. AD. D. 柏倉瑛子　Eiko Kashiwakura
　　CD. 安藤僚子　Ryoko Ando
　　CL. 73 (ななみ) 和食ダイニング
　　Dining Bar 73
　　PT. DIN Condensed

312 Corporate design
TD. Atelier mit Meerblick
　　Mehtap Avci
　　CL. ABK Stuttgart
　　PT. Yeni Zaman

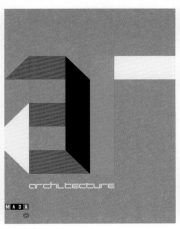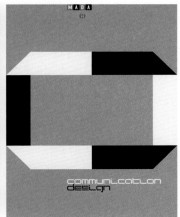

313

314

315

316

315 Mark & Logo / Brochure
TD. CD. Benny Au
 CD. Teresa Chan
 P. Studio TM
CL. Antalis(HK)Limited
PT. Custom-made for the project /
 AW Conqueror

313 Mark & Logo / Poster
TD. MADA LAB. / John Warwicker
CL. MADA
 (Monash Art, Design & Architecture)
PT. Custom-made for the project

314 Mark & Logo / Corporate stationery
TD. Vanessa Eckstein
CL. Furlined

316 Mark & Logo
TD. 宮川 宏　Hiroshi Miyakawa
CL. Piece to Peace

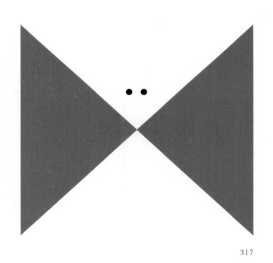

317

318

319

デザインあ

©NHK

320

317 Mark & Logo
TD. AD. 佐野研二郎　Kenjiro Sano
　D. 石黒篤史　Atsushi Ishiguro
CL. 東京アートディレクターズクラブ
　　Tokyo Art Directors Club
P T. Clarendon

318 VI
TD. AD. D. 大森 剛　Tsuyoshi Omori
　CL. 羽場太郎建築設計事務所
　　Taro Haba Architects

319 Logotype
TD. 原 健三　Kenzo Hara
CL. kilk records

320 Logotype
CD. AD. TD. 佐藤 卓　Taku Satoh
MO-DI. TD. 中村勇吾　Yugo Nakamura
　　MU. コーネリアス　Cornelius
　　CH. 日本放送協会　NHK
PRO. CL. NHK エデュケーショナル
　　　　NHK Educational
　　PT. Custom-made for the project

321

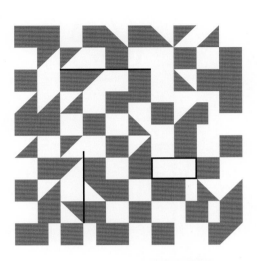

322

Health Care Camp

SHISEIDO

323

青山見本帖

324

322 Logotype
TD. AD. 植原亮輔   Ryosuke Uehara
   D. 斎藤 純   Jun Saito
   PR. 中岡美奈子   Minako Nakaoka
   CL. SEMPRE
   PT. Custom-made for the project

321 Mark & Logo
TD. AD. D. 松原秀祐 Shusuke Matsubara
   CL. トポス

323 Mark & Logo
TD. D. 柴田賢蔵   Kenzo Shibata
   AD. 佐藤益大   Masuhiro Sato
    D. 伊藤親雄   Chikao Ito
    C. 松井孝典   Takafumi Matsui
   CL. (株)資生堂
      Shiseido Co., Ltd.
   PT. Custom-made for the project

324 Mark & Logo/Corporate stationery
TD. AD. D. 高田 唯 Yui Takada
   CL. (株)竹尾
      Takeo Co., Ltd.
   PT. Original Font

TOYOTA 86

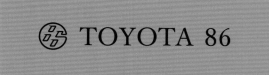

325

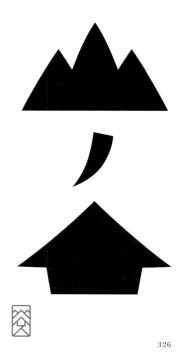

326

327

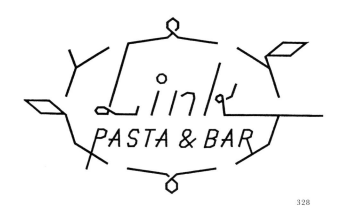

328

325 Mark & Logo
TD. AD. 葛西 薫　Kaoru Kasai
AD. 小島潤一　Junichi Kojima
CD. 前田知巳　Tomomi Maeda
D. 増田 豊　Yutaka Masuda
藤田佳子　Kako Fujita
CL. (株)トヨタマーケティングジャパン
Toyota Marketing Japan Corporation
PT. Bodoni

326 Mark & Logo
TD. 山本和久　Kazuhisa Yamamoto
CL. 山ノ家プロジェクト
Yamanoie Project

327 VI
TD. D. Hao, Ma
CL. ShangHai DAWN Film &
Television communication Co., Ltd.
PT. Custom-made for the project/
Garamond/Qi Ti simple

328 Mark & Logo
TD. AD. D. 安部洋佑　Yosuke Abe
CL. pasta & bar Link
PT. Original

野らぼー

合同会社
美術通信
社

330

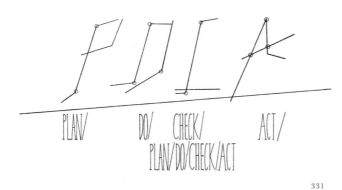

PLAN/　　DO/　CHECK/　　ACT/
PLAN/DO/CHECK/ACT

331

なし世界

江口宏志

text & photograph by Hiroshi Eguchi
typography & illustration by Daijiro Ohara

332

329 Mark & Logo
TD. CD. AD. D. 宮川和之　Kazuyuki Miyakawa
　　CD. 鈴木祐介　Yusuke Suzuki
　　CL. (有)善通寺フーズ
　　　　Zentsugi Food
　　PT. Custom-made for the project

330 Logotype
TD. AD. D. 伸條正義　Masayoshi Nakajo
　　CL. 美術通信社　Bijutsu Press
　　PT. Custom-made for the project

331 Logotype
TD. AD. D. 竹内佐織　Saori Takeuchi
　　CL. PDCA
　　PT. Custom-made for the project

332 Mark & Logo
TD. 大原大次郎　Daijiro Ohara
CL. (株)木楽舎　Kirakusha, inc.
PT. 筑紫ゴシック

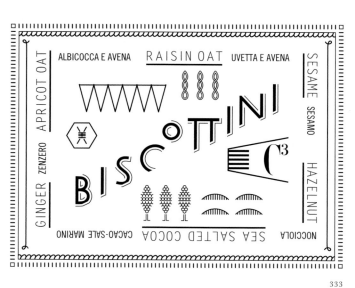

333

334

軽井沢千住博美術館

HIROSHI SENJU MUSEUM KARUIZAWA

335

333 VI
TD. AD. D. 増永明子　Akiko Masunaga
　　C. 山村光春　Mitsuharu Yamamura
CL. (株)アッシュ・セー・クレアシオン
　　H.C.Création Co., Ltd.
PT. Custom-for the project/
　　Trade Gothic / Letter Gothic

334 Logotype
TD. AD. D. 三宅宇太郎　Utaro Miyake
　　CL. (株)東本三郎 YOROZU 相談室
　　　Tomoto Saburo YOROZU Advice Co., Ltd.
PT. Custom-made for the project

335 Logotype
TD. AD. D. 菊地敦己　Atsuki Kikuchi
　　CL. 公益財団法人 国際文化カレッジ
　　　International Cultural College Foundation
PT. Custom-made for the project

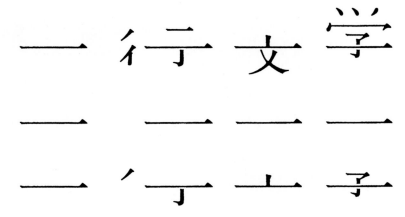

336

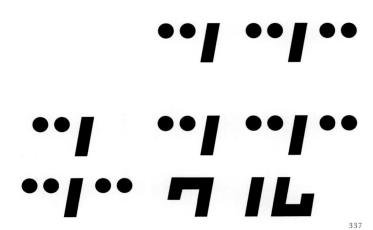

337

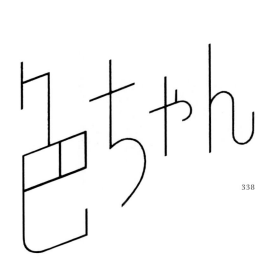

338

339

336 Logotype
TD. AD. D. 小杉幸一　Koichi Kosugi
　　CL. 一行文学

337 Logotype
TD. AD. D. 小杉幸一　Koichi Kosugi
　　CL. ツヅクル　Tsuzukulu

338 Logotype
TD. D. 福岡南央子　Naoko Fukuoka
　　CL. 色ちゃん
　　PT. Custom-made for the project

339 Logotype
TD. AD. D. 田頭慎太郎　Shintaro Tagashira
　　CD. 村松秀俊　Hidetoshi Muramatsu
　　CL. AD ROOM
　　PT. Custom-made for the project

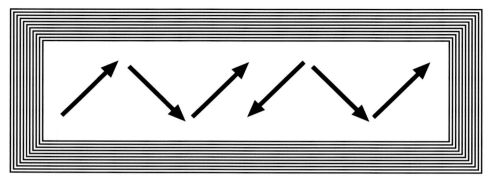

340

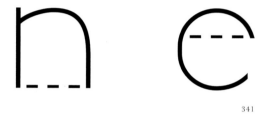

341

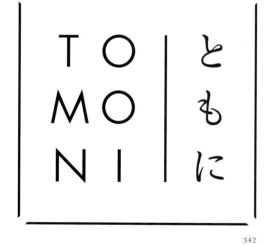

342

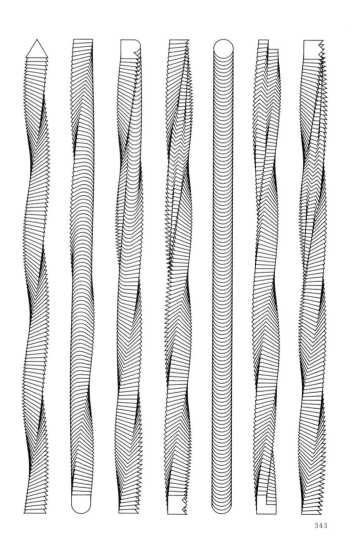

343

342 Mark & Logo
TD. AD. 中田卓志　Takushi Nakada
D. スズキカヨ　Kayo Suzuki
CD. 松崎武史　Takeshi Matsuzaki
C. 柴田秀信　Hidenobu Shibata
CL. (株)中三　Nakasan Co., Ltd.
PT. Futura / はなぶさ /
custom-made for the project

341 Mark & Logo
TD. AD. D. 樋口寛人　Hiroto Higuchi
CL. ネ　ne
PT. Custom-made for the project

340 Mark & Logo
TD. D. Guo Guo Guang
CL. NAPEK ElectronicTechnology Co., Ltd.

343 Mark & Logo
TD. 原 健三　Kenzo Hara
CL. kilk records

344

345

SUN-AD

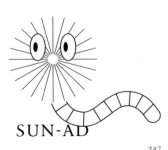

SUN-AD

346

347

344 Logotype / Corporate stationery
TD. AD. D. 安部洋佑 Yosuke Abe
　　CL. 奥原工芸 Okuhara Kougei
　　PT. Original

345 Logotype
TD. AD. D. 平野篤史 Atsushi Hirano
　　CL. (株)LEWS 纏
　　PT. Custom-made for the project

346 Mark & Logo
TD. AD. D. I. 渡邉良重 Yoshie Watanabe
　　CL. (株)集英社 Shueisha Inc.

347 Mark & Logo / Stationery
TD. D. I. 高井 薫 Kaoru Takai
　　CL. (株)サン・アド
　　SUN-AD Co., Ltd.

19

DESIGN SCHOOL

348

349

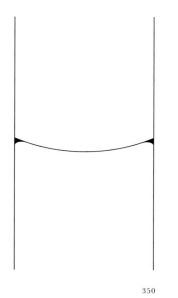

350

351

349 CI
TD. AD. 植原亮輔　Ryosuke Uehara
CD. 青木むすび　Musubi Aoki
D. 天宅 正　Masashi Tentaku
C. 国井美果　Mika Kunii
CC. 後藤 工　Takumi Goto
CL. (株)ルミネアソシエーツ
　　Lumine Associates
PT. Custom-made for the project

348 Logotype
TD. AD. 浅葉克己　Katsumi Asaba
D. 石原千明　Chiaki Ishihara
CL. 桑沢デザイン研究所
　　Kuwasawa Design School
PT. Custom-made for the project

350 VI
TD. AD. D. 大森 剛　Tsuyoshi Omori
CL. Masao Hayashi

351 Mark & Logo
TD. AD. D. 大原健一郎　Kenichiro Ohara
CL. 4COLORS
PT. Copperplate Gothic

Signage & Display,
Package Design

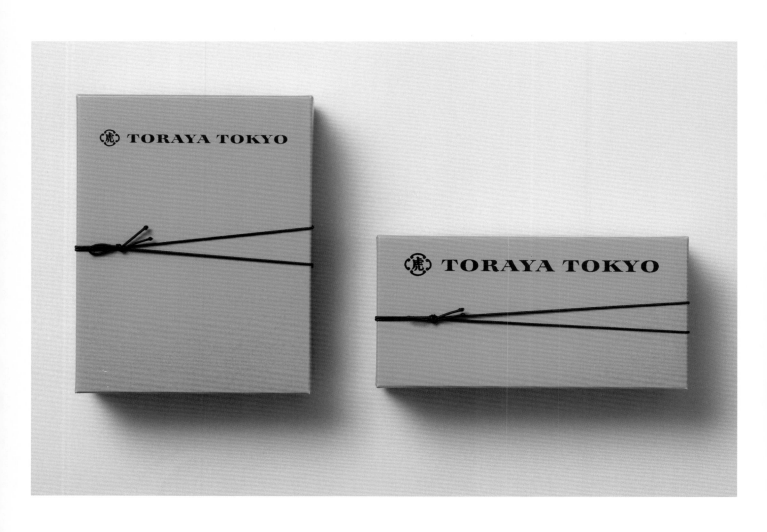

Prize Nominee Work

352 Packaging
TD. AD. CD. 葛西 薫　Kaoru Kasai
　　　 D. 徳田祐子　Yuko Tokuda
　　　CL. (株)虎屋
　　　　　　 Toraya Confectionery Co., Ltd.
　　　 PT. Custom-made for the project

新しくなった東京駅の南口にオープンしたこの
店は、建築家・内藤廣氏の設計によるもので、
往時のレンガがむき出しの、非常に個性的なイ
ンテリアである。そのレンガ色を基調に、古さ
のなかに新しい虎屋の表情を作ろうと思った。

This new shop on the south side of the renewed Tokyo Station was designed by Mr. Hiroshi Naito (architect). It features a very distinct interior design, accentuated by bare brickwork, evoking a feeling of the past. I then thought of creating a new concept for Toraya by touching on such "antiquity," thus using brick color as the basic tone.

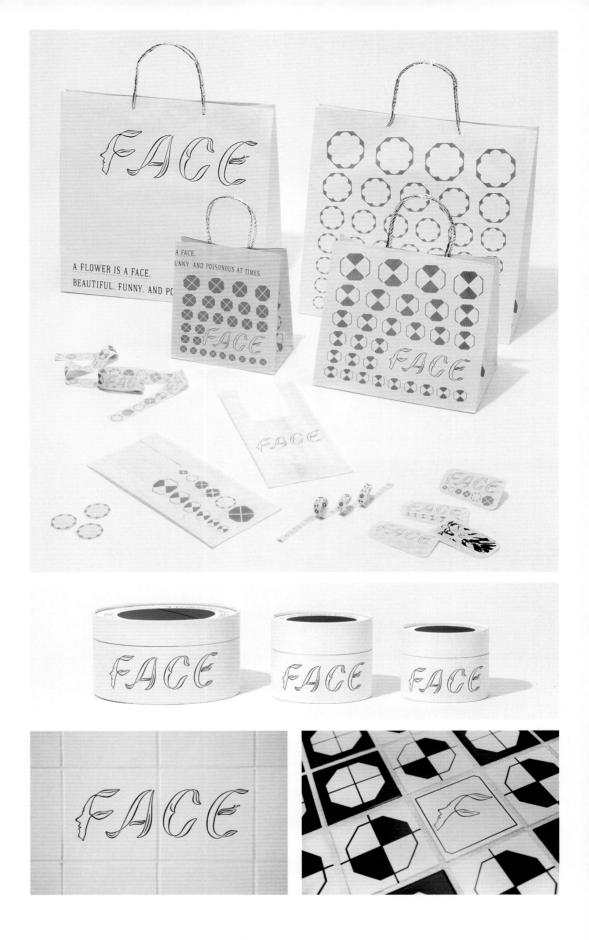

Prize Nominee Work

353 Signage & Display / Packaging
TD. AD. 植原亮輔　Ryosuke Uehara
　　CD. 青木むすび　Musubi Aoki
　　　D. 天宅 正　　Masashi Tentaku
　　　ID. イーエム　e.m.
　　　CC. 後藤 工　　Takumi Goto
　　　CL. (株)ルミネアソシエーツ Lumine Associates
　　　PT. Custom-made for the project

有楽町ルミネの一階にオープンした花屋さんのグラフィックです。「花は顔。美しく、毒々しく、いとおしい」という考え方のもと、クリエイティブディレクターの青木むすびさんと一緒にイメージを考え、僕は、グラフィック、空間、WEBのアートディレクションを担当しました。

These are graphics for a flower shop that opened on the first floor of LUMINE Yurakucho. With the idea that "flowers are like faces; they are beautiful and sometimes appear both angry and sweet," Ms. Musubi Aoki (creative director) and I thought of an idea, and I took charge of graphics, spacing, and Web art direction.

Prize Nominee Work

354 Exhibition
TD. AD. D. 植原亮輔　Ryosuke Uehara
　　　渡邉良重　Yoshie Watanabe
CL. ギンザ・グラフィック・ギャラリー
　　ginza graphic gallery

キギ展は、2012年5月にgggギャラリーで開催されました。キギは、私たち（植原亮輔と渡邉良重）が2012年1月に設立した会社です。主にドラフト時代に手掛けた企業やショップ等のブランディングの仕事からD-BROSのプロダクト、個人的な作品に至るまで約14年間のクリエイションを凝縮して展示しました。

The KIGI Design Exhibition was held at the ginza graphic gallery (ggg) in May 2012. We (Ryosuke Uehara and Yoshie Watanabe) established the company (KIGI) in January 2012. Our work, spanning about 14 years, was displayed in a condensed manner, ranging from those for corporations and shop branding (produced when we belonged to DRAFT Co., Ltd.) to D-BROS products and personal artwork.

355

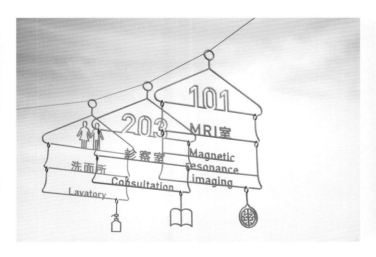

356

356 Signage & Display
TD. AD. 廣村正彰　Masaaki Hiromura
D. 黄 善佳　Fang Son Ga
ID. 橋本夕紀夫　Yukio Hashimoto
P. （株）ナカサアンドパートナーズ
Nacása & Partnars Inc.
CL. 医療法人心和会
Healthcare Corporation Shinwakai
PT. 新ゴR／DIN R

355 Exhibition
TD. AD. 中島英樹　Hideki Nakajima
CL. （株）大和プレス
Daiwa Press

357

358

359

357 Signage
TD. AD. D. 菊地敦己　Atsuki Kikuchi
　　CL. 公益財団法人 国際文化カレッジ
　　　　International Cultural College Foundation
　　PT. Custom-made for the project

358 Signage & Display
TD. 榮 良太　Ryota Sakae
CL. （株）集英社　Shueisha Inc.
PT. Hand writing

359 Signage & Display
TD. AD. 居山浩二　　Koji Iyama
　　 D. 渡辺真由子　Mayuko Watanabe
　　　　杉村武則　　Takenori Sugimura
　　　　柴田沙央里　Saori Shibata
　　CL. カモ井加工紙（株）Kamoi Kakoshi Co., Ltd.
　　PT. Custom-made for the project

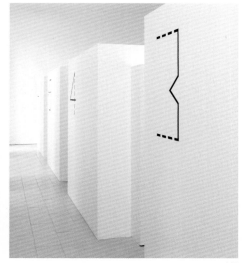

361

360

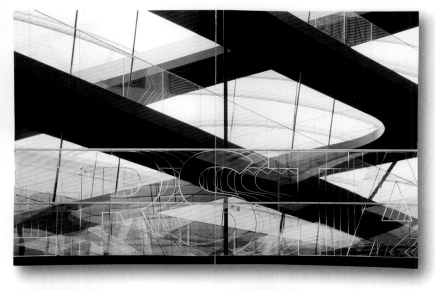

362

360 Signage & Display
TD. AD. D. 丸橋 桂　Katsura Marubashi
　P. 伊東祥太郎　Shotaro Ito
　CL. (株)資生堂　Shiseido Co., Ltd.
　PT. Custom-made for the project

361 Signage & Display
TD. AD. D. 長嶋りかこ　Rikako Nagashima
　D. 矢後直規　Naonori Yago
　CL. 壬生歯科　Mibu Dental Clinic
　PT. Custom-made for the project

362 Signage & Display
TD. Carolin Himmel
　　Andreas Uebele
　P. Christian Richters
　CL. Adidas Ag
　PT. AdiHaus

363

364

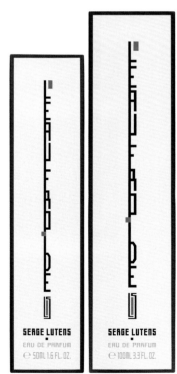

365

363 Packaging
 TD. artless Inc.
AD. D. 川上 俊　Shun Kawakami
 D. (Assistant) 杉 怜　Ryo Sugi
PM. 若松 牧　Maki Wakamatsu
CL. ヨシモリ（株）Yoshimori Inc.
PT. artless grotesk (Original Font)

364 Packaging
 TD. Serge Lutens
TD. AD. D. 和久井裕史　Hiroshi Wakui
CD. 平戸絵里子　Eriko Hirato
CL. Les Salons Du Palais Royal Shiseido - Sli
PT. Original-made for the project

365 Packaging
 TD. Serge Lutens
TD. AD. D. 和久井裕史　Hiroshi Wakui
CD. 平戸絵里子　Eriko Hirato
CL. Les Salons Du Palais Royal Shiseido - Sli
PT. Original-made for the project

366

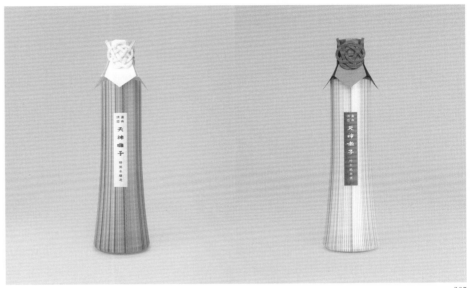

367

368

366 Packaging
TD. AD. D. 中本陽子　Yoko Nakamoto
　CD. AD. 葛西 薫　Kaoru Kasai
　　　I. Philippe Weisbecker
　　PR. 坂東美和子　Miwako Bando
　　　　常木宏之　Hiroyuki Tsuneki
　　CL. Toraya Tokyo
　　PT. RcP本明朝 - M新小がな

367 Packaging
TD. AD. D. 黒柳 潤　Jun Kuroyanagi
　　CO. 桑原康介　Kousuke Kuwabara
　　CL. 魚沼酒造（株）
　　　　Uonuma Sake Brewery Co., Ltd.
　　PT. Custom-made for the project /
　　　　金陵

368 Packaging
TD. AD. CD. 植原亮輔　Ryosuke Uehara
　　　D. 岩永和也　Kazuya Iwanaga
　　CL. （株）ダイドーインターナショナル
　　　　Daidoh International Ltd.

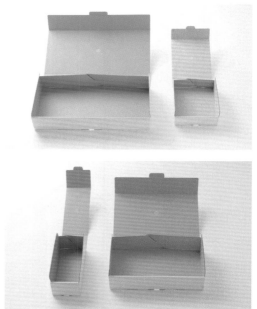

20

369

370

371

372

369 Packaging
TD. AD. D. 竹内佐織　Saori Takeuchi
　　TD. 寺島響水　Kyosui Terashima
　　C. 牧田智之　Tomoyuki Makita
CL. 濱田醤油
　　Hamada Syoyu Coporation
PT. Custom-made for the project

370 Packaging
　　TD. AD. 植原亮輔　Ryosuke Uehara
　　TD. AD. I . 渡邉良重　Yoshie Watanabe
　　D. 小山麻子　Asako Koyama
CL. (株)スマイルズ
　　Smiles Co., Ltd.

371 Packaging
　　TD. AD. D. 石川 耕　　Ko Ishikawa
　　CD. 佐藤可士和　Kashiwa Sato
CL. (株)ユニクロ
　　Uniqlo Co., Ltd.
PT. Custom-made for the project

372 Packaging
　　TD. D. 増永明子　Akiko Masunaga
CL. モリタ(株)
　　Morita Corporation
PT. Custom-for the project/
　　News Gothic / Letter Gothic

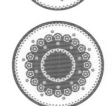

373

374

375

376

373 Packaging
TD. AD. 細島雄一　Yuichi Hosojima
D. 齋藤可奈子　Kanako Saito
小松崎裕寿　Yuji Komatsuzaki
CL. メリーチョコレート
Mary Chocolate
PT. Custom-made for the project

374 Packaging
TD. AD. D. 松原秀祐　Shusuke Matsubara
CL. 北島酒造(株)　Kitajima Shuzo
PT. A-OTF正楷書CB1 Std

375 Packaging
TD. AD. D. 黒栁 潤　Jun Kuroyanagi
CL. (株)越後鶴亀
Echigo Tsurukame Co., Ltd
PT. ヒラギノ /
Custom-made for the project

376 Packaging
TD. AD. D. 増永明子　Akiko Masunaga
C. 山村光春　Mitsuharu Yamamura
CL. (株)アッシュ・セー・クレアシオン
H.C.Création Co., Ltd.
PT. Custom-for the project /
Trade Gothic / Letter Gothic

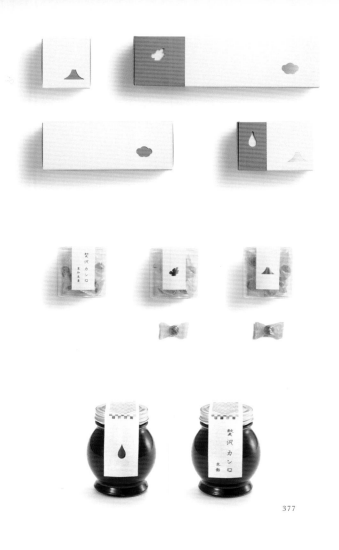

377

378

379

380

377 Packaging
TD. AD. 関本明子　Akiko Sekimoto
　　D. 岩永和也　Kazuya Iwanaga
　PR. 川又俊明　Toshiaki Kawamata
　　　細田幸子　Sachiko Hosoda
　　　中岡美奈子　Minako Nakaoka
　　　藤村るり子　Ruriko Fujimura
　CL. カンロ（株）　Kanro Co., Ltd.
　PT. Custom-made for the project

378 Packaging
TD. AD. D. C. E. 黒柳 潤　Jun Kuroyanagi
　　　　　A. 伊藤睦子　Mutsuko Ito（Wooden stamp）
　C. E. PM. 村山 薫　Kaoru Murayama
　　　PM. 桑原康介　Kousuke Kuwabara
　　　CL. 東下組農産物加工所
　　　　　Higashishimogumi Agro processing plant
　　　PT. Custom-made for the project

379 Packaging
TD. AD. 廣村正彰　Masaaki Hiromura
　　AD. 柴田文江　Fumie Shibata
　PR. 中川政七商店 十三代 中川淳
　　　Nakagawa Masashichi Shoten,
　　　The 13th president Jun Nakagawa
　CL. （株）タダフサ　Tadafusa Co., Ltd.
　PT. Custom-made for the project

380 Packaging
TD. Chris Bolton
CL. Anton + Anton
PT. Sackers Gothic Std /
　　Futura Condensed

Advertising

Prize Nominee Work

381 Poster
TD. D. Philippe Apeloig
  CL. Théâtre National de Toulouse
  PT. Bespoke typeface

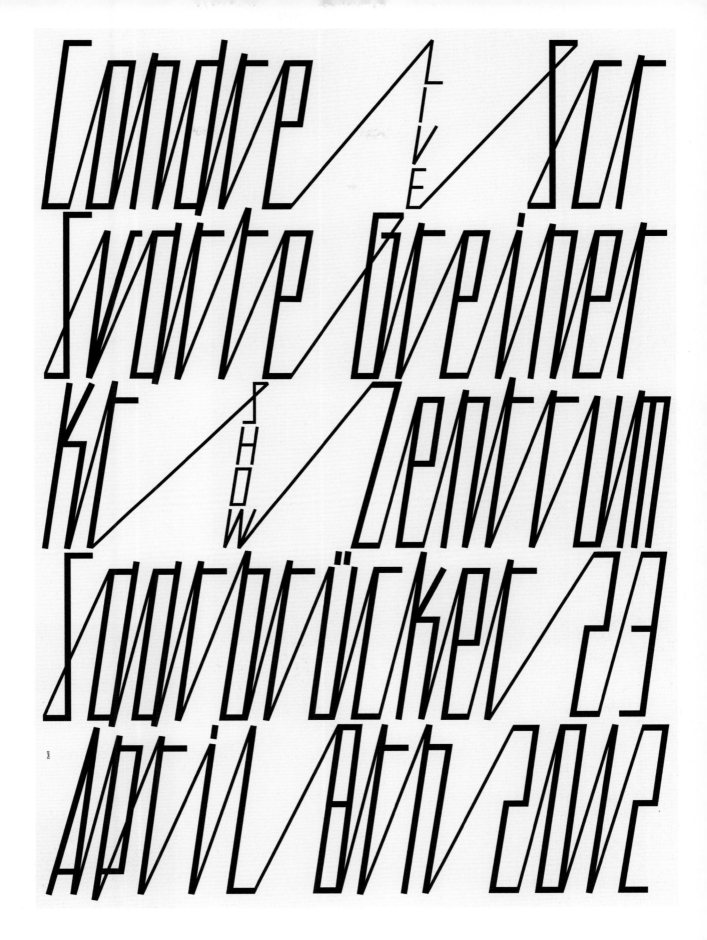

タイポグラフィのみのこのポスターは、テクスチャが豊かでアンビエントな音とクリアな楽器音が混成された音楽のライブのために制作された。かすかな実際のブレーク(間)を伴う連続的かつエッジーな音のように、単独の文字をつなげてタイポグラフィの混成を作ることにした。

The exclusively typograhic poster was made for a triple-live-show of rich textured ambient sounds and crystal clear instrumental noise. Like the continuous and edgy sounds with minor real breaks we decided to connect the solo letters to form a typographic concoction.

Prize Nominee Work

383 Poster
TD. AD. D. 草谷隆文 Takafumi Kusagaya
CL. Unite本部 Unite Headquarters
PT. Adobe Caslon Pro Regular

自身が参加している東日本震災支援のプロジェクトのひとつである玉川学園UNITE本部の支援ライブの告知ポスターである。支援プロジェクトと名がつくと"ある顔つき"に偏ってしまいがちだが、極力暖かさと厳しさを同時に感じさせるビジュアルになるように気を配った。

This is a poster advertising a concert organized by the Tamagawa Gakuen "UNITE" Headquarters, one of the support projects for those affected by the Great East Japan Earthquake in which I participate. Support projects tend to take on a "certain feeling," so I tried in earnest to ensure that the poster would encompass both warmth and severity as much as possible.

Prize Nominee Work

384 Poster
TD. AD. D. 草谷隆文　Takafumi Kusagaya
CL. 草谷デザイン　Kusagaya Design Inc.
PT. Custom-made for the project

ここ2年ほど何か機会があればマジックインキを使った表現を試みている。事務所の年賀状をこの表現で続けている。草谷の「K」とデザインの「D」をモティーフに使い、今までならマジックで描いた後に色加工をしたが、ストレートに原画のまま引き延ばした。

I have tried to create a concept using felt pens over the past two years or so, whenever I have an opportunity, including the time when I made the New Year's card for our office. I usually apply color after drawing lines with felt pens, but, this time, I continued solely with the original strokes, using the "K" of "Kusagaya" and the "D" of "Design" as a motif.

Prize Nominee Work

385 Poster
TD. 渋谷克彦　Katsuhiko Shibuya
CL. （株）資生堂　Shiseido Co., Ltd.

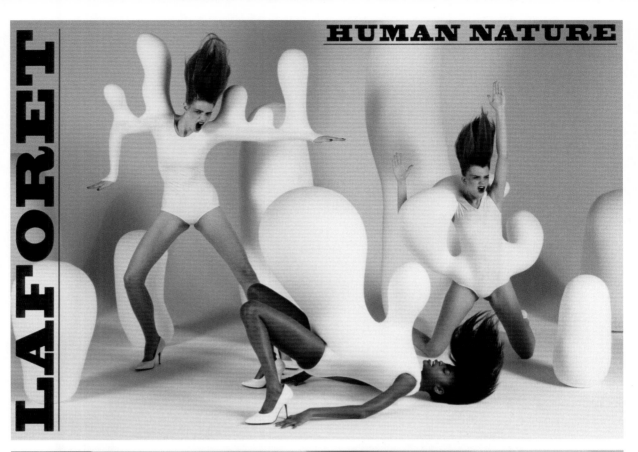

Prize Nominee Work

386 Campaign
TD. AD. D. 長嶋りかこ　Rikako Nagashima
D. 矢後直規　Naonori Yago
P. 戎 康友　Yasutomo Ebisu
HM. 加茂克也　Katsuya Kamo
ST. 伊藤佐智子　Sachiko Ito
CL. 森ビル流通システム㈱
Mori Bldg. Ryutsu System Co., Ltd.
PT. Custom-made for the project

人間がもともと持っている、目に見えないけど
みんなの内にあるであろう、「生命力みたいなも
の」をカタチにした。震災後のラフォーレをひ
っぱってくれるようなものを、とのオーダーだ
った。昭和期のような得体のしれない熱量がほ
しくて、写真や文字の見え方に時代感を入れた。

Here, I tried to bring the idea of "vitality" — something almost invisible but inherent in all humans — into physical form, in response to a request to create something that will support Laforet's business after the earthquake disaster. I wanted to express an unknown energy, along with something akin to the Showa Period, and then tried to add a sense of that time period in the photographs and letters.

Prize Nominee Work

387 Poster
TD. AD. D. 上西祐理　Yuri Uenishi
CD. 小郷拓良　Takeru Kogo
CL. 上野風月堂　Ueno Fugetsudo
PT. Times New Roman/
　　Custom-made for the project

カステラのふわふわしたスポンジ感や、特徴的な直方体の形状をテーマに制作しました。細かな暗い色面はよく見ると、細かい文字で出来ていたり、砂糖の粗目やスポンジを表すような様々なトーンで出来ています。ふとカステラいいな、食べたいなと思ってもらえると嬉しいです。

I created this using a theme featuring soft sponge textures and the characteristic cuboid shapes of Castella cake. If you look carefully, you will find that the minute dark color surface is composed of very small letters in various tones, expressing coarse sugar and sponge cake. Actually, I would be ecstatic if this makes you feel like eating a piece of Castella cake.

388

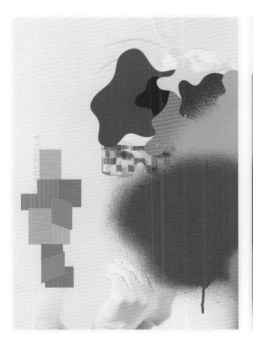

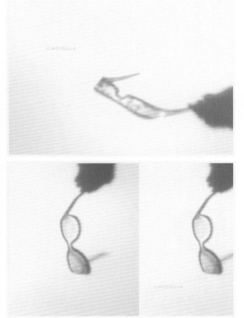

389

388 Poster
TD. AD. 葛西 薫　Kaoru Kasai
AD. 小島潤一　Junichi Kojima
CD. 前田知巳　Tomomi Maeda
D. 増田 豊　Yutaka Masuda
　　藤田佳子　Kako Fujita
P. 五條伴好　Banko Gojo
CL. (株)トヨタマーケティングジャパン
　　Toyota Marketing Japan Corporation
PT. Custom-made for the project

389 Poster
TD. 榮 良太　Ryota Sakae
CL. マジックタッチジャパン
　　Magic Touch Japan
PT. Raoul Transport

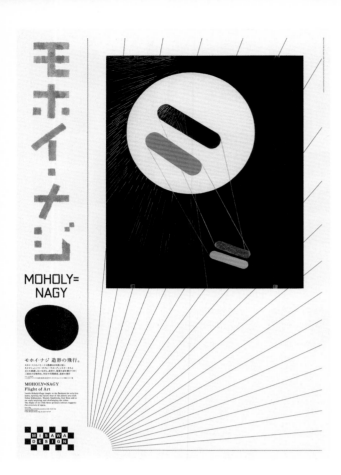

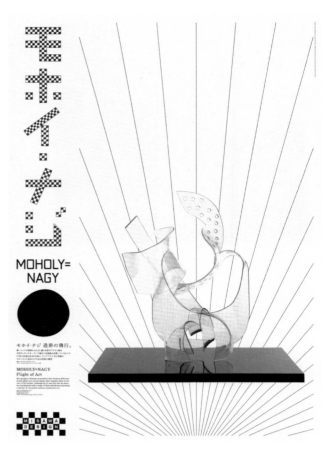

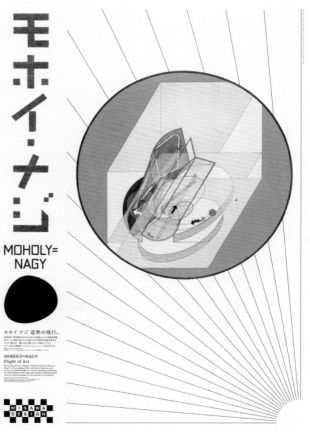

390 Poster
TD. AD. 浅葉克己　Katsumi Asaba
　　CD. 長岡 潤　Jun Nagaoka
　　PR. 城井廣邦　Hirokuni Shiroi
　　　C. 新藤真知　Makoto Shindo
　　　D. 石原千明　Chiaki Ishihara
　　CL. ミサワホーム　Misawa Homes Co., Ltd.
　　PT. 游明朝体 / Custom-made for the project

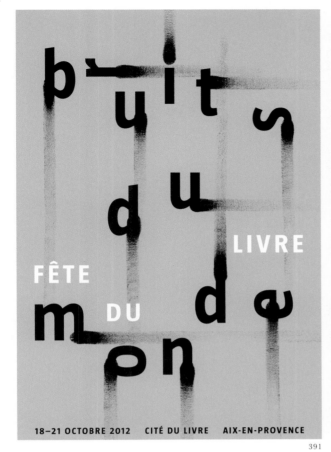

18–21 OCTOBRE 2012   CITÉ DU LIVRE   AIX-EN-PROVENCE

391

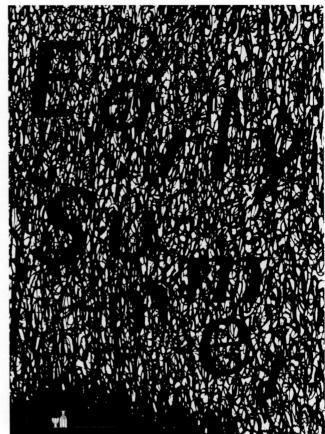

392

393

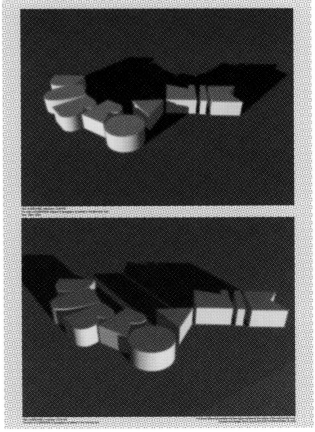

394

391 Poster
TD. D. Philippe Apeloig
   CL. Fête du Livre – Aix-en-Provence
   PT. Taz Bold

392 Poster
TD. AD. D. 栗林和夫 Kazuo Kuribayashi
   CL. (株)ヴィノテーク Vinothèque Co., Ltd.
   PT. Custom-made for the project

393 Poster
TD. AD. D. 上田真未 Mami Ueda
   CL. Non-commercial work
   PT. Helvetica Neue Light

394 Poster
TD. D. I. Boris Ljubicic
   I. Igor Ljubicic
   CL. Studio International
   PT. Strand

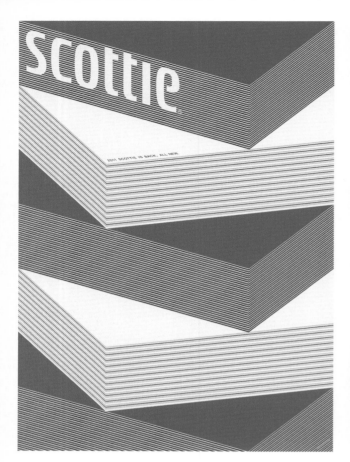

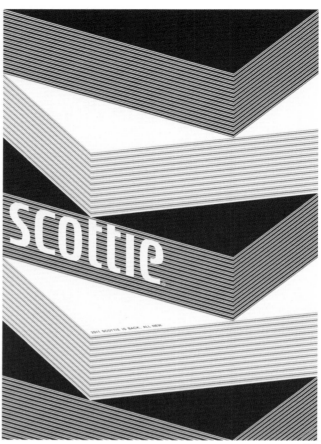

395

396

395 Poster
TD. AD. D. 松永 真　Shin Matsunaga
　　　　D. 松永真次郎　Shinjiro Matsunaga
　　　　清川萌未　Moemi Kiyokawa
CL. 日本製紙クレシア（株）
　　Nippon Paper Crecia Co., Ltd.
PT. Custom-made for the project

396 Campaign
TD. AD. 佐野研二郎　Kenjiro Sano
　　　D. 市東 基　Motoi Shito
　　　P. 森本美絵　Mie Morimoto
CL. LUMINE
PT. Custom-made for the project

Hiraka Express

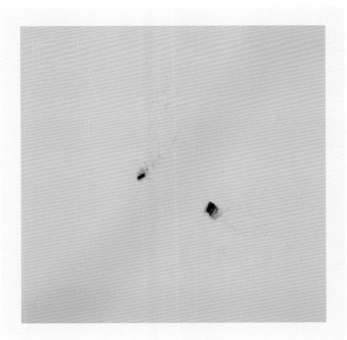 

398 Poster
TD. AD. 玉置太一　Taichi Tamaki
　　　P. 宇禄　　　Uroku
　　　C. 歓崎浩司　Koji Kanzaki
　　　CL. Hair Salon uecology
　　　PT. 本明朝

397 Poster
TD. AD. D. 竹村真太郎　Shintaro Takemura
　　　CL. 平賀運送　Hiraka Express
　　　PT. Custom-made for the project

399

400

399 Poster
TD. AD. 八木義博　Yoshihiro Yagi
　　CD. 高崎卓馬　Takuma Takasaki
　　 C. 一倉 宏　Hiroshi Ichikura
　　　　坂本和加　Waca Sakamoto
　　 D. 畠山大介　Daisuke Hatakeyama
　　　　小林るみ子　Rumiko Kobayashi
　　 P. 藤原康利　Yasutoshi Fujiwara
　　CL. 東日本旅客鉄道 (株) East Japan Railway Company
　　PL. Futura / 小塚ゴシック

400 Campaign
TD. AD. えぐちりか　Rika Eguchi
TD.　D. 今村 浩　Hiroshi Imamura
　　 D. 福永耕士　Kohji Fukunaga
　　　　飯村卓也　Takuya Iimura
　　 I. 山根 Yuriko 茂樹　Yamane Yuriko Shigeki
　　 C. 渡辺潤平　Junpei Watanabe
　　CL. チーム青森×青森市　Team Aomori × Aomori City
　　PT. Hand Writing

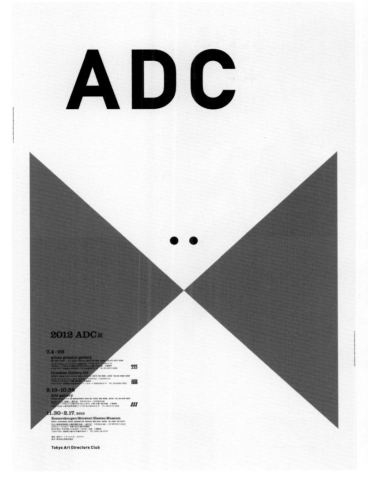

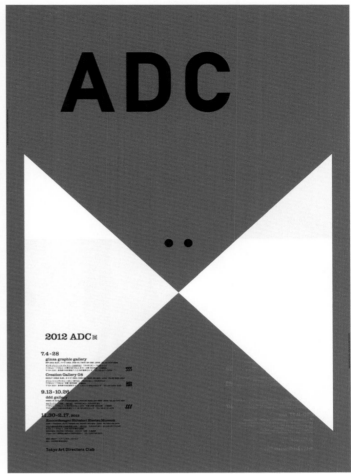

401

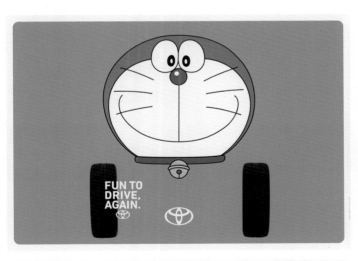

402

402 Campaign
TD. AD. 佐野研二郎　Kenjiro Sano
　　CD. 佐々木 宏　Hiroshi Sasaki
　　C. 澤本嘉光　Yoshimitsu Sawamoto
　　D. 石黒篤史　Atsushi Ishiguro
　　P. 瀧本幹也　Mikiya Takimoto
　CL.（株）トヨタマーケティングジャパン
　　　Toyota Marketing Japan Corporation
　PT. Din next

401 Poster
TD. AD. 佐野研二郎　Kenjiro Sano
　　D. 石黒篤史　Atsushi Ishiguro
　CL. 東京アートディレクターズクラブ
　　　Tokyo Art Directors Club
　PT. Clarendon

403

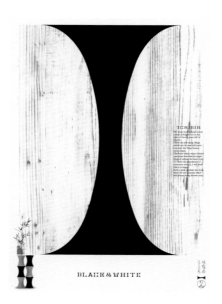
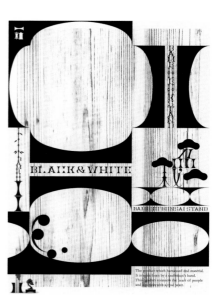

404

403 Advertising
TD. AD. D. 長嶋りかこ　Rikako Nagashima
　　　D. 藤本大生　Taisei Fujimoto
　　　P. 田島一成　Kazunali Tajima
　　HM. 加茂克也　Katsuya Kamo
　　　ST. 野口 強　Tsuyoshi Noguchi
　　CL. キングレコード（株）
　　　　King Record Co., Ltd.
　　　PT. Custom-made for the project

404 Advertising
TD. AD. D. 対馬 肇　Hajime Tsushima
　　　D. P. 對馬由紀子　Yukiko Tsushima
　　　　D. 野田高杉　Takasugi Noda
　　　　　藤本聖二　Seiji Fujimoto
　　CL. （株）北辰製機所　Hokushin Factory
　　　PT. リュウミン

221

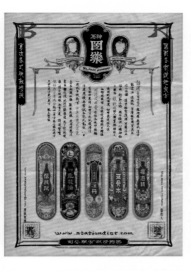

405

406

407

405 Advertising
TD. D. I. Zhan Wei
　CL. Challenge Skateboard Co., Ltd.
　PT. Custom-made for the project

406 Poster
TD. AD. D. 前川景介　Keisuke Maekawa
　CL. Bistro Paisen
　PT. Miso /
　　Custom-made for the project

407 Poster
TD. Stefan Sagmeister
　CL. Les Arts Decoratifs, Paris

408

409

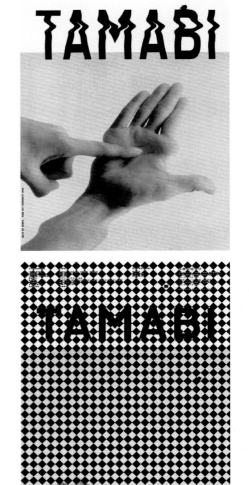

410

408 Newspaper Ad.
TD. AD. 葛西 薫　Kaoru Kasai
　　AD. 小島潤一　Junichi Kojima
CD. C. 前田知巳　Tomomi Maeda
　　 D. 増田 豊　Yutaka Masuda
　　　　藤田佳子　Kako Fujita

P. 五條伴好　Banko Gojo
　上原 勇　Isamu Uehara(Person)
CL. (株)トヨタマーケティングジャパン
　　Toyota Marketing Japan Corporation
PT. 游明朝体／たおやめ

409 Poster
TD. 相澤千晶　Chiaki Aizawa
　D. 福原奈津子　Natsuko Fukuhara
CL. (株)八海山　Hakkaisan
PT. Linotype Univers

410 Campaign
TD. AD. 佐野研二郎　Kenjiro Sano
TD. D. P. 石黒篤史　Atsushi Ishiguro
CL. 多摩美術大学
　　Tama Art University
PT. Custom-made for the project

223

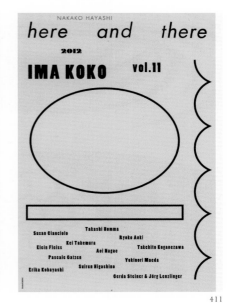

411

412

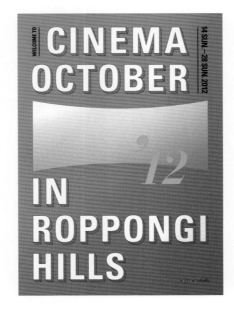
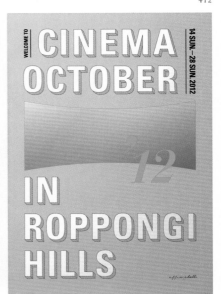

413

411 Poster
TD. AD. D. 服部一成　Kazunari Hattori
CD. 林 央子　Nakako Hayashi
P. ホンマタカシ　Takashi Homma
CL. Nieves
PT. Poplar Std Black

412 Poster
TD. AD. D. 菊地敦己　Atsuki Kikuchi
CL. (株)ニューヨーカー
Newyorker Ltd.
PT. Custom-made for the project /
OCRB

413 Poster
TD. AD. D. 高谷 廉　Ren Takaya
P. 新谷真博　Mahiro Shintani
PR. 森ビル(株)タウンマネジメント事業室
Town Management Division Mori Building Co., Ltd.
CL. 森ビル　Mori Building Co., Ltd.
PT. Custom-made for the project

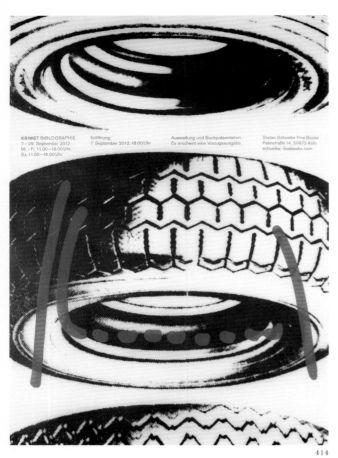

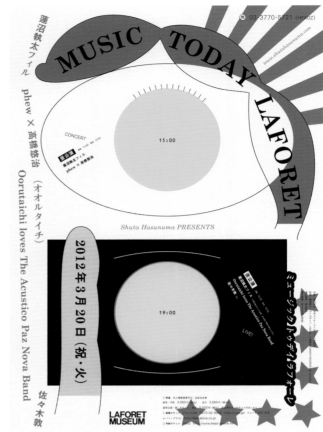

414

415

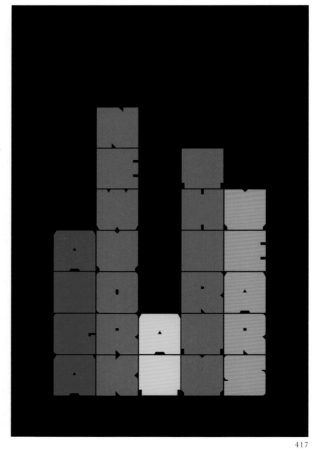

416

417

414 Poster
TD. tino grass
PRI. Jürgen Flechsenhaar/
　　Werkstatt für Serigrafie
CL. Stefan Schuelke Fine Books
PT. Akzidenz Grotesk

415 Poster
TD. AD. D. 菊地敦己　Atsuki Kikuchi
CL. 蓮沼執太　Shuta Hasunuma
PT. A-OTF見出ゴ/A-OTF見出ミン/
　　Century Schoolbook

416 Poster
TD. AD. D. 石川 耕　Ko Ishikawa
CD. 佐藤可士和　Kashiwa Sato
CL. 国立新美術館
　　The National Art Center, Tokyo
PT. Custom-made for the project

417 Poster
TD. D. Ivan Chermayeff
　　Chermayeff & Geismar
CL. AIGA New York
PT. Custom-made by -
　　Ivan Chermayeff called "Hint"

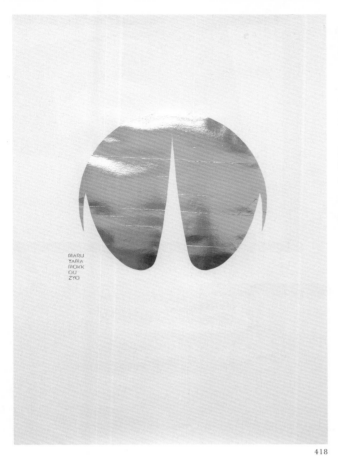

418

419

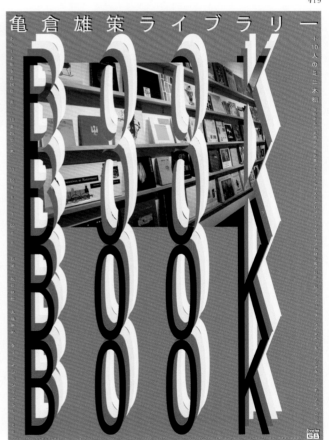

420

421

418 Poster
TD. AD. D. 丸山 建　Ken Maruyama
CL. (有) 丸山木工所
　　Maruyama Mokkouzyo
PT. Maruyama Mokkouzyo Original Font

419 Poster
TD. AD. D. 岩田勇紀　Yuki Iwata
CL. Hair Makalu
PT. Trade Gothic /
　　Custom-made for the project

420 Poster
TD. D. Chen Pingbo
CA. Huang Zhicheng
CL. SGDA

421 Poster
TD. AD. D. 服部一成　Kazunari Hattori
CL. クリエイションギャラリーG8
　　Creation Gallery G8
PT. MSゴシック

422

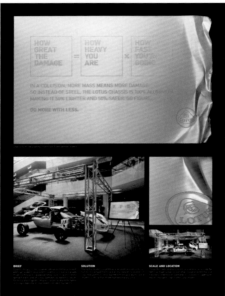

423

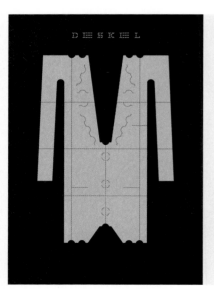

424

425

422 Poster
TD. AD. D. ST. 竹内佐織　Saori Takeuchi
D. 中谷亜美　Ami Nakaya
P. 島村朋子　Tomoko Shimamura
HM. 梅澤優子　Yuko Umezawa
CL. Gas As Interface
PT. Custom-made for the project

423 Poster
TD. Ean-Hwa Huang/
Jerome Ooi / Vince Lee
C. Szu-Hung Lee /
Randy Lee / Kevin Teh
PR. Jimmy Ong
CL. Lotus Cars Malaysia
PT. DIN / Custom-made for the project

424 Poster
TD. AD. D. 藤田純平　Junpei Fujita
CL. タッカ（株）T'acca Inc.
PT. Stamp Font

425 Poster
TD. AD. D. 藤田純平　Junpei Fujita
CL. タッカ（株）T'acca Inc.
PT. Stamp Font

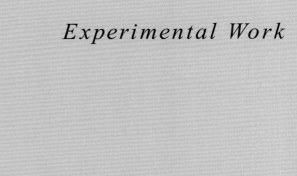

Experimental Work

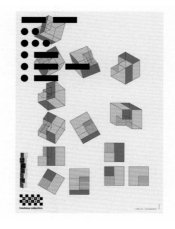

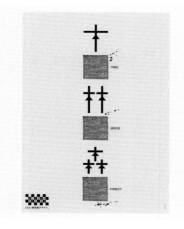

426

427

426 Exhibition
TD. AD. 浅葉克己 Katsumi Asaba
　D. 石原千明 Chiaki Ishihara
CL. バウハウス ドイツ展 2012
PT. Custom-made for the project

427 Experimental work
TD. 宮田絵里子 Eriko Miyata
CL. Non-commercial work
PT. Hand writing

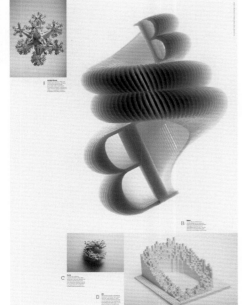

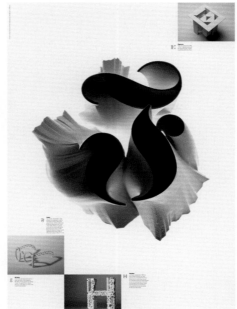

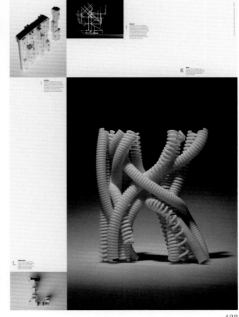

428

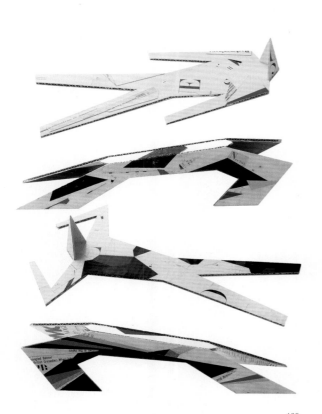

429

430

428 Experimental work
TD. Michael Johnson
CL. Ravensbourne College

429 Experimental work
TD. 山口 馨　Kaoru Yamaguchi
　A. カーク！ヤン？　Kirk! Yang?
CL. Non-commercial work

430 Experimental work
TD. Seul Gi, Gu
CL. Non-commercial work
PT. Custom-made for the project／
SMsinsinmyeongjo10tt

431

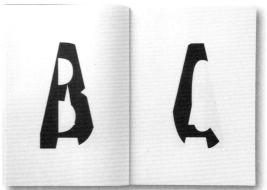

432

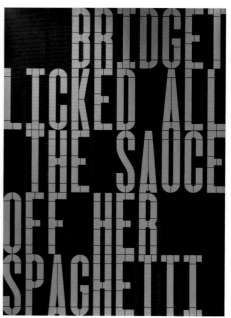

433

432 Experimental work
TD. Fraser Muggeridge
    Giorgio Sadotti
Technical assistance.
    Emma Williams
    Ben Jones
CL. Giorgio Sadotti

431 Experimental work
TD. AD. D. C. SUNDAY PROJECT
    CL. Sketch
    PT. Helvetica

433 Experimental work
TD. tomato, Dylan Kendle
CL. Non-commercial work

231

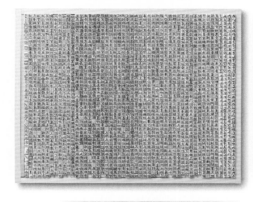

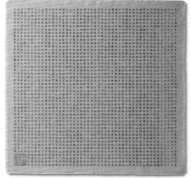

434

435

436

434 Experimental work
TD. AD. D. 千葉菜々子　Nanako Chiba
　CL. Non-commercial work
　PT. Custom-made for the project

435 Experimental work
TD. 安齋朋恵　Tomoe Anzai
　CL. Non-commercial work

436 Experimental work
TD. Grace Kim
CL. Non-commercial work
PT. Modified Clarendon for the project

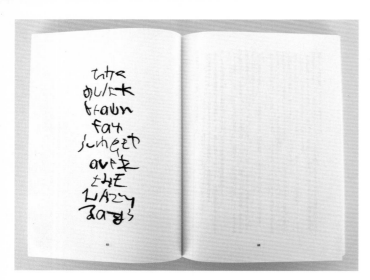

437

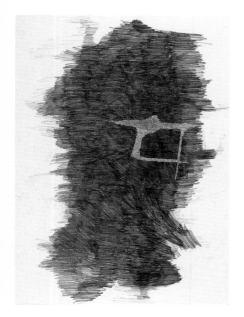

438

439

437 Experimental work
TD. D.W. 伊東友子　Tomoko Ito
　CL. Non-commercial work
　PT. 本明朝

438 Experimental work
TD. AD. D. よつやなつみ　Natsumi Yotsuya
　CL. Non-commercial work
　PT. リュウミン L-KL

439 Experimental work
TD. 谷岡茂樹　Shigeki Tanioka
　CL.（株）岸本吉二商店
　Kishimoto-kichiji syouten Co., Ltd.

RGB

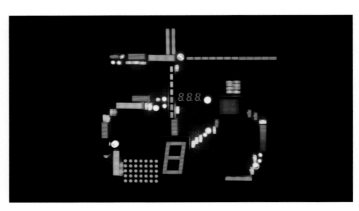

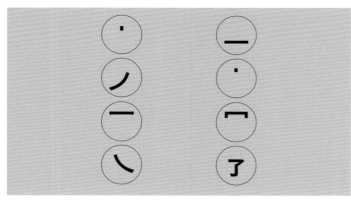

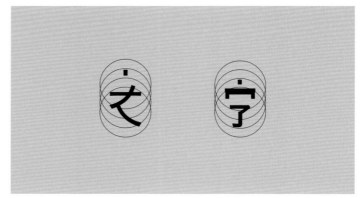

©NHK

Prize Nominee Work
440 TV program
CD. AD. TD. 佐藤 卓　Taku Satoh
MO-DI. TD. 中村勇吾　Yugo Nakamura
MU. コーネリアス　Cornelius
CH. 日本放送協会　NHK
PRO. CL. NHK エデュケーショナル
　　　　 NHK Educational
PT. Custom-made for the project

これからは、全ての人にデザインマインドが必要だ。その想いが、子どものためのデザイン番組制作を実現させた。子どもは未来の大人。大人になると、デザインと関わりのない仕事は何一つないということに気付く。子どもの時からデザインマインドを育むことが今、とても大切である。

In the future, I think that everybody will have the need to think in a "design-oriented" way. This idea led to the production of a design program for children. As time passes, children grow into adults. When we grow up, we notice that every job has something in common with design. Thus, cultivating a "design-oriented" mind during childhood is very important.

Prize Nominee Work
441 Web site
TD. AD. 大来 優　　Yu Orai
　　AD. 鎌田貴史　Takashi Kamada
　　　D. 庄司さやか Sayaka Shoji
　　　C. Nadya Kirillova
　　CD. 菅野 薫　　Kaoru Sugano
　E-PR. 中島正雄　Masao Nakajima

CL. (株)エフエム東京
　　Tokyo FM Broadcasting Co., Ltd.
PT. 丸アンチックU / DIN Round /
　　丸丸ゴシックALr
http://www.tfm.co.jp/smile/petiteco/

「あのね プチェコ」は、クルマのラジオパーソナリティ「プチェコ」との会話を楽しめるサイト。プチェコに話しかけると、過去の取材データとウェブ上のみんなの会話から学習した言葉を組み合わせた人工知能を使って返事をする。このやりとりは、番組のコンテンツとも連動していく。

"Hey Petiteco!" is a website where everyone can enjoy dialogs with Petiteco the car radio-personality. Talk to Petiteco and it will answer back using AI developed by combining footage from the past trips and all open conversations on the internet. These dialogs are integrated into future episodes of the radio show.

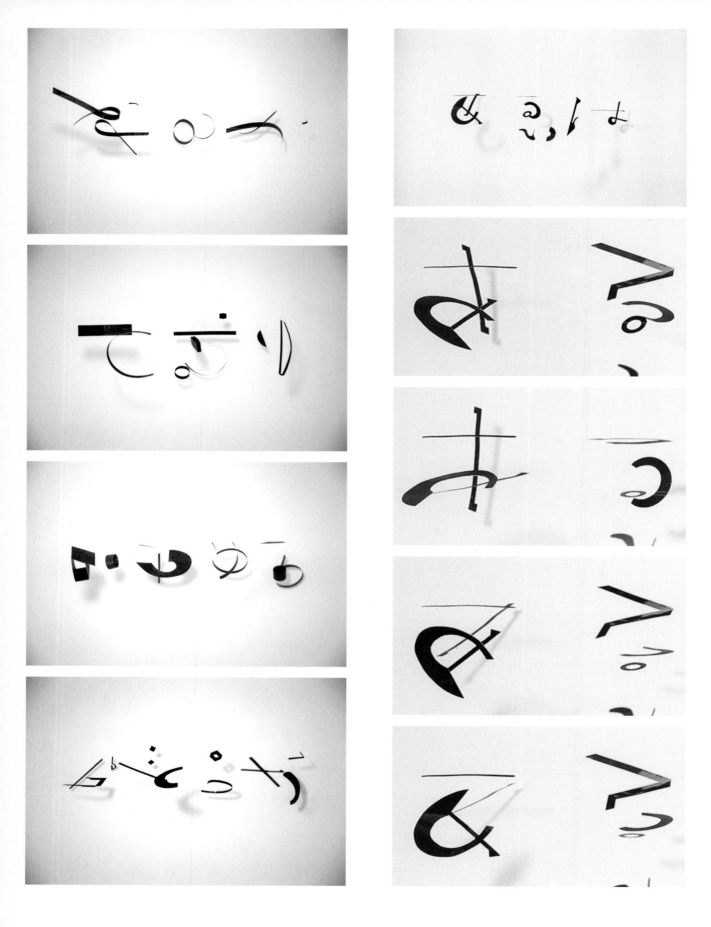

Prize Nominee Work

442 Experimental work
TD. AD. 大原大次郎　Daijiro Ohara
　　　P. 五十嵐一晴　Kazuharu Igarashi
　　　CL. Non-commercial work

『もじゅうりょく』は、文字、モジュール、重力を掛け合わせた造語である。ある文字を分解し、モビールとして再構成したものを定点でビデオ撮影。分解された文字のモジュール群は定着することなく動き続け、ある一瞬重なり合い、意味をもつ言語として知覚される。

"Typogravity" is a term coined by combining "type," "module," and "gravity." To illustrate this, I deconstructed a letter and restructured it as a mobile. Then, I shot a video from a fixed point. The module pieces of the deconstructed letter keep moving, fit each other momentarily, and are perceived as a word with a meaning.

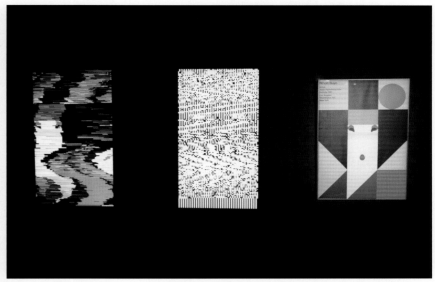

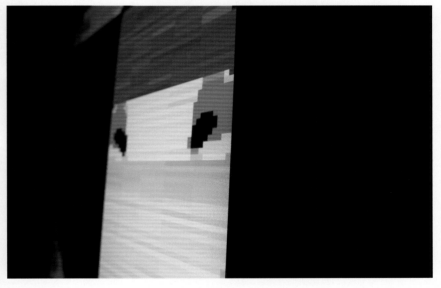

Prize Nominee Work

443 Art work
TD. 田中良治　Ryoji Tanaka
T-DI. 菅井俊之　Toshiyuki Sugai
PRG. 柴田祐介　Yusuke Shibata
CL. 21_21 design sight

この作品はインターネットの影響下で生まれる（グラフィック）イメージについて考えるインスタレーションです。田中一光氏のポスターを暗号化した画像に変換（カラフルなタイル状のイメージ）し、その画像を逆変換をして元のイメージに復元するという仕組みになっています。

This is an installation aimed at sparking contemplation regarding (graphic) images created under the influence of the Internet. Mr. Ikko Tanaka's poster is converted into an encrypted picture image (a colorful tile-shaped image), and then the image is reconverted into the original image.

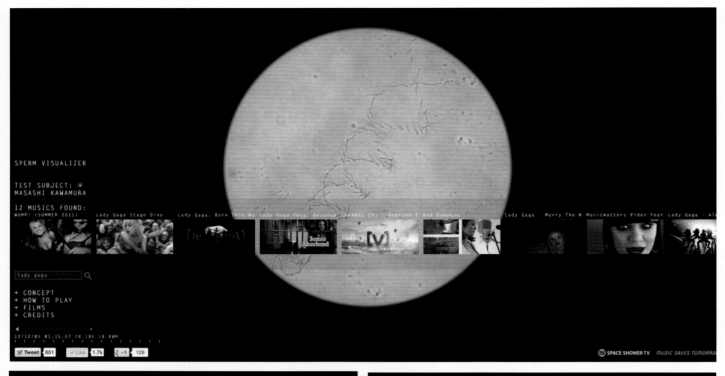

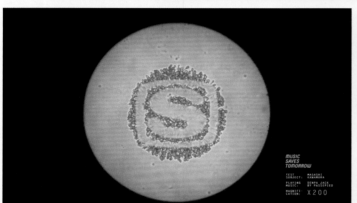

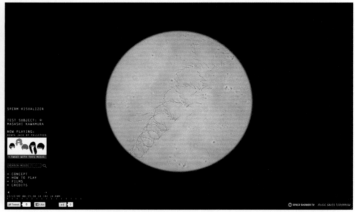

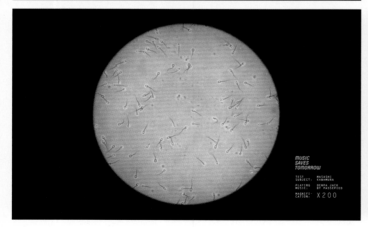

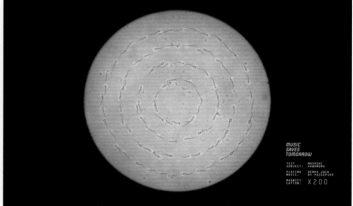

444 Web site/PV

TD. CD. F-DI.	川村真司 Masashi Kawamura	IN-D. 梅津岳城 Takeshiro Umetsu	CL. (株)スペースシャワーネットワーク
TD. CD. T-DI.	清水幹太 Qanta Shimizu	W-DI. 萩原裕一 Yuichi Hagiwara	Space Shower Networks Inc.
PL.	真鍋大度 Daito Manabe	AG. PARTY	http://sperm.jp/
T-DI.	中村大祐 Daisuke Nakamura	Filming Support. (株)タイムラプスビジョン	
PR.	岡田行正 Gyosei Okada	Timelapse Vision Inc.	
PM.	丹羽克宏 Katsuhiro Niwa	Film PRO. puzzle inc.	
VFX PR.	大林 謙 Ken Obayashi	Interactive PRO. mount inc.	
AD.	Jeong-Ho Im	VFX. FLAME	

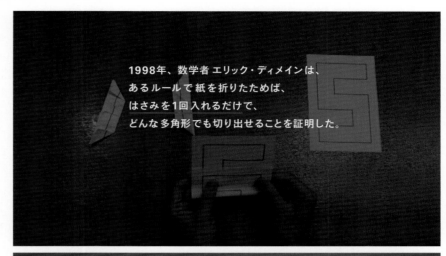

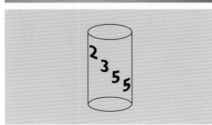

445

446

445 Web site/PV
TD. 川村真司　Masashi Kawamura
　　清水幹太　Qanta Shimizu
　　関 和亮　Kazuaki Seki
A. IN-DI. 築地ROY良　Roy Ryo Tsukiji
D. 石塚美帆　Miho Ishizuka
　　渡部大輔　Daisuke Watanabe
T-DI. Front-end Engineer
　　高橋智也　Tomoya Takahashi

PR. 高橋 聡　Satoshi Takahashi
　　相原幸絵　Sachie Aihara
　　佐渡島康平　Yohei Sadoshima
CL. (株)キューンミュージック
　　Ki/oon Music Inc.
　　(株)講談社
　　Kodansha Company Ltd.
PT. Custom-made for the project
http://ucbros.jp/

446 TV program
TD. 山本晃士ロバート／貝塚智子／佐藤 匡／
　　うえ田みお／石川将也／米本弘史／時田亜希子／
　　菅 俊一／湧川晶子／廣瀬隼也／大島 遼
　　Kohji Robert Yamamoto／Tomoko Kaizuka／
　　Masashi Sato／Mio Ueta／Masaya Ishikawa／
　　Hirofumi Yonemoto／Akio Tokita／
　　Syun'ichi Suge／Masako Wakigawa／
　　Junya Hirose／Ryo Oshima

CD. 佐藤雅彦　Masahiko Sato
PR. 岡本美津子　Mitsuko Okamoto
　　伊江昌子　Akiko Ie
AG. ユーフラテス　Euphrates
CL. 日本放送協会　NHK
PT. Gill Sans/
　　Custom-made for the project

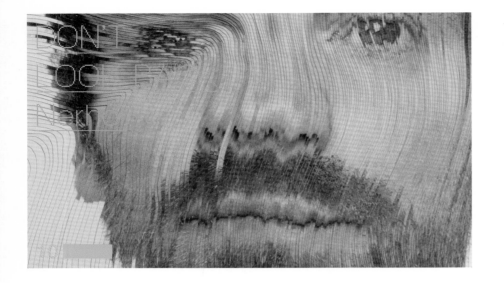

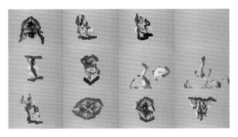

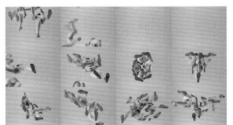

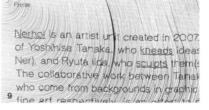

447

448

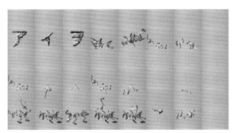

447 Web site
　TD. 田中良治　Ryoji Tanaka
PRG. 萩原俊矢　Shunya Hagiwara
A. CL. Nerhol
　PT. Custom-made for the project
http://nerhol.com/

448 Web site
TD. CD. 大八木 翼　Tsubasa Oyagi
　TD. OK Go
　　Pilobolus
　DI. Damian Kulash
　　Trish Sie
CL. Google
http://www.allisnotlo.st/index_ja.html

特集：TDC DAY レポート
仲條正義 × 葛西 薫

Feature story from the design forum TDC DAY :
Masayoshi Nakajo × Kaoru Kasai

2013年4月6日 / 女子美術大学杉並キャンパス

The following are excerpts from a discussion between Masayoshi Nakajo and Kaoru Kasai
held on April 6, 2013 at the Suginami Campus of Joshibi University of Art and Design.
Mr. Nakajo won a 2013 Tokyo TDC Special Prize for composites of four series of his
posters initially shown at an exhibition of his works. Mr. Kasai won the same award for
his book design of the Japanese-language edition of Peter Zumthor's *Architektur Denken*.

葛西：はからずも賞をいただきまして、こうして仲條さんと一緒にたくさんの方の前で話すことになりました。10年ぐらい前に後藤繁雄さんと三人で話したことがあって、そのときは後藤さんを頼りながら仲條さんに関わるというふうでした。今日も誰かをとちょっと思ったんですが、普段は仲條さんと雑談はしているんですけれども、こうやって向かい合って二人でちゃんと話すことを思い切ってやってみようと。どうなるかわかりません。楽しい話になればうれしいというぐらいで、進め方も考えていなくて、お互いに茶々を入れながらやっていきたいと思います。最初に、仲條さんの受賞作について仲條さんから、あまり手短かにならないようにお話をしてもらって（笑）、続いて僕も自分の作品に触れて、それから二人であれこれ話していきたいと思います。

1

仲條：このあいだ葛西さんに「仲條さん、TDC DAYどうしますか」と聞かれましてね。「きっとみなさん、最後のほうには疲れ果てているから、二人で適当に話してりゃ時間はすぐ経っちゃうからいいんだよ」と答えました。そういうずるいことを考えています。本当に同時に私たちが賞をいただいたのはうれしいですね。私が大尊敬している葛西さん、年齢は十何歳か下なんですけども。先日もあるところで、「葛西さんっていうのは、もう名人だね」って僕は言ったんです。名人という呼び名は、落語でも歌舞伎でも、なかなか人は使わないんですが、葛西さんのお仕事は名人というふうに思っております。

葛西：仲條さんにそう言われたら、もうお終いかなという感じがしていまして（笑）、そういうふうになりたくはないけど、でもなりたいような。

仲條：葛西さんとは時々お会いしているんです。食事の席だったり、大勢いるところでいろいろ話をしたことがあります。葛西さんとゆっくり話したいな、話したいなと思っているんだけど、なんか照れちゃうんですよね、男同士なのに照れちゃうということがあって。相手がもっと若い人だと半分ぐらい相手に悪口言ってりゃ、それも一つの親しくなる方法なんですけど、葛西さんに悪口を言うわけにいかない。それで今までゆっくりお話したことがないものですから。

2

葛西：仲條さんに褒められてうれしかったのが、ついこのあいだ、銀座で焼き鳥をご馳走になったときに、ものすごくおいしくて、僕があんまりうれしそうに食べていたら、「本当においしそうに食べるね」と褒められました。それはそれはご馳走さまでした、おいしかったです。
　　さて今回の受賞は、昨年夏に資生堂ギャラリーで開催された「仲條正義展　忘れちゃって EASY 思い出して CRAZY」という展覧会、その作品をめぐっての賞だったんですけれども。

仲條：このグリーンのものは[1]、もともとは9枚のシリーズで、ダイジェスト版では2点はずしてます。それからブルーのシリーズ[2]。赤いもの[3]。そしてもう1種[4]。昨年の展覧会のためにこれら4系列の作品を作ったんです。展覧会では一点一点が独立している作品で、だいたい一つについて1メーター×2メーターというサイズです。持ち運べるような大きさではない。それで、みなさんに見てもらいたいから、ダイジェストにしてB全のポスターに印刷したものが賞をいただきました。一つはロゴだったり[3]、一つは人間の身体のようなもの[2]、これはもう風景のようなものです[1・4]。
　　私はTDCの活動に設立当初から参加していますから、みなさん若い人たちの成長というのをずっと見てきました。だから僕なんかがもう出る幕じゃないと重々分かっているんです。TDC賞の審査会はなかなか刺激的な会でして、新しいものをいろいろ見るのが好きで、そういう刺激を受けたいから行くんです。しかし私がこの賞を獲ったというので、「ちょっとおかしくねえか」「TDC間違っているんじゃないの」というようにそのときは思ったんです。だけどこれからこういう展覧会はもう何回もできないので、有り難くいただくことにしました。
　　作品自体は説明の仕様がないようなものなんです。これが目だとか、口だとか、人体だとか、耳と思うとか、そんなようなものがテーマです。これはまた別のものでして[4]、とにかく風景のつもりで書いたら、だんだんだんだん骸骨が増えてきちゃって、そのまま冥土の世界みたいに一つの流れにしたらどうかと。これはもとは縦が4メーターの大きさがあるんです。こちらは9枚のシリーズで[14]、これは口です[5]（笑）。

3

葛西：口がでかいですよね（笑）。

Nakajo: The works for which I won this award are composites based on four series of posters I created for my solo exhibition, held in summer 2012 at the Shiseido Gallery, titled "Forgetting makes things easy; remembering drives you crazy." The original posters each stood on their own and were generally 1 × 2 meters in size. But since this is a size too big to carry around and I was eager to have everybody see them, I printed them as composite images on posters of B-1size [1030 × 728 mm] — and these are what I received the award for. This one[3] features various logos; this one[2] suggests parts of the human body; and these two[1・4] resemble scenery. This one[4] is 4 meters tall in the original version. Because this was likely to be my last exhibition on this scale, I chose the title I did. "Forgetting makes things easy" would actually have sufficed; I added "remembering drives you crazy" in the hope that, occasionally, people might think of me.

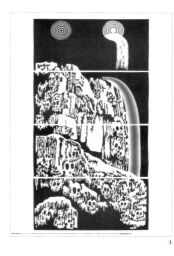

4

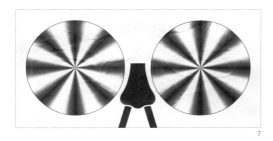

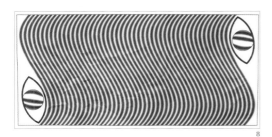

葛西：「忘れちゃって EASY 思い出して CRAZY」という展覧会のタイトルは先にあったんですか。

仲條：いえいえ。こういう展覧会をやるときのテーマは、これまでも、たとえば骸骨だとか、富士山だとか思いつくんですが、決めちゃった後で困ることがいっぱいあるんですよね。そこから離れられなくなってしまって。今回タイトルを決めてくれとギャラリーに言われて。まあこれで最後かもしれないから、「忘れちゃって EASY」というつもりで、たまには「思い出してくれい、じー（CRAZY）」というつもりで付けたんです。

葛西：仲條さんの言葉をめぐる話は多くて、あとでその話をしたいなと思っていたんですが、このタイトルを見ただけで、半分以上見ることができたという感じがしたんですけどね。

それで今、急に思い出したんですが、20年ぐらい前に俳優の小林薫さんに出ていただいて、サントリーのお中元の広告を作りまして、そのコマーシャルソングはスリーグレイセスというグループが歌うんですけれど、曲名が「思い出してウクレレ」というんですよ（笑）。すごくいいタイトルだなあと思いました。

仲條：そっちの方がいいですね。

葛西：語呂がいいということと、タイポグラフィにしたときと、意味のあることと無いことの間にあるような心地よさ、含蓄の無さがすごくいいと思っていて、僕が好きなものは、あるいは仲條さんの作られるものはそういうことと関係しているかもしれないと思うんです。

仲條：僕はいつもただ思いつく。さっきは口を書いたから今度は喉を書かなきゃいけないとか[6]、脈絡がない。耳を書いてなかった、耳はむずしいからどうしようかなとか、「お前、真剣にやってるのか」なんて怒られそうな作り方ばかりしているんです[14]。

葛西：グラデーションの終わるところに、波なんですかね、エッジをそれに沿ってこう波形にカットしてますよね。どんな場合でもこういうところ、面白いですね。

仲條：僕の事務所の白鳥さんがわりと奇麗に仕上げをやってくれたんだけど、その出力したものを濡らして、皺にして、それをまた複写しています。奇麗に仕上がったらどうしようもないんでね。

葛西：この色は、何か思いがある色なんですか。

仲條：こういう色はわりと好きなんです。どこか古典的ですよね、スタンダードというか。そういうやつをデザインの中に必ず一個忍ばせておくと安心するんですね。

葛西：これは鼻ですね[7]。これは目[8]。目の中を見ると、いままで平行線だったグラデーションがちゃんと球体になっていますね。

仲條：僕が二カ所は定規を使ったりして、あとは鉛筆でグラデーションをつけて、それをもとに白鳥さんが加工してくれたんです。あまり奇麗すぎちゃってるとダメだということで、下手に。

葛西：もんだり、濡らしたり。

仲條：まあ、ずるい。

Nakajo: I always just follow what pops into my mind. For example, after I've drawn a mouth[5], it might occur to me that next I should then draw a throat[6]. There's no logical connection involved, but that's how I always work, even though people could well berate me and tell me to "get serious"[14]. I take printed works and deliberately wet them, crumple them up, and then photocopy them. If something comes out too pretty, I just can't leave it alone. I'll take a sphere with gradations, and in two places I'll use a ruler and then pencil to add gradations. Then I'll have my assistant process this on a computer. I make sure the job isn't done too skillfully, because being too pretty is no good. The work has to be rubbed, made wet, whatever. Underhanded of me, I know.

葛西：これが一番わからなかったんですけれども、人体なんですか[9]。

仲條：これはむずかしいんだけど、太ももなんです。

葛西：太ももですか（笑）。今日は何しろこれを質問したかったんです。

仲條：太ももがいっぱい並んでいるところです。

葛西：太ももですかー。僕は真ん中からちょっと何かが出ている感じがしたので、そっち方向かなとずっと思っていたんですけど（笑）。では、その真ん中のこうモヤモヤと下に下がっているものは何ですか。

仲條：これはむずかしい（笑）。

葛西：ああ（笑）。

仲條：最初は柱のような、ギリシャの絵みたいなものを描きたいと思ったんですね。いくつか並べてみたら面白い。でも身体に置き換えることがなかなかね、「君の太ももだよ」みたいな。

葛西：今ようやくわかりましたね。そしてこれ、僕が一番好きなのがこれなんです[10]。

仲條：ええ。

葛西：理由は自分でも分かりませんけど、これは耳ですよね。左の円錐が重なり合って四つあって、その間に逆さまに刺さっている一つがありますけど、そのまったく理由のない組み合わせの感じと耳との関係とか。これを見たときに僕なりの日本的な見方かもしれないけれど、サーカスを思い出しましたね。テントかな、何か、そういうふうな目で見ると、すべてが少しサーカス的な気がしたんです。

仲條：僕も子供のときサーカスを見ました。テントのサーカスでした。僕はそういう、昭和というよりは大正というようなものが好きですね。僕の体質だと思います。

葛西：僕もサーカスによく連れて行かれまして、あれは何の教育もないし、ただ驚かせているだけですよね。それがすごく楽しい。それからトランプのマーク、ダイヤだとか、ハートとか、クラブとか、あれも見るとサーカスを思い出すんですね。

仲條：ピエロですかね。

葛西：ああピエロ。仲條さんがさっきおっしゃった古典的なとか、何かこうベーシックのものとか、そういうものとも少し関係しているのかなと。

仲條：そうだね。だから、たとえば新しい文学よりも古い文学の方が好きですから。

葛西：僕も古い文学が好きなんですけど、でもこのあいだ仲條さんから贈っていただいたのは『重力とは何か』という本ですね。すごく面白かったんです。古いものが好きというよりも、やっぱり奥の奥にあるようなものが。

仲條：そうね、不思議なものが好きなのかもしれないですね。宇宙とか、原始の話とか、どう考えたって分かるものじゃないんだけど、こう遠く、遠く、光ってるものが何だろう、ぐらいのことは知りたいと思う。

9

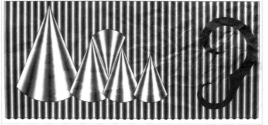

10

Kasai: This is the one I least understood [9] What is it, a human body?

Nakajo: They're thighs. At first, I had in mind to drawn in Grecian style, like pillars. I thought it would be interesting to line up a number of them.

Kasai: This is an ear, isn't it[10]. On the left you've placed four overlapping cones, with another one lodged in between, upside down. What's the connection between that utterly meaningless grouping and the ear? When I saw this, to me there seemed to be something circus-like in it.

Nakajo: Like so many people, when I was a child I saw a circus, in a tent. I'm fond of things like that, things that were popular during the first quarter, say, of the twentieth century. It's just the way I am.

Kasai: I was often taken to the circus too. There's nothing educational in it; its only purpose is to surprise, which is really entertaining. Another thing that reminds me of the circus are the suits of a deck of playing cards: diamonds, hearts, clubs and so on.

Nakajo: Maybe it has something to do with clowns.

Kasai: Or maybe it's connected in some way to something classical — you know, something very basic.

Nakajo: Could be. And that's why, for example, I prefer old literature to new literature.

Kasai: The other day, though, you gave me the book *Jūryoku to wa nani ka* [What is gravity?]. More than liking old things, I'd say you like things that lurk in the deepest recesses.

Nakajo: You may be right. I like things that are out of the ordinary. What I want to know, I think, are the things we can't comprehend but that glow in the very farthest distances — things like the universe, or primordial sagas.

葛西：これはかわいいですね [11]。こちらは [12] 姿勢が悪いなと思って（笑）。

仲條：これは広げるとだめで [12]、折ってみたらちょっといいかと。僕はやっぱり半分は偶然に頼っているというか、偶然じゃないと創造というのはなかなかラクにはできない。サイコロみたいだと考えて、転がして、丁か半かみたいなところはありますね。

葛西：思わぬカタチやレイアウトって、僕はMacでは作れないです。モニターをにらんでいると、あまりにも不自由で胸が苦しくなってくる（笑）。それよりは、紙の上で要素をハサミで切ったり貼ったりして、置いてみて、瞬間にすごくいいなあとなったときに、メンディングテープで押さえつけて、それをコピーして同じことをくり返す。あの楽しみは若いみなさんはきっと知らないんじゃないかと思う。あれは楽しい時間ですよね。

仲條：葛西さんはペンで書くお仕事が多いですよね。

葛西：このごろ少し。フリーハンドというのは自分が出るのが恐くて、定規を使うと定規のせいにできるので、「これ、俺じゃない」と言える、そういうふうに思っていたんですけど、最近はだんだん気持ちがいい加減になってきたのか書いていて、しかもたくさん書かないで、「最初に書いたものがもうこうなったんだからしょうがないじゃないか」と自分に言い聞かせて、そのまま出していくような感じになりましたね。

仲條：だんだん神がかってきた。

葛西：神がかってきたのかな（笑）。諦めがついてきたというんですかね。深くまとめていくとある方向に行くんですけれど、やっぱりつまらなくなりますので。

仲條：今回受賞のご本のタイトルのロゴは作ったんですか。葛西さんが作っているんだろうなと。

葛西：いえいえ、あれはありものなんです。すいません、仲條さんの話をもっと聞きたいので、またあとでその話をしたいと思います。この右側のまつげについているのは涙ですよね [13]。

仲條：はい。

葛西：あれも形がなかなかきれいだなと、明朝体のレタリングの点の形にちょっと似ていて、すごくきれいですね。

仲條：これは楕円定規を使っています。楕円定規でつなげるのが上手いんですよ。

葛西：僕も上手いですよ。そんなことで張り合ってもしょうがないですけど（笑）。カーブからカーブへつなぐとか、楽しいですね。

仲條：まつげの方は全部、雲形定規で書いてます。

葛西：これは左右まったく対称ではないですね。

仲條：そうです。

葛西：かわいいですよね。

11

12

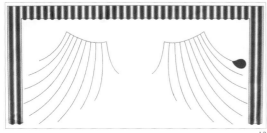

13

Kasai: This one has bad posture, I'd say.[12]

Nakajo: It's bad when you open it out, but if you fold it, it's just right. I rely half on chance occurrence; without just letting things happen by chance, I'd have a hard time being creative. I think of it like rolling dice: you just have to let the dice roll and see what ends up.

Kasai: I do the same as you, albeit to a lesser extent. When things don't go as I want them to on my monitor, my Mac, I cut up things by hand and place them on the monitor —— and in an instant everything goes really well. If I gingerly remove my hands, what I've fixed to the monitor moves and creates something different again. For a second I think, "Oops, it got away." But then in the next instant, I say, "It may have gotten away, but this is really good too." Then I labor to recreate the whole thing inside my Mac, getting the precise positions between the various parts. I think fun like that is surely unknown to young people today.

Nakajo: Many of your works use materials done in pencil, don't they.

Kasai: Some of my recent works, yes. Earlier, I used to use a ruler. I was scared to do things freehand, because if I used a ruler I could blame things on the ruler and say, "It's not my doing." Lately, though, I've gradually loosened up a lot. What's more, I don't draw a lot; instead I just go with the way I drew it the first time, saying, "Well, that's just the way it turned out, so there's nothing to be done about it." When you put something together logically, you proceed in a given direction, but the end product ultimately becomes boring and trite.

仲條：もう葛西さんの話をしたらいいんじゃないですか。

葛西：え、そうですか。ではこの『建築を考える』という本の話に。著者のペーター・ツムトアという名は本国での読みで、通称ピーター・ズントーと呼ばれてます。装丁の仕事は自分の仕事の中の一部なんですけれども、ピーター・ズントーという名前とその建築物を知った最初は、スイスのこの教会ですね[15]。僕は実際に見たことはないんですが。ずっと前からピーター・ズントーが大好きだった人が会社におりまして、その人のお陰で他の建築物もいろいろ教えてもらったんですね。それで僕の興味が深まってきて、もう10年ぐらい前の話ですけれども。

これはそのピーター・ズントーのアトリエの入口です[16]。素朴な田舎の方にあるそうなんですけれども、この入口のこの鉄でできているステップ、地面から宙に浮いているんですね。これを見てものすごくうれしくなってしまいまして。この下に箒が入って、庭の掃除をするのが楽だろうなと（笑）。細部を見ると、いろいろなことが頭に浮かぶんです。この周りに散る落葉はきれいだろうなとか。

これ、アトリエの窓なんですけれども[17]、よく見ると三重に枠をとっているこの木の組み合わせとかが、一見素朴だけどなかなかあちこちに気持ちが張り巡らされていて、そのことに説明できない惹かれるものがあったんですね。この教会もなんかこう風景と建物の関係が反しているような[18]、そういう土地との関係とか、肌合いとか、とにかく説明のできない、他の建築家にはない、明らかにこの人だけは違うという感じがします。

仲條：これは実際に今もあるものなんですね。

葛西：ええ、実際に立ってるものなんですよ。建築物は少ないそうですけどね。それから彼が自分の建物に付けた書体はこれです[19]。装丁するにあたってヒントになりました。そんなわけで、遠いところからすごく尊敬をしてます。僕より6つ年上だということが分かって、6年前は今の僕と同じ歳だったのかと思うとなんかため息が出てきます。

そういう人の仕事がなぜできたかということなんですが。みすず書房に小川純子さんという若い編集者の方がおられて、その方がだいぶ前から僕と一緒に仕事ができたらということをおっしゃっていたんです。その小川さんがピーター・ズントーの、人も好きだし、建築物も好きで、直接本人に会いに行って、すでにドイツ語と英語で出版されている『建築を考える』という本を、「日本で出したいので、そのときはぜひ私にやらせてください」と頼んだそうなんです。で、後から連絡がきて、結構ですということになったのが7年前だったんです。それで、彼女が彼に会いに行く前に、「葛西さん、もしこの人の本が実現することになったら装丁をしませんか」ということを言われて、びっくりして、「もちろん、やりますよ」ということがきっかけだったんですね。

18

19

Kasai: This is the entrance to Peter Zumthor's studio[16]. The step at the entrance floats on something made of iron sticking up out of the ground. When I first saw it, I thought it was really cool, and the whole thing made me really happy. I kept envisioning how, with a broom tucked underneath that step, how easy it would be to clean that garden. You could keep it clean and it would never get messy. I also pondered how pretty the wood would look as it progressively decayed.

Then there's the window of the studio[17]. Normally a window has a singular frame, but this one has a triple, "layered" frame design that reveals the attention given even to the smallest details — which I found attractive in a way I can't explain in words. Here again[18], where we have a contrary relationship between the scenery and the building, I sensed that here was an architect like no other — the way the land accompanies the scenery, the texture, it's just impossible to explain. Having such respect for Zumthor from afar, I discovered he's five or six years older than me, and when I then realized that six years ago he was the age I am now, it made me shiver. That's the kind of man Zumthor is.

20

21

葛西：これはその本の箱のデザインです²⁰。僕は「会ったこともないピーター・ズントーが僕のデザインを見てどう思うかな」ということだけが心配で、何々をしたいというよりも、「これを見たら彼はどう思うだろうか」というようなことばかり思っていました。

　それと別に、このみすず書房という出版社が僕は大好きで、建築の世界でのピーター・ズントーみたいに、「非常に変わった唯一の出版社」というイメージがあって、とりわけこのみすず書房の古風な独特な書体のロゴが、どなたが作ったかは知らないんですけれども、これが使えるのがすごくうれしかったんですね²¹。それで、少し大きめにレイアウトしました。

　それからこちらは、安藤忠雄さんの推薦の言葉による帯なんですけれども²²、日本で出す本なので縦組みでいこうかなと。「ピーター・ズントーが縦組みを見たらどう思うかな」、「スイスの人が日本の組みを見たらどう思うかな」と想像しながらデザインしました。縦組みにしたらこのぐらいの幅の帯が必要になりこんなに太くなってしまいました。

　そこで、この白地の多さで思ったんです。ピーター・ズントーについてはいろんな人がいろんな目で見ているはずだから、何人かの人に推薦文を書いてもらってはどうだろうと。で、あるとき図書新聞に深澤直人さんが長い文章を寄せていたことを知ったんです。それが素晴らしい文章で、その文章から僕がこの一節を帯にしてはと小川さんに提案して、こういう形になりました²³。

仲條：帯というのは邪魔な感じで作ってありますよね。これは邪魔じゃなくて必要で美しい。

葛西：それからズントーの建築を想うと、色を使うのがすごく恐かったんですね。そうしたら小川さんが、「実は、彼は結構、色が好きなんですよ」と、向こうで出した本のいくつかを見せてくれたんです。それは真っ赤だったり、紫色だったり。「ああ、色を使えるんだ」というふうに思って、それで、表紙は紫と青の間ぐらいの色でやりました²⁴。

　この書体は「BANJO」という書体です²⁵。一緒にデザイナーをしている増田豊くんがフィニッシュをやってくれているんですけれども、彼の手元に古いレタリングの本があって、その中にこの書体を使ったものがありました。書き文字だろうと思っていたら、そうじゃなくて、いくつかの文字がこういう細長だったり、左右が極端に長かったりというフォントであることが分かったんです。名前のどこを大きくするかというのを楽しく悩んで組んでみました²⁶。

仲條：昔の書体ですか。

葛西：おそらく昔の書体だと思うんですけど、誰か知っている人がいたら教えてほしいですね。彼がこれを見たら「デザインしすぎじゃないか」と思われるんじゃないかと心配だったんですけど、喜んでくれたみたいで助かりました。運良くいい書体に巡り合ったと思いました。

仲條：葛西さんの書体だと思っていたんですけど。

葛西：そんなわけで、そうじゃないんですよ。

22

23

24

25

26

Kasai: The only thing I'm concerned about is what Peter Zumthor, whom I've never met, might think if he were to see my designs. It was with that thought in mind that I went about my design work.

Kasai: Since the book was to be published in Japan, I was insistent that the text be laid out vertically. If Tadao Ando's recommendation blurb were to be printed vertically as well, I thought a fairly large "obi" would be necessary, and I just went ahead and designed it as big as I wanted. Then I found out that Naoto Fukasawa had written a long, brilliant piece about Peter Zumthor, and I selected an excerpt and put that on the obi[23].

Nakajo: Obis usually seem extraneous, but in this case, far from being extraneous, the obi's both necessary and beautiful.

Kasai: For the book title I used a typeface called "Banjo"[25]. I played around a lot with where I should put the book title in big letters[26].

Nakajo: I thought you had created the typeface.

Kasai: No, that's not the case.

仲條：だいたい葛西さんがやる場合、字をいじらないことが多いですね。

葛西：若い頃はそうではなかったんですけれども、確かにそうですね。でも最近は、それもどうかなとちょっと思うようになってきました。

仲條：レタリングのタイポグラフィは外れるとバカみたいになったりするので、わりと気を付けてやっているんですけどね。ちょっと外れると過剰になったり、バカみたいになる。

葛西：いえいえ。仲條さんのを見ていても、危ないなという感じがするときもあって、むしろ危ないから、そういうところが、こう何ですかね、温かみだとか、近づきたくなるツボなんだろうなとか。もちろん、ある程度通過した結果、そうなってると分かっているんですけども。

　　本を開くと、杉本博司さんが撮った彼の建築の写真が出てきたり[27・28]。これは目次ですね[29]。本文はこういうスタートを切ります[30]。本文中、よくこんなふうに数字の1、2、3が入ったり、空きを作らなきゃいけないんですね[31]。この辺りの組み方が難しいというか。そういう組みの設計をすることが楽しかったですね。数字は3行アキのど真ん中に2を置けば済むんですけども、2は次の文章に所属している2なので、ちょっとだけど3行アキの真ん中より左に寄せるとか、そんなことを楽しんで組み版を考えました。

　　本文は精興社の明朝体です[32]。もともと精興社にこの活字があって、退職した精興社の職人の人たちがMacの技術を覚えて、活版印刷の清刷りを全部取り込んで復刻したそうです。その書体を使っています。仲條さんも『文体練習』という本でこの書体を使っていますね。字間ベタで組むと、ふつう漢字が続くと重たくなっちゃいますよね。この書体の特色は、正方形の中に入っている漢字が一般の書体の95％ぐらいかな、ちょっと小さいんですよ。普通の9ポイントが、8.5ポイントという感じで。ですから字面が明るいです。

仲條：これは活字の復刻だったんですか。

葛西：そうなんです。すごく読みやすいんですよね。この活字を知った時にとりこになっちゃいまして大好きになったんですよ。

仲條：我々は使いたくなりますよね。

27

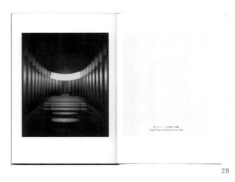

28

29

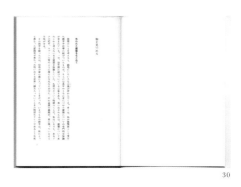

30

31

小さな山のホテルのおもだった部屋には隣り合ってふたつ、板壁のラウンジ

2

かで考えるようにしてみたい。をしてみようと思う。そのさい、建物のこの問題が頭を去らないので、仕事に象化しようとすると個々の建物は輝きをかどうかはいずれも一瞬でわかるが、概物であることに私たちは気づく。そうした性質を持ち、なにか特別なものが記憶す。知っている建物を順々に検討してい何週間かして、私は妻のアンナリーゼもろもろの観点からしても、面白いんで

32

Nakajo: Generally, you don't play around with the typeface, do you.

Kasai: You're right, although that's not true of when I was young. Lately, though, I've come to wonder about the wisdom of using a typeface without any modifications.

Nakajo: If what we aim for with lettering typography misses the mark, you can really make a fool of yourself, so I'm a bit cautious in that respect. If we're not careful, you can overdo it and look foolish.

Kasai: When I see your designs, there are times when I sense you're in dangerous territory, but I figure that's precisely where their warmth lies or what makes them so approachable. Of course, I know that in your case it's a position you've come to after having passed through so many things.

Kasai: The text body uses "Seikosha's Minchotai" typeface[32]. Originally it was a typeface used in metallic typesetting, but when the company that invented it broke up, some retired pros at Seikosha learned how to work on a Mac and they reproduced it inputting the letterpress photo proofs. That's the typeface I use, because it's so easy to read. Once I became familiar with it, I was captivated. I really like it.

Nakajo: It's a typeface we begin wanting to use ourselves, too.

葛西：嬉しいことに、みすず書房から布製の特装版を作ろうという話になって、時間がずいぶんかかったんですが実現しました。布の
デザイナーの須藤玲子さんがピーター・ズントーについてすごくご存知で、ご縁があって「この本のために布を作ってくれませ
んか」と頼んだら、「喜んでやります」ということになったんです。4種類ぐらいの布を作ってくれたのでそれらを束見本にしてピー
ター・ズントーに送りました。その中から「これが一番好きだ」と選ばれたものが、僕も須藤さんも一番やりたかった布だったの
で、すごくうれしかったですね。[33]

仲條：本ではピーター・ツムトアという名前になっていますね。

葛西：ご本人が日本で出すときはドイツ語の発音通りにしてほしいということで。それから英語版とドイツ語版が先に出ていたわけで
すけれど、「ドイツ語版の方が自分の気分が伝わっている」と言ったそうです。日本で出す本は学術書的なものではなくて、エッ
セイとか、あるいは小説的なものでありたいので、文学畑の人に翻訳をとお願いされたそうで、それで選ばれたのが鈴木仁子さ
んという方です。何カ月もかけて、ようやく訳が完成したそうなんです。

　　もうそろそろ仲條さんの話に戻りましょう。これ、仲條さんがデザインをされた『文体練習』という本です[34]。もちろんご存知
の人も多いと思うんですけども、この装丁がすごい。これが中の本文組みのごく一部なんですけども[35]、どうということのない
話をさまざまな文体で書くということを、タイポグラフィを変えながらいろんな組み方でしているんです。

仲條：もっと書体を変えた英語の本があるんですよ。日本語ではこんなことできないはね。

葛西：ええ。本当に全編に違うんですけれども、これは英語のもともとあったものとはまったく別で、仲條さん流ですね。このスペー
スというんですかね、重心の低さというか、なんでこんなに文字組の周りを空けるのかと思うところがあるんだけど、それがす
ごくのどかで気持ちいい。ぜんぶ精興社の明朝体で組まれていて、結局なんだかんだ言っても文字組としてのオーソドックスと
いうものが元にしっかりあるものだから、その上で仲條さんが暴れているから恐ろしい（笑）感じがするんですね。

33　　　　　　　　　　　　34　　　　　　　　　　　　35

Kasai: Ultimately talk arose of working up a specially bound version, and we had a textile designer named Reiko Sudo create for this. She
came up with about four textile designs, and I prepared dummies and sent them off to Peter Zumthor. The one he chose as most to
his liking was the fabric I and Sudo-san were both most eager to do — although there was another one we liked that was slightly more
delicate, like silk — so we were very happy[33].

Nakajo: I see that the book refers to Peter Zumthor by the German pronunciation of his name transliterated into Japanese, rather than the
conventional rendering based on an English pronunciation.

Kasai: Mr. Zumthor said that since the book was to be released in Japan, he wanted it to follow the German pronunciation, which of course is
the way his name is actually pronounced in Germany. For the translation also, he said that with his book for release in Japan he didn't
want it to be a scholarly work but rather like an essay or somewhat like fiction, and since that was what he was aiming for, he requested
that the translation be done by someone with a background in literature. That's the kind of atmosphere I put into the book design, too.

Kasai: There's an old book you designed, *Exercices de style*[34]. The book design is amazing. Here is just a sample of the body text[35], and
you've taken content that's in no way special and printed it in a humorous style, changing the typography as you go along. It's very
typical of your style. All this white space… The low center of gravity, if that's an appropriate description… Why, I wonder, have you
left so much blank space; and yet, it's very calming and soothing. You've used the same Minchotai of Seikosha's as I chose, so after all
is said and done, the underlying basis is solid, orthodox. That's why I sense very well that if you, the solidly based designer that you
are, allow yourself to run free, there's no telling what might happen.

Kasai: Here we have a collection of your works[36]. It contains a remark I'm most fond of[37]. In response to the question, "What do you consider
the greatest joy of being a designer?" this is what you reply: "The joy derived from missing a catch in the outfield on purpose and then
putting the runner out at home base." It's exactly what I'd expect from you, although I think perhaps you're just being evasive.

Nakajo: So you think I'm a cunning guy, do you?

葛西：こちらは仲條さんの作品集です[36]。その中に、僕が一番大好きな仲條さんの言葉があります[37]。後藤繁雄さんが質問されていて、「デザイナーであることの愉びを何と心得る？」と聞いたら、「外野フライをワザとはずしてホームで刺す愉び。」と。ものすごく仲條さんらしいというのか、あるいは何かをかわしているんだろうなと思うんですけど、このようなことについて今日はゆっくり説明をしていただきたいと思います。

仲條：あはは、僕はずるい人間ですね。

葛西：もうちょっと何か（笑）。

仲條：10年ぐらい前に、富士山をテーマに資生堂ギャラリーで展覧会をやっていただいたんです。歳をとると富士山を描くようになる。もうそろそろ富士山を描いてもいいかなと冗談を言ってたんです。富士山は台形ですから、あの形は自由勝手にできない。その展覧会の作品集に後藤さんに評論を書いてもらうことになって、だけどインタビューする、質問するから答えてよ、ということになりましてね、一晩で回答を書いた、そういうものなんです。

葛西：10年ぐらい前にこの本をいただいたわけなんですが、久しぶりに見てみたら、当時気になる言葉に自分でサイドラインを引いてたんですね。それは「人生の歓び、いずこにありや？」という問いに[38]、「宇宙物理の本を見ても理解できないが、今ここに居る自分は奇跡である。従って創造主は自分自身であることがわかる。」と仲條さんが答えている。すごいこと書いていたんですよ。そのとき僕は「仲條さんを見た」という気がして、サイドラインを引いたと思うんです。このときの仲條さんの思いをいま語るとしたら、どうですか。

仲條：先ほど言ったように、後藤さんが原稿を書かない、リトルモアからすぐ出版しなければならないからと。それで舞台には立ったけど、申しわけないんですけど（笑）。

葛西：仲條さんの言葉とデザインとの関係をいつも思うんです。両方ともデザインだなという気もしたり、両方とも言葉だなという気がしたり、しかも言葉もロジックとかじゃなくて、詩のようなものなのか何か分からないんですけれども、そこでは解決していない言葉かもしれない。だけど、やられちゃった感が強い言葉が多いんですよね。

仲條：詐欺師みたいなもんだね。

葛西：『Künel』という雑誌がいつも届くんですが、今回、詩の特集なんです。僕は詩というものは全然分からないんだけど、その中に、谷川俊太郎さんが「詩とは犬の遠吠えのようなものである」と書いている。要するに、意味というよりも、心の中を形そのままに吐露したのが詩であると。谷川さんとご縁があって話をする機会があったときに伺ったんですが、谷川さんは模型工作が大好きなんですよ。ラジオを作ったり、スポーツカーにも乗る。おっしゃったのは、言葉というのは部品のようなものであって、ビスやナットみたいに、その並べ方を変えると結果的に言葉の流れができてきて、リズムが生まれる。そういうことで、むしろ感情は後からやってくると。それを聞いてうれしくなったんですね。仲條さんのデザインを見ても、その点でオーバーラップして。何なんですかね、仲條さんは現実に生きているんですけれども、生きなきゃならないんですけど、どこかで遠くの、実は向こうから自分を見ているような距離感をすごく感じましたね。

36

仲條　外野フライをワザとはずしてホームで刺す愉び。

後藤　デザイナーであることの愉びを何と心得る？

37

仲條　宇宙物理の本を見ても理解できないが、今ここに居る自分は奇跡である。従って創造主は自分自身であることがわか

後藤　人生の歓び、いずこにありや？

38

Kasai: I received this book around 10 years ago, and when I took a look at it for the first time in a long while, I discovered that I'd "underlined" something in it. You were asked where the joy of life exists, to which you replied: "I can look at a book on astrophysics and I won't be able to understand it. But my being here is a miracle, so I understand that I'm my own Creator"[38]. I must have underlined that thinking that I'd come to see who you are.

Kasai: I always think about the connection between your words and your designs. Sometimes I have the feeling both are "designed," while at other times they both seem like words to me — what's more, not words for the sake of logic but words that are like poetry or something — and maybe it's there that words exist that have no resolution.

Nakajo: Like a con artist.

Kasai: Shuntaro Tanikawa, the poet, wrote that poetry is like the distant howling of a dog. He says that rather than having meaning, poetry is a pouring out from the heart, in unadulterated form. Tanikawa-san is very fond of making scale models. "It's not that I don't have an interest in words," he has said, "but it's more the form of things that I'm interested in. Like screws and nuts, when you alter how they're arranged, the result is that words start to flow. I think things like rhythm, arrangement and such are what come later, as expressions of emotions." When I heard that, it made me happy, and in that respect this overlaps with how I feel when I see your designs. In real life you're alive, and you have to be; but I strongly feel a sense of distance, as if you're looking at me from someplace far, far away.

仲條：もうじき80歳になるんですけど、実は80だろうと、90だろうと、物事なんて悟れないんですね。人間なんて完成などとてもできるものじゃないと最近わかった。だから、まだまとめるのは早いかなと。普通は、絵をやるとしても、役者でも、年齢に達してくれば完成に向かって固まってくるというか、整理整頓して、巨匠になっておられるんだと思うけど、どうもそういうことがあまり好きじゃない。いつもデタラメが出てきちゃうんですけど、いろんな流れでできちゃったんだからいいかと、わりと諦めつくというものでもある。だから、偉い人になりたいとか、立派な人になりたいとかいうのがない。かっこよくはいきたいとは思うけど、かっこよくったって、そこだけ言っていても良くないし。

葛西：僕は今日、何か言わなきゃいけないなと思って、思い付いた言葉をちょっとメモなんかしていたら、仲條さんと同じで、「どうせ、もともと俺なんか何もなかったんだから」とある。いま話を聞いてうれしくなったんですけど、無責任かもしれないけれど、デザインをする喜びというのは、無いものからカタチにできたり、そのあと消えていきますけれども、それがやっぱり楽しいということが基本にある。ついもっともらしい話になっちゃうこともあるけれど、そういう破れかぶれなところがどこかあって、たまたまこの仕事をしていると。線を引くのが好きだとか、そういうことだけで仕事がカタチになるというのは有り難いことだなとよく思うんですね。

仲條：葛西さんは会社の役員にもなって、社会的にも責任があるからちゃんとしないといけないけど、僕なんかはね。

葛西：仲條さんの言葉の中で最近一番感動したのがこれなんですよ[39]。すごいなあと思って、倒れそうになったんですけれども（笑）。このあいだ、仲條さんの展覧会が勝どきの青木克憲君のbtfギャラリーで開催されたときに、見たことのないポスターがあり、そこに仲條さんが書いたと思われる文章が載っていて、それが「IN & OUT 飲 と 嘔吐」。いいですよね。何のためのポスターだったんですか。

仲條：これは太陽印刷のね。

葛西：何人かの競作の。

仲條：そうです。B0サイズ6枚とか作って、10年ぐらい前かな。

葛西：読んでもあまり意味の分からない言葉が書いてあるんですけど、これだけは忘れられなくて。

仲條：久しぶりに引っぱり出してみてね。

葛西：「忘れちゃって EASY 思い出して CRAZY」と共通で、その語呂といい、本当に意味もあって。なんかこういうところに一番感動してしまう。

　　　最後に仲條さんに質問ですけど、TDCには日本人だけではなくて世界中から作品が集まっているんですけれども、何か感じられることはありますか。

仲條：僕は昔から負けちゃいけないと思ってる。だけれども海外に開かれているTDCには大賛成で、これをやるところはなかなかないのでね。随分いろんな作品が来ていますよね。ただ昔はみんながお見それした過去の外国のデザイナーはいっぱいいるんだけど、いまの実感としては僕らとそんなに違うかね、ということかな。グラフィックデザインという考え方というのはあちらが始まりなんだと思うけれども、見て理解して伝えるみたいなものが、海外ではそんなことをしたら通用しないよというものを日本人はいっぱい作るんです。結構フリーにいい変化を持っているなと思うんですよ。逆に言えば、その中には社会的にあまり役に立たないポスターもいっぱいあるんだろうと思いますけど。

IN & OUT

飲 と 嘔吐

39

Nakajo：I'll soon be turning 80, but whether we're 80 or 90 or whatever, we never become enlightened about things. Lately I've come to comprehend that humans can never reach a state of perfection. That's why I think it's still early to wind things up. Normally, if you're an artist who paints or maybe an actor, when you reach a certain age you steadily approach perfection, things fall into place, and you become a "great master" of your art. That's something I don't take a fancy to, myself. I always let things just take their course, and if they happen to flow in all which ways, so let it be, I think. It's relatively easy to reconcile things that way. I have no aspirations to become a "great" or upstanding person. I want to do things in style, yet even if I achieve that, talking only in terms like that won't do, either.

Kasai：I'm the same as you. My interpretation may be that "well, I started out having nothing anyway." It may sound irresponsible, but the joy of designing is, fundamentally, in creating something from nothing; and even though it later vanishes, it's still enjoyable after all. When we get talking about design, we sometimes get into major discussions, but at our most basic we have an aspect of desperation, and by chance this is the job we happen to be doing. I often think how fortunate we are to be able to make a living simply from having a fondness for drawing lines and such.

Q & A

（会場から）お二人はよく本を読まれると思いますけど、愛読書なり、好きな作家がいたら教えていただけたら。

葛西：読むんですけども頭に入ってこないことが多い。一冊本を読むのにも3カ月かかったりすることもあるんですけどね。最近読んだ中で面白かったのは、このペーター・ツムトアの本を依頼してくださった小川さんから教えてもらったんですけど、『赤めだか』という立川談志の弟子の立川談春が書いた本です。3年ぐらい前ですか、立川談志が亡くなったあとに出版された。落語家が書いたエッセイ、苦労話というのか、立川談志との関係の話とか、一代記みたいなものなんですね。文章もすごく楽しくて、強くて、面白かったです。面白いと思うのは5年に一つぐらいしかないんですけれども、読んでいてわーという気分になりました。それと『へうげもの』という漫画。仲條さんが教えてくれましたね。千利休の時代についても、一般的なことしか知らなかったんですが、強烈な漫画を読んだという感じでした。それでちょっと火がついて、ちょうどその時代のもので、山本兼一の『利休にたずねよ』、映画化されますね、その本を読みました。

仲條：僕は、映画も本を読むのも、時間の無駄じゃないかというように思う極端な人間なんですよ。だから本は楽しむために読んでいます。面白ければ映画も見るようなタチなので、「こういう系列の本を読んでます」とか、歴史物が好きです、などということはないんです。面白ければ読みます。したがってあまり難しい本は読まない。

葛西：先ほど話した『重力とは何か』は最近夢中になった本ですね。

仲條：わかんないんだけど、あれっ！、ということが書いてあるので。

葛西：僕も『生物と無生物の間』という有名な本があったので読んでみたら、自分の働いている研究所に行くまでのアメリカの当時の状況、そこに行くまでの道すがらの風景描写が文学的ですごくいいんですよ。ところが本番の話になったら何がなんだかだんだん分からなくなってきちゃって、でも、ああいう科学者が書く、科学を取り巻く話の言葉遣いがすごく良かったなあと。

仲條：ものすごく分かりやすいですよね。気持ちいい人がいい。だから僕は新しい作家の本がベストセラーになって評判になっていても、1ページ読んで身体にすっと入ってこないと、もう読まない。

葛西：たまたまリービ英雄という人のものを読み始めたら、日本人の血と外国人の血が入ってるんですが、誰よりもと言ったら言い過ぎかもしれませんが、この人の日本語が好きで、僕は意味を読むという以上に、言葉の流れ、言葉遣いとかにすごいエクスタシーを感じるというのか、なんか入っていきます。

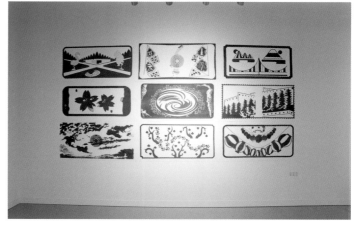

「仲條正義展 忘れちゃってEASY 思い出してCRAZY」 資生堂ギャラリー・2012
撮影：ジェイソン・エヴァンス／写真提供：資生堂 企業文化部

TDC Saturday School 希望塾　仲條正義 講義から
2011年11月26日／ギンザ・グラフィック・ギャラリー3F

TDCDAYの仲條正義・葛西薫両氏の対談をレポートするにあたり、2011年11月に行われた
希望塾（＝TDCが主催するデザイン塾）での仲條正義氏講義の一部をあわせて収録いたします。

＊ 希望塾ではあらかじめ塾生に数字のフォント制作の課題が出されました。
　本講義はその講評の前に行われたもので、仲條氏自身のカレンダー作品も解説いただきました。

Complementary to this Special Feature, the Japanese-language edition contains part of a talk
Masayoshi Nakajo gave at "Kibo-juku," a design workshop organized by Tokyo TDC, in 2011.
On that occasion, Mr. Nakajo introduced the series of calendars (size: 728×1030mm) he has
personally been creating for two decades. For his calendars, every year he has created a new set of
numbers of original design. Here, we present an English translation of his closing remarks, as they
are indicative of Mr. Nakajo's approach to design.

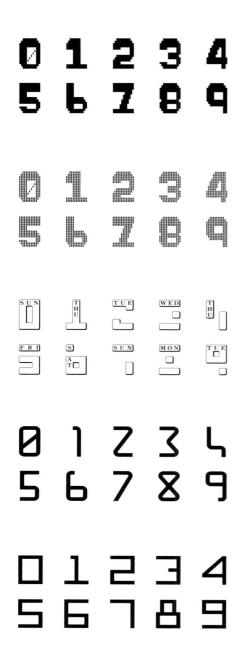

仲條：希望塾でみなさんに課題をやっていただきました。短時間でいろいろ作業なさるには、大げさなテーマでは大変だろうと思って、なるべく単純でつめられる仕事ということで数字のデザインを選びました。算用数字は歴史が長いものですから、現代の我々が簡単にリニューアルできるものじゃないと思う。でも貯金通帳を見たり、あるいは請求書などを見ればそこにある。馴染んだ、見慣れたカタチだと思います。

　僕はもう20年ぐらい、カレンダーをデザインしています。B全紙のカレンダーは昔は商店街なんかで配るとか、でかいカレンダーを貼るところがいっぱいあって、結構役に立っていたらしいんです。だけど僕が頼まれる頃になると、邪魔っけだ、みたいなことになっていました。カレンダーには、12枚ものとか、6枚ものとか、いろいろジャンルがあります。しかし相変わらずB全1枚のカレンダーというジャンルもあるんですよ。年末が近づくとカレンダーコンクールがあって、そこに出品するために京都印刷が僕に最初に依頼してから、かれこれ20何年続けています。その間にスポンサーがいろいろ変わったんですが、最近は資生堂の文化部のレストランのおまけに差し上げているというものです。

　作り始めた頃から、カレンダーにしては分かりづらい、使い道にならないとずっと言われてきました。事実そうなんですが、「時々見てくれればいいんじゃないの」という厚かましい方針で今までやってきました。毎年やっていると、どんどん上手くなるのかと皆さん思うかもしれないけれど、なかなかそうはいかなくて、当たり外れ、出来不出来があります。

　グラフィックデザイナーの基本は形ということ、形でコミュニケーションする、伝達する仕事だとすると、どうしても書体とか活字、文字が基本になる。それで一応は常識的な勉強を学校でもするし、社会に出てもそこそこやるんです。でも僕はどうも学ぶということが子どもの頃から体質的にだめで、教わっても頭に入らない。もちろん成績もあまり良くないし、どうにか学校は過ごしてきましたけど。ですから書体の一つ一つ、カタチを見ているうちに、「俺がやらなくてもいいだろう」のようなことになってしまいました。書体について専門家の人がいるから、私たちはそれを利用すればいいと。「使う人」と「作る人」がいるわけですね。

　「使う人」にも上手い人がいて、葛西薫さんとか服部一成くんなんかは見事に使いこなすから、人が作った書体だけれども個性的な表現ができる。活字というのは横に並べたり縦に並べたりして組み立てますから、字の空きとか、行の空き、あとはレイアウトで、なんとなく作家性というのが出てくる。また書体はその選択においてやはりセンスがすごく大事みたいです。無限大ということはないけれども、相当の種類のフォントというか書体があるわけです。和文、欧文、それを組み立てて「えっ、いいね」なんて思わせるのは、やはりかなりの修練と、修練だけではなくてセンスというか才能が必要だと思います。学べばなんでも上手になるのだと思うんですが、やはりひらめきというか、個性があって、文字についてこれができる人はなかなか少ない。私や、浅葉克己さんなんかに、「あいつは字が分かるね」とか、「あいつは字が分からないからデザイナーとしてだめだね」と、けんもほろろに否定されてしまう。表立って見えないんだけど、そのきらめきというのかな。料理屋さんで言えば、うまく調理するよりも、鼻が利いて鮮度が分かって味が分かるみたいな、基本のようなことなんです。その点、僕の場合はもともと特に優れていたとは思わないんですが、そこは修練みたいなものも確かにあって、いいものを見ていると、少しずつ身に付いてくるのかなという気もするんです。

　僕は55年くらい前に、芸大を卒業してから資生堂の宣伝部に入りました。入ると1年ぐらいはいろんな工場見学に行ったり、販売の現場を見に行ったりする。それと同時に、資生堂の書体というのがありまして、明朝体とゴシックの中間みたいな書体なんですけれども、その字を書かされるんです。お給料をもらって勉強させてくれるんだからありがたいけれど、どうもその作業がだめで、僕はほとんど拒否したみたいにして書かなかった。その後、資生堂をやめて社会に出ました。人間が従順じゃないものだから結局いられなかったんだと思うんです。

その時々でゴシック体が流行ったり、ゴシック体を変形して平体にしたり、字間をうんと詰めたり、流行りというのはある。リズムとかメロディーみたいなもの、フォークだ、ロックだというように。2、3年あるいは3、4年、音楽の流行と近いのかな。音楽が変わるように時代の空気が変わると、書体の選び方が変わってくる。その辺が面白い。また、音楽が変わればスターが出てくるように、デザイナーもそんなふうにひょこっと出てくるような気がします。そうなると、デザインも音楽も食べ物も、時代の風潮に流されているのかもしれない。

フォントはそのまま並べれば読めるし、会社のロゴにはなります。たとえばソフトバンクのロゴは大貫卓也さんという優秀な人が手がけましたが、何ていうことない書体を使っているんだけど、彼もなかなか活字の選び方は素晴らしい人だと思う。ソフトバンクはあまり字をいじってないかもしれないけれど、いわゆるロゴタイプは塊にして印象的な一つのメッセージにする、社標にする。ＡＢだとしたら、そのＡＢは街中にいっぱいあふれているけれど、うちのＡＢは特別であるというふうにするために、ちょっと癖を付けるというか、主張を持たせる。そこら辺にオリジナリティというものが加わる。だけど、一文字だって字は難しいのだけれど、二つ並ぶともっと難しくなる。三つ四つになるともっと。そのうちにあまり癖を付けてしまうと、逆にいいものができなかったりする。

僕が世の中を見て歩いて腹が立つのは、変なロゴタイプのお店の名前、ひどいのがあって、やはり日本人は横文字には弱いのかな、などと思うんです。地方都市の駅前なんか行くと、ひどいものだなと思うことがある。昔のほうが良かったよね。戦前ぐらいの頃の、筆で書いた看板なんかのほうがよほど良かった。やはり文化というか、育ち方が違うわけですからね。みなさんがグラフィックデザインをやるか、あるいは広告をやるか、他のいろいろなデザインのお仕事をするにしても、やはり字というのは基本であるということ。それを学ぶことは何の仕事をしても頼りになると思います。

話を戻すと、僕は資生堂の書体をやらなかったばかりに苦労することになるんです。ある時、ある美術館のロゴのコンペティションがあって、4、5人のデザイナーが参加しました。参加費というのはもらえるんですけど、1等賞になると10倍ぐらいいいのかな。名誉なことだし、歴史に残らないかもしれないけれど、しばらくはみんなの目の前にあるなと思って気分がいいものだから、一生懸命やるわけです。ロゴマークを作る以外に、「なんとか美術館」という字を作らなきゃならない。そうすると、だいたいコンペティションというのは3種類ぐらいデザインを出してくださいとなる。5人でやれば3×5＝15ぐらい集まるわけですね。それを社内で選んだり、第三者の偉い人たちが選ぶ場合もあります。

マークはみんな得意というか、一晩で1個ぐらいできるんだけど、美術館名はすごく大変だよね。特に僕の場合は資生堂時代に文字を書くことを拒否したものだから、字を書いたことがない。もちろん活字を並べてしまったって構わないんだけど、ロゴマークを個性的に作っていくと、日本字の美術館名が浮いてしまう、合わなくなってしまう。あるいは最初に日本字の美術館名をやると美術館名が勝ってしまって、肝心のマークのほうがおろそかになる。それで僕はその美術館のコンペの時に、オリエンテーションの会場で手を挙げて、「マークが通った人に、美術館名を書かせたらどうですかね」と提案したんです。そうしたら、「そういたしましょう。いいことを言ってくれましたね。」と感謝されました。1種類を書くのだって大変なんだから、本当に苦労しました。その時に書いた字はまだ気に入らないんだけど、今さら直すわけにいかない。すべて昔やったものは直すわけにいかないんです。

先ほど言った大貫卓也とか、あるいは葛西薫とか服部一成とかはほとんど字を作らない。僕は実を言うと、字を作るよりも、書体を選んで世界を組み立てるデザイナーのほうが偉いと思うんですよ。そうなると葛西さんや服部くんに負けたことになってしまう。これはしょうがない。そのほうがセンスとして上等なんじゃないかなと。

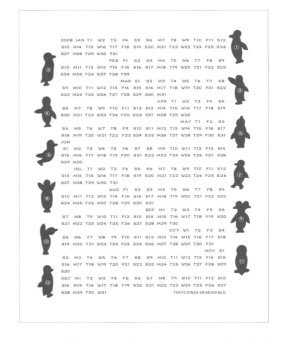

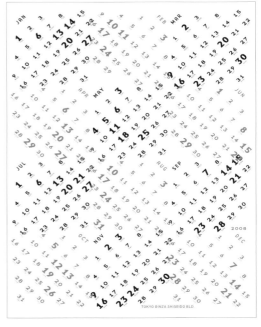

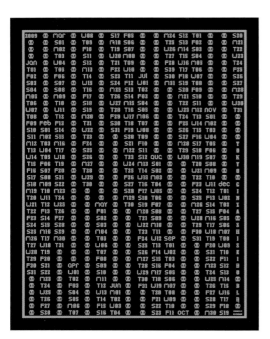

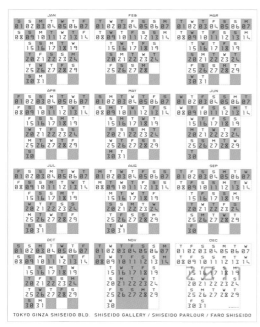

TOKYO GINZA SHISEIDO BLD. SHISEIDO GALLERY / SHISEIDO PARLOUR / FARO SHISEIDO

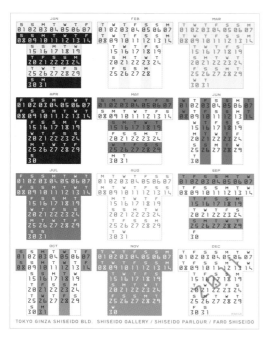

TOKYO GINZA SHISEIDO BLD. SHISEIDO GALLERY / SHISEIDO PARLOUR / FARO SHISEIDO

　僕は78歳なので、皆さんが考えられないような昔の勉強をしている。戦前も知っているし、東京大空襲も知っているような世代ですから、勉強の仕方が違っていました。僕が子どもの頃は戦時中でナチスがどうしたと言っている頃です。日本はドイツの味方だったけど、実際は街中でそういったことが我々の目に触れる時代ではなかった。戦後になると、ロシア・アヴァンギャルドだ、バウハウスだというようなわりと合理的というか、ロシア・アヴァンギャルドは合理的とは思えないけれども、近代的な造形というものを追求した時代でした。写真のメッセージ性、字のメッセージ性、プロパガンダ、言葉を伝えるために努力した時代です。カタチを、いわゆる昔の装飾過多な時代からどこまでそぎ落とすことができるか。20世紀の初めぐらいからそういうのがあって、戦後もずっと続いたわけです。だからどんどんカタチはシンプルになって、誰でも読める、誰でも分かるようなことになった。そういう時代、ことさら強烈な時代に生まれているから、何しろあまり複雑な、飾りが多いものはどうも体験がない。若い頃に身についたものというのは、いつまでもその影響から抜けられないものです。あなたたちはきっといろんな様式とかいろんなジャンルの音楽から、映画から演劇から、多様なものを体験できて、もっと豊かな展開があるだろうと思うんだけど、僕はわりと狭い路線で来てしまった。そのためにあまり迷わなくて来られたのだとも思うんです、これは言い訳ですけれど。

　全部そろっているから数字だと思うけれど、1個だけ取り出してぽっと見ると、「これ、なんていう字かな」となかなか分かりづらい。ありがたいことに、活字というのは前後の言葉とかお話、ストーリーに合わせて読んだり書いたりできますから、なんとなく「Aの次はBだろう」、「Bの次はCに決まっている」という分かり方で、これを文化と言うんだろうと思います。僕がつくった数字を見ていただくとあまり単純とは言えないけれど、だいたいがこんなレベルの書体を作ってきたんです。

　カレンダーは、1年が365日。来年は確か閏年だったね366日だ、1日多い。1カ月が30日前後で、1週間が7日でという区切りがあって、お休みの日が日曜日というふうに、みんなの生活ができていますよね。その生活のリズムが迷わないように、1週間単位というのがカレンダーの基本です。葛西さんが作っているカレンダーは端正、その基本のカレンダーで、とてもきれい。それが一つあればいいかみたいなことです。それにどこの家に行っても同じカレンダーがあるというのもちょっとさみしい。また、1週間で切ると5行か4行がバラバラあるだけで、分かりやすくていいんだろうけど、何かちょっと面白くしてみようかとなるとそれが邪魔になってしまう。僕のカレンダー、B1の紙1枚で1年間の日にちを並べるということ自体が、おおよそ馬鹿げたことだと思うんですけれど、建築家みたいに、3カ月とか半年とか、そういう長いスパンでお仕事をなさる方には、1年のカレンダーが便利かなとも思います。一方でお店のカレンダーなんかは1年分ある必要はないよね。1週間とか1カ月単位でいいと思います。ご覧になっただけで、いかに僕のカレンダーが役に立たないかという側面がある。だけどそこは日にちと曜日を一緒にくっつけてしまえばいいのではないのかと。「12月の11日は、あれっ、何曜日だっけ？」とこう探せば分かるわけ。そういう暇な人もいたっていいだろうと。

　おととしはサッカーの年でもあったので、よく分からないくせに、こんなのを作った、ユニフォームのつもりなんです。サッカーのユニフォームは、イタリアだとかスペイン、ブラジルと結構個性的で、ブルーのストライプだったり、いいものだなと思う。ところが一時期、10年ぐらい前か、コンピューターでいかにもやりましたというようなユニフォームが流行った時期があった。僕はそれが嫌いで、サッカーを見なかった時期もあるくらい。やっとクラシックなスタイルに戻ってくれました。ユニフォームを見るとグラフィックの基本だと思うんです。敵味方がまじって乱れるから、あまり複雑な柄や、たくさんの色数が向かないんだと思う。

　僕は陸運局の自動車のナンバープレート、アルミにプレスしてあるあの字がわりと好きなんです。どこへ行くとああいうフォントがあるものなのかね、使えるのかな。字と

いうのは不思議で、みなさんは頭からお尻まで一つのセンス、感覚でピッと通っている書体が基本であるとお勉強したと思います。美しくて偉い。だけど僕が好きなその陸運局のやつなんかは、ちょっと破たんがあるんだろうと思う。サッカーのユニフォームの数字も破たんがある。これは自分勝手な言い分だけれど、そのあたりが味があるというのかな、「あいつは欠陥があるから面白い」という。あまり人格的に完成された人というのは、付き合っても面白くないじゃないかというような。やはりデザインでも、でき上がったものは一つの人格のようなものがありますから。

僕は失敗してもさらけ出したほうがいいと思っているんです。「こう直せばもっと良くなるかもしれないけど、まあ、こっちのほうがいいか」というようなことで決めてしまうことが多い。だからいつまでたっても一流になれないというか、あやふやな。まあ、あやふやだったから長持ちしたのかもしれない。スポンサーもあやふやだったかもしれない。それから書体の組み合わせでも、さっき葛西さんや服部くんが本当に上手いとお話しましたが、服部くんの字の組み合わせなんていうと、やはり活字と活字がつっこんだりボケたりするという遊びをやっているから、楽しい空間が生きているのでね。葛西さんだって、この字とこの絵と、不思議な組み合わせをする。それはやっぱりボケとつっこみじゃないけれど、笑いとか漫才のようなユーモアかもしれない。

僕は自分で自分を壊していたからね、壊しながら作ってきた。それをまともに頭から最後までビシーッとやっていたら、きっとそんなに面白くなかったかもしれない。成績がいいから生きやすいというわけでもなくて、生きやすいようにみんな生きるから長持ちする。だからあまりビクビクしないで勝手なことをやればいいと思う。

Writing systems are somewhat strange. In school I think you have all learned that the fundamental rule to follow when writing Japanese is to create characters in a clean, neat sweep from top to bottom. Therein lies their beauty, their greatness, you've been told. Personally, though, I'm fond of characters that have "imperfections," like those we find on our vehicle license plates, or the numbers that adorn our soccer uniforms. This is just my personal opinion, but it's imperfections of that sort that make them interesting. It's the same with people. We say somebody is interesting because he has certain faults; it's no fun hanging around with someone who is "too perfect" in character.

Design too has a kind of personality, in its final form. I think that even if you fail at something, it's best not to hide it. I often make decisions with the notion in mind that my design might perhaps be better if I were to make some adjustment to it, but I ultimately just feel like going with what I already have. That's why my work has never made it up there among the top ranks and is neither here nor there. Then again, maybe that equivocality is the reason for my longevity. Perhaps my clients have been equivocal too.

When it comes to putting typefaces together, Kaoru Kasai and Kazunari Hattori are truly brilliant at that. In Hattori's case, he plays around with type — letting one serve as a foil to the other — and in doing so he creates spaces filled with fun. In Kasai's case, I often marvel at the odd way he combines a certain form of lettering with a visual — again letting one play the foil to the other, with the same humor we find in comedians.

I've always worked while breaking my own mold. Had I instead aimed for perfection — that neat sweep from start to finish — the result would surely not have been very interesting. Life isn't made easy by performing brilliantly; longevity comes from everyone trying to lead an easy life. That's why I think we should do whatever we feel like and not worry too much what others will think.
(Masayoshi Nakajo)

東京TDC会員名簿
2013年8月末日現在

Tokyo TDC Members List
The list dates from August 2013

TDCのWebサイトで会員の代表作およびプロフィールをご覧いただけます。
You can refer to the TDC website for the major works and profiles of the members :
http://www.tdctokyo.org/

法人会員　Corporate Members

アンタリス・ジャパン株式会社　Antalis Japan Co., Ltd.
〒151-0051　東京都渋谷区千駄ヶ谷 5-26-5　代々木シティホームズ 301
Tel. 03-5360-1203　Fax. 03-5360-1820
http://www.antalis-asiapacific.com/

公益財団法人DNP文化振興財団　DNP Foundation for Cultural Promotion
〒104-0061　東京都中央区銀座 7-7-2　DNP銀座ビル
Tel. 03-5568-8224　Fax. 03-5568-8225
http://www.dnp.co.jp/foundation/

株式会社竹尾　Takeo Co., Ltd.
〒101-0054　東京都千代田区神田錦町 3-12-6
Tel. 03-3292-3611　Fax. 03-3292-9202
http://www.takeo.co.jp/

株式会社電通　Dentsu Inc.
〒105-7001　東京都港区東新橋 1-8-1
Tel. 03-6216-5111（main）
http://www.dentsu.co.jp/

株式会社ピラミッドフィルム　Pyramid Film Inc.
〒105-0022　東京都港区海岸 1-14-24　鈴江倉庫 5F
Tel. 03-3434-0916　Fax. 03-3434-0827
http://www.pyramidfilm.co.jp/

株式会社モリサワ　Morisawa Inc.
〒556-0012　大阪市浪速区敷津東 2-6-25
Tel. 06-6649-2151（main）　Fax. 06-6649-2153
http://www.morisawa.co.jp

個人会員　　Members

青木克憲　Katsunori Aoki
バタフライ・ストローク・株式會社　butterfly・stroke inc.
〒104-0041　東京都中央区新富 1-8-2　八丁堀北島ビル 6F
Tel. 03-5541-0061　Fax. 03-5541-0085
shintomi@btf.co.jp
http://www.butterfly-stroke.com/
http://www.shopbtf.com/

秋元克士　Yoshio Akimoto
秋元克士制作室　Yoshio Akimoto Office
〒174-0043　東京都板橋区坂下 3-20-1-213
Tel. 03-5918-9128　Fax. 03-5918-9128
yazyo3@u04.itscom.net

秋山カズオ　Kazuo Akiyama
株式会社 Deluxe　Deluxe Co., Ltd.
〒107-0062　東京都港区南青山 5-4-6　パレ・ロワイヤル南青山 103
Tel. 03-6427-4381　Fax. 03-6427-4382
a@dx-d.jp
http://dx-d.jp/

秋山具義　Gugi Akiyama
デイリーフレッシュ株式会社　Dairy Fresh
〒150-0034　東京都渋谷区代官山町 20-20　モンシェリー代官山 3F
Tel. 03-5457-1500　Fax. 03-5457-1501
info@d-fresh.com
http://www.d-fresh.com/gugi/

浅葉克己　Katsumi Asaba
株式会社浅葉克己デザイン室　Asaba Design Co., Ltd.
〒107-0062　東京都港区南青山 3-9-2
Tel. 03-3479-0471　Fax. 03-3402-0694
http://www.asaba-design.com/

味岡伸太郎　Shintaro Ajioka
有限会社スタッフ　Design Studio STAFF
〒441-8011　愛知県豊橋市菰口町 1-43
Tel. 0532-32-4871　Fax. 0532-32-7134
shintaro@ajioka3.com
http://www.ajioka3.com

阿部一秀　Kazuhide Abe
http://www.kazuhideabe.com/

阿部克昭　Yoshiaki Abe
ワイディー（阿部克昭デザイン室）　yd (yoshiaki abe design room)
〒151-0051　東京都渋谷区千駄ヶ谷 3-3-8　第 5 スカイビル 403
Tel. 03-3475-4677　Fax. 03-3475-4633
yd-abe@amy.hi-ho.ne.jp
http://ydabe.com/

天野幾雄　Ikuo Amano
天野幾雄クリエイティブ・スタジオ INC.　Amano Ikuo Creative Studio Inc.
〒157-0066　東京都世田谷区成城 6-29-14
Tel. 03-3482-8866　Fax. 03-3482-4588
amano@amanoikuocs.com

荒木優子　Yuko Araki
有限会社ランドサット　Landsat Inc.
araki@landsat.jp

有山達也　Tatsuya Ariyama
ariyama design store
〒103-0001　東京都中央区日本橋小伝馬町 20-4　東洋ハットビル 2 F
Tel. 03-3808-1414　Fax. 03-3808-1313

池越顕尋　Akihiro Ikegoshi
有限会社 GWG　GWG Inc.
info@gwg.ne.jp
http://www.gwg.ne.jp/

池田充宏　Mitsuhiro Ikeda
DRAWER inc.
〒150-0001　東京都渋谷区神宮前 6-35-3　コープオリンピア 508
Tel 03-6427-2041 Fax 03-6427-2042
ikeda@drawer.co.jp
http://www.drawer.co.jp/

石﨑悠子　Yuko Ishizaki
TOY
〒939-1119　富山県高岡市オフィスパーク 5 番地
富山県産業高度化センター 2 F
Tel. & Fax. 0766-88-2371
toutetsu1@gmail.com

石田直久　Naohisa Ishida
株式会社ライトパブリシティ　Light Publicity Co., Ltd.
Tel. 03-3248-3115　Fax. 03-3248-3122
ishidana@lightpublicity.co.jp
http://www.lightpublicity.co.jp/

石橋政美　Masami Ishibashi
masami ishibashi design inc.（id）
midesign@fuga.ocn.ne.jp
http://tdctokyo.org/jpn/?member=masami_ishibashi/

伊勢克也　Katsuya Ise
女子美術大学短期大学部　Joshibi University of Art and Design

板倉敬子　Keiko Itakura
イッカクイッカ株式会社　IKKAKUIKKA Co., Ltd.
info@keikoitakura.com

市川絵里子　Eriko Ichikawa
ウクナ株式会社　uQuna Inc.

糸井重里　Shigesato Itoi
東京糸井重里事務所　Tokyo Itoi Shigesato Office
http://www.1101.com/

井上嗣也　Tsuguya Inoue
ビーンズ　BEANS
〒106-0041　東京都港区麻布台 1-1-20　麻布台ユニハウス 502
Tel. 03-3586-8005　Fax. 03-3588-1003

井上庸子　Yoko Inoue
〒107-0061　東京都港区北青山 3-1-6-405
Tel. 03-5785-2556　Fax. 03-5785-2556
inoueyok@io.ocn.ne.jp
http://www.inoueyoko.com/

後 智仁　Tomohito Ushiro
株式会社 WHITE DESIGN
〒107-0062　東京都港区南青山 6-3-14-204
Tel. 03-6805-1320　Fax. 03-6805-1321
info@whitedesign.jp

大杉 学　Gaku Ohsugi
株式会社ナナマルニ・ワークス　702 Design Works Co., Ltd.
〒151-0064　東京都渋谷区上原 3-6-6　オークハウス 1-A
Tel. 03-3468-9702　Fax. 03-3468-9797
gaku@702design.co.jp
http://www.702design.co.jp/

大橋清一　Seiichi Ohashi
クリエイティブコミュニケイションズ株式会社レマン　C.C. LES MAINS, Inc.
〒150-0002　東京都渋谷区渋谷 1-19-25　エスタビル
Tel. 03-3407-1013　Fax. 03-3407-1598
info@cc-lesmains.co.jp
http://www.cc-lesmains.co.jp/

大原健一郎　Kenichiro Ohara
NIGN（株式会社ナイン）　NIGN Co., Ltd.
info@nign.co.jp
http://www.nign.co.jp/

岡室 健　Ken Okamuro
株式会社博報堂　HAKUHODO Inc.
〒107-6322　東京都港区赤坂 5-3-1　赤坂 Biz タワー
Tel. 03-6441-8153

奥村靫正　Yukimasa Okumura
TSTJ inc.
〒141-0031　東京都品川区西五反田 1-32-8　ぐれいぷハウス 2F
Tel. 03-5434-8031　Fax. 03-5434-6212
oua@tstj-inc.co.jp
http://www.tstj-inc.co.jp/

尾崎伸行　Nobuyuki Ozaki
株式会社百舌／モズデザイン　MOZU Co., Ltd.
〒150-0013　東京都渋谷区恵比寿 2-17-5
Tel. 03-5449-7716　Fax. 03-5449-0024
nozaki@mozu.co.jp

葛西 薫　Kaoru Kasai
株式会社サン・アド　SUN-AD Co., Ltd.
〒107-0061　東京都港区北青山 2-11-3　青山プラザビル
Tel. 03-5785-6800　Fax. 03-3796-3850

笠井則幸　Noriyuki Kasai
kasai@gdc.name

柏本郷司　Satoji Kashimoto
株式会社リクルートマーケティング局クリエイティブセンター Recruit Co., Ltd.
kashimo@r.recruit.co.jp

梶山かつみ　Katsumi Kajiyama
有限会社インテグラルプラス　Integral-Plus Inc.
〒150-0001　東京都渋谷区神宮前 5-38-8
Tel. 03-3797-3531　Fax. 03-3797-3532
kajiyama@integral-plus.jp
http://integral-plus.jp/

葛本京子　Kyoko Katsumoto
株式会社視覚デザイン研究所　Visual Design Laboratory, Inc.
〒559-0034　大阪府大阪市住之江区南港北 2-1-10
アジア太平洋トレードセンタービル ITM 棟 10F
Tel. 06-6615-0800　Fax. 06-6615-0801
http://www.vdl.co.jp/

加納佳之　Yoshiyuki Kano
株式会社アイデアスケッチ　ideasketch
information@ideasketch.jp
http://www.ideasketch.jp/

河北秀也　Hideya Kawakita
株式会社日本ベリエールアートセンター　Japan Belier Art Center Inc.
Tel. 03-5565-5641　Fax. 03-5565-5563
kawakita@belier.co.jp
http://www.belier.co.jp/

菊地敦己　Atsuki Kikuchi
株式会社菊地敦己事務所　Atsuki Kikuchi Ltd.
studio@akltd.jp
http://atsukikikuchi.com/

木住野彰悟　Shogo Kishino
6D
〒107-0062　東京都港区南青山 5-12-4　泰平南青山ビル 8F
Tel. 03-6427-3752　Fax. 03-6427-3753
info@6d-k.com
http://www.6d-k.com/

北川一成　Issay Kitagawa
GRAPH Co., Ltd.
〒150-0033　東京都渋谷区猿楽町 29-8　E22
Tel. 03-5489-6931　Fax. 03-5489-6933
info@moshi-moshi.jp
http://www.moshi-moshi.jp/

北澤敏彦　Toshihiko Kitazawa
株式会社ディスハウス　DIX-HOUSE Inc.
〒150-0001　東京都渋谷区神宮前 5-1-7
Tel. 03-3406-6631　Fax. 03-3486-4940
http://www.dix-house.co.jp/

木下勝弘　Katsuhiro Kinoshita
株式会社デザイン倶楽部　DESGIN CLUB Inc.
〒171-0021　東京都豊島区西池袋 2-22-8　目白第二欅マンション 304
Tel. 03-5952-7487　Fax. 03-5952-7489
design-club@nifty.com
http://www.design-club.jp/

金田一 剛　Kou Kindaichi
金田一デザイン／株式会社チーム　Kindaichi Design / Team Co.

草谷隆文　Takafumi Kusagaya
有限会社草谷デザイン　Kusagaya Design Inc.
〒168-0082　東京都杉並区久我山 4-9-3
Tel. 03-5938-9493　Fax. 03-6761-9493
kusagaya@kt.rim.or.jp
http://www.kusagayadesign.com/

工藤青石　Aoshi Kudo
コミュニケーションデザイン研究所　Communication Design Laboratory
〒107-0051　東京都港区元赤坂 1-2-5　TANEDA Bldg,7F
Tel. 03-3478-9777　Fax. 03-3478-4777
info@cdlab.jp
http://www.cdlab.jp/

工藤強勝　Tsuyokatsu Kudo
デザイン実験室　Design Laboratory
〒107-0062　東京都港区南青山 2-22-4　秀和南青山レジデンス 208 号
Tel. 03-3479-1670　Fax. 03-3479-1850

工藤規雄　Norio Kudo
有限会社グリフ　Griffe Inc.
〒150-0001　東京都渋谷区神宮前 4-7-7　ゼルコーヴァ表参道 201
Tel. 03-5785-2477　Fax. 03-5785-2478
n-kudo@japan.email.ne.jp

國定勝利　Katsutoshi Kunisada
花王株式会社 作成センター ビューティケア広告作成部
Creative Department, Kao Corporation
〒103-8210　東京都中央区日本橋茅場町 1-14-10
Tel. 03-3660-7169　Fax. 03-3660-7983
kunisada.katsutoshi@kao.co.jp
http://www.kao.com/

郡司龍彦　Tatsuhiko Gunji
gunji@08772.com
http://www.08772.com/

小磯裕司　Yuji Koiso
北京大思広告有限公司
郵編 100027　中華人民共和国 北京市朝陽区工体北路 8 号院
三里屯 SOHO 商場 53 層 5305
Tel. +86-10-8527-0483　Fax. +86-10-8527-0493
koiso@ndc.co.jp
http://www.ndc.co.jp/koiso/

小島潤一　Junichi Kojima
株式会社サン・アド　SUN-AD Co., Ltd.
〒 107-0061　東京都港区北青山 2-11-3　青山プラザビル
Tel. 03-5785-6800　Fax. 03-3796-3851
j-kojima@sun-ad.co.jp

小島利之　Toshiyuki Kojima
小島デザイン事務所　Kojima Design Office Inc.

後藤繁雄　Shigeo Goto
有限会社アートビートパブリッシャーズ　artbeat publishers Inc.
〒 135-0062　東京都江東区東雲 2-9-13 2F　G/P ＋ g3gallery
Tel. 03-6426-0624　Fax. 03-6426-0625
〒 150-0013　東京都渋谷区恵比寿 1-18-4
NADiff A/P/A/R/T 2F G/P gallery
Tel. 03-5422-9331　Fax. 03-5422-9331
info@gptokyo.jp
http://gptokyo.jp/　http://g3gallery.jp/　http://a-b-p.jp/
http://superschool.jp

後藤 宏　Hiroshi Goto
株式会社イメージゲート　Image Gate Co., Ltd.
〒 815-0035　福岡県福岡市南区向野 2-13-29 秀巧社印刷株式会社内
Tel. 092-707-1651　Fax. 092-541-4001

小西啓介　Keisuke Konishi
小西啓介デザイン室　Keisuke Konishi Design Room
〒 106-0031　東京都港区西麻布 3-21-20　霞町コーポ 1009
Tel. 03-3404-8251　Fax. 03-3404-4257
kkonishi@za2.so-net.ne.jp

権田雅彦　Masahiko Gonda
株式会社電通 第 CR プランニング局　Dentsu Inc.
〒 105-7001 東京都港区新橋 1-8-1
Tel. 03-6216-8659
masahiko.gonda@dentsu.co.jp

近藤一弥　Kazuya Kondo
株式会社カズヤコンドウ　Kazuya Kondo Inc.
〒 150-0001　東京都渋谷区神宮前 4-19-8　アロープラザ 321
Tel. 03-3423-7051　Fax. 03-3423-7052
info@kazuyakondo.com
http://www.kazuyakondo.com/

七種泰史　Yasushi Saikusa
株式会社デザインシグナル　Design Signal Inc.
〒 216-0035　神奈川県川崎市宮前区馬絹 576-1-203
Tel. 044-854-9822　Fax. 044-854-9822
yes-c@design-signal.co.jp
http://design-signal.co.jp/

齋藤 浩　Hiroshi Saito
有限会社トンプー・グラフィクス　tong-poo graphics
〒 154-0017　東京都世田谷区世田谷 4-14-34　欅ハウス 302
saito@tongpoographics.jp
http://tongpoographics.jp/

斉藤正明　Masaaki Saito
株式会社ライトパブリシティ　Light Publicity Co., Ltd.

寒河江亘太　Kota Sagae
株式会社 SAGA　SAGA Inc.
〒 107-0052　東京都港区赤坂 2-23-1　アークヒルズフロントタワー RoP 9F
Tel. 03-6459-1600　Fax. 03-6459-1601
info@sagainc.co.jp
http://www.sagainc.co.jp/

坂元 純　Jun Sakamoto
〒 180-0004　東京都武蔵野市吉祥寺本町 3-11-3　SOLA Court C 号室
sakamoto@gekkodo.co.jp

坂本尊徳　Takanori Sakamoto
takanori.sakamotoz@gmail.com
http://tdctokyo.org/jpn/?member=takanori_sakamoto/

佐藤可士和　Kashiwa Sato
SAMURAI
〒 150-0011　東京都渋谷区東 2-14-11-1F
Tel. 03-3498-3601　Fax. 03-3498-3602
samurai@samurai.sh
http://www.kashiwasato.com/

佐藤晃一　Koichi Sato
佐藤晃一デザイン室　Koichi Sato Design Studio
〒 113-0033　東京都文京区本郷 4-12-16-402
Tel. 03-5804-7655　Fax. 03-5804-7656

佐藤 卓　Taku Satoh
株式会社佐藤卓デザイン事務所　Taku Satoh Design Office Inc.
〒 104-0061　東京都中央区銀座 3-2-10　並木ビル 6F
Tel. 03-3538-2051　Fax. 03-3538-2054
tsdo@tsdo.co.jp
http://www.tsdo.co.jp/

佐藤直樹　Naoki Sato
株式会社アジール　ASYL inc.
contact@asyl.co.jp
http://www.asyl.co.jp/

沢田耕一　Koichi Sawada
株式会社電通 コミュニケーション・デザイン・センター
Communication Design Center, Dentsu Inc.
koichi.sawada@dentsu.co.jp

澤田泰廣　Yasuhiro Sawada
澤田泰廣デザイン室　Yasuhiro Sawada Design Studio
〒 150-0034　東京都渋谷区代官山町 4-1　代官山マンション 710
Tel. 03-5459-3383　Fax. 03-3463-4822
sy28@apricot.ocn.ne.jp

SUNDAY PROJECT
sketch@sundayproject.jp
http://sundayproject.jp/

篠塚大郎　Taro Shinozuka

澁谷克彦　Katsuhiko Shibuya
株式会社資生堂　Shiseido Co., Ltd.
http://www.shiseido.co.jp/

シマダタモツ　Tamotsu Shimada
有限会社シマダデザイン　Shimada Design Inc.
http://www.shimada-d.com/

清水正己　Masami Shimizu
有限会社清水正己デザイン事務所　Shimizu Masami Design Office
〒 150-0002　渋谷区渋谷 1-15-15　テラス渋谷美竹 1203
Tel. 03-5467-0581　Fax. 03-5467-0584
info@shimizu-design.co.jp
http://www.shimizu-design.co.jp/

新谷秀実　Hidemi Shingai
株式会社圖庵　Zuan, Inc.
〒 104-0041　東京都中央区新富 1-13-19　櫻正宗東京支店ビル 2F
Tel. 03-3537-0845　Fax. 03-3537-0846
shingai@zu-an.co.jp
http://www.zu-an.co.jp/

末広峰治　Mineji Suehiro
パワーデザイン　Power Design
Alameda de Urquijo 35, Bilbao Spain

杉崎真之助　Shinnoske Sugisaki
真之助事務所　SHINNOSKE Design
shinn@shinn.co.jp
http://www.shinn.co.jp/

関根慎一　Shinichi Sekine
関根慎一デザイン室　Shinichi Sekine Design Room

祖父江 慎　Shin Sobue
有限会社コズフィッシュ　cozfish
〒153-0061　東京都目黒区中目黒 3-11-13 1F
Tel. 03-3793-2225　Fax. 03-3793-2226
tamao@cozfish.jp

大日本タイポ組合　Dainippon Type Organization
〒150-0041　東京都渋谷区神南 1-5-14　三船ビル 303
Tel. 03-6804-3353　Fax. 03-6804-3352
dainippon@type.org
http://dainippon.type.org/

高岡一弥　Kazuya Takaoka
株式会社ディーケイ　DK Co., Ltd.

髙橋正実　Masami Takahashi
有限会社マサミデザイン　MASAMI DESIGN
〒131-0033　東京都墨田区向島 3-3-1　チューブマンション 1101 号室
Tel. 03-5619-1550　Fax. 03-5619-1554
info@masamidesign.co.jp
http://www.masamidesign.co.jp/

高橋善丸　Yoshimaru Takahashi
株式会社広告丸　Kokokumaru Co., Ltd.
〒530-0052　大阪府大阪市北区南扇町 7-2　ユニ東梅田 608
Tel. 06-6314-0881　Fax. 06-6314-0806
yoshimaru@kokokumaru.com
http://www.kokokumaru.com/

高原 宏　Hiroshi Takahara
有限会社高原宏デザイン事務所　Hiroshi Takahara Design Office
〒107-0062　東京都港区南青山 1-15-22　ヴィラ乃木坂 305
Tel. 03-3404-9963　Fax. 03-3404-9727
YRL03026@nifty.ne.jp
http://takahara.fri.macserver.jp/

竹内佐織　Saori Takeuchi
株式会社博報堂　HAKUHODO Inc.
〒107-6322　東京都港区赤坂 5-3-1　赤坂 Biz タワー
Tel. 03-6441-8151　Fax. 03-6441-8227
SAORI.TAKEUCHI@hakuhodo.co.jp

竹村真太郎　Shintaro Takemura
株式会社 ADK アーツ　ADK Arts Inc.
〒104-0045　東京都中央区築地 4-1-1　東劇ビル 2F
Tel. 03-3545-1881　Fax. 03-3545-6167
takemura@adk-arts.jp
http://www.adk-arts.jp/

立花ハジメ　Hajime Tachibana
株式会社立花ハジメデザイン　Tachibana Hajime Design

立花文穂　Fumio Tachibana
立花文穂プロ．　TACHIBANA FUMIO PRO.
〒165-0034　東京都中野区大和町 1-5-10
Tel. 03-5373-2858　Fax. 03-5373-2858

タナカノリユキ　Noriyuki Tanaka
TANAKA NORIYUKI Activity
tna@tnamail.jp

田中北斗　Hokuto Tanaka
ホクトデザインルーム　Hokuto Design Room
〒171-0021　東京都豊島区西池袋 1-26-5　東山ビル 4F
Tel. 03-5953-2723　Fax. 03-5953-2724
hdr@sepia.ocn.ne.jp

玉置太一　Taichi Tamaki
株式会社電通 第 5 クリエーティブ局　Dentsu Inc.
Tel. 03-6216-8654　Fax. 03-6217-5800
taichi.tamaki@dentsu.co.jp

塚田男女雄　Minao Tsukada
ツカダデザイン　Minao Tsukada Design
〒123-0843　東京都足立区西新井栄町 3-1-1-811
Tel. 03-3848-0831　Fax. 03-3848-0831
minao.t@tokyo.email.ne.jp
http://www.ne.jp/asahi/minaotsukada/design/

塚本 陽　Kiyoshi Tsukamoto
tkmt@xf6.so-net.ne.jp
http://eraplatonico.tumblr.com/

土屋孝元　Takayoshi Tsuchiya
有限会社土屋孝元事務所　TSUCHIYA TAKAYOSHI Inc.
tsucci@me.com
http://tsucci.cj3.jp/
http://members3.jcom.home.ne.jp/tsucci/

永井裕明　Hiroaki Nagai
株式会社エヌ・ジー　N.G. inc.
〒107-0062　東京都港区南青山 5-4-19　南青山コート 403
Tel. 03-3486-0800　Fax.03-3486-3509
ng@nginc.jp
http://www.nginc.jp/

中島英樹　Hideki Nakajima
有限会社中島デザイン　NAKAJIMA DESIGN Inc.
〒154-0002　東京都世田谷区下馬 1-8-5 1F
Tel. 03-5430-1081　Fax. 03-5430-1082
info@nkjm-d.com
http://www.nkjm-d.com/

中島祥文　Shobun Nakashima
ウエーブクリエーション　Wave Creation Inc.
〒107-0062　東京都港区南青山 6-15-13-503
Tel. 03-5778-9711　Fax. 03-5778-9712
jdw06140@nifty.ne.jp

仲條正義　Masayoshi Nakajo
株式会社仲條デザイン事務所　Nakajo Design Office
〒106-0041　東京都港区麻布台 1-1-20-308
Tel. 03-5570-9093　Fax. 03-5570-9095

長友啓典　Keisuke Nagatomo
株式会社ケイツー　K2 Inc.
〒106-0032　東京都港区六本木 7-18-7　内海ビル 4F
Tel. 03-3401-9266　Fax. 03-3403-4180
k-two@k2-d.co.jp
http://www.k2-d.co.jp/

中村至男　Norio Nakamura
中村至男制作室　Norio Nakamura Studio
〒150-0002　東京都渋谷区渋谷 4-1-23-802
Tel. 03-5468-2655　Fax. 03-5468-2662
contact@nakamuranorio.com
http://nakamuranorio.com/

中村勇吾　Yugo Nakamura
tha ltd.
〒107-0062　東京都港区南青山 5-3-5　南青山ミル・ロッシュビル 3F
Tel. 03-3400-0490　Fax. 03-3400-0492
yugo@tha.jp
http://tha.jp/

中森陽三　Yozo Nakamori
中森デザイン事務所　Nakamori Design Office
〒165-0032　東京都中野区鷺宮 4-41-1

南部俊安　Toshiyasu Nanbu
有限会社テイスト　Taste Inc.
〒572-0825　大阪府寝屋川市萱島南町 18-10
Tel. 072-824-5538　Fax. 072-824-5583
tasteinc@osk.3web.ne.jp
http://www.tasteinc.net/

西村 武　Takeshi Nishimura
株式会社コンプレイトデザイン　Completo Design Inc.
〒107-0062　東京都港区南青山 2-15-6　ループ青山ビル B1F
Tel. 03-6427-0435　Fax. 03-6427-0436
info@completo.co.jp
http://www.completo.co.jp/

西村佳也　Yoshinari Nishimura
株式会社ウエストビレッジ コミュニケーション・アーツ
West Village CA Co., Ltd.
〒140-0002　東京都品川区東品川 2-2-43
Tel. 03-3740-0331

野村高志　Takashi Nomura
株式会社カチドキ　KACHIDOKI

畑野憲一　Kenichi Hatano
株式会社電通 第 1CR プランニング局　Dentsu Inc.
〒 105-7001　東京都港区東新橋 1-8-1
Tel. 03-6216-4510　Fax. 03-6217-5692
kenichi.hatano@dentsu.co.jp

服部一成　Kazunari Hattori
有限会社服部一成　Kazunari Hattori Inc.
〒 106-0031　東京都港区西麻布 3-20-13　木村ビル 5F
Tel. 03-3478-2591　Fax. 03-3478-2592
hattori@flyingcake.com

浜田武士　Takeshi Hamada
h@hamada-takeshi.com
http://www.hamada-takeshi.com/

林 規章　Noriaki Hayashi
HAYASHI DESIGN
hayashid@me.com

針谷建二郎　Kenjiro Harigai
ANSWR Inc.
〒 154-0001　東京都世田谷区池尻 2-32-2　デパール池尻ビル 1F
Tel. 050-8882-0088　Fax. 03-5433-1138
harigai@answr.jp
http://www.answr.jp/
http://www.kenjiroharigai.com/

日高英輝　Eiki Hidaka
株式会社グリッツデザイン　gritzdesigninc.

日比野克彦　Katsuhiko Hibino
株式会社ヒビノスペシャル　HIBINO SPECIAL Co., Ltd.
〒 150-0002　東京都渋谷区渋谷 3-3-10　秀和青山レジデンス 401
Tel. 03-5485-8832　Fax. 03-3407-7530
special@hibino.to
http://www.hibino.cc/

平野湟太郎　Kotaro Hirano
有限会社平野湟太郎デザイン研究所　Kotaro Hirano Design Laboratory
〒 639-3432　奈良県吉野郡吉野町大字窪垣内 515
Tel. 0746-39-9176
yoshino@hiranodesign.jp
http://www.hiranodesign.jp/

平林奈緒美　Naomi Hirabayashi
PLUG-IN GRAPHIC
info@plug-in.co.uk
http://www.plug-in.co.uk/

平松聖悟　Seigo Hiramatsu
キャリアデザイン・エンタープライズ、デザイン墨道・聖墨会
Career Design Enterprise
〒 815-0001　福岡県福岡市南区五十川 2-36-48
Tel. 092-406-0262　Fax. 092-406-0262
seigohiramatsu@w7.dion.ne.jp
http://sei5.com/

廣村正彰　Masaaki Hiromura
株式会社廣村デザイン事務所　Hiromura Design Office
http://www.hiromuradesign.com/

福島 治　Osamu Fukushima
福島デザイン　Fukushima Design
〒 135-0045　東京都江東区古石場 3-11-17
Tel. 03-5621-3036　Fax. 03-5621-3026
fukushima-design@gol.com
http://www.fukushima-design.jp/

福田秀之　Hideyuki Fukuda
有限会社スタジオ福デ　studio Fuku-De
〒 150-0011　東京都渋谷区東 3-17-16　第二今井ビル 5F
Tel. 03-5778-4705　Fax. 03-5778-4706
fukude@fsinet.or.jp

藤井陽一郎　Yoichirou Fujii
株式会社トースターズ　Toasters Inc.

Blood Tube Inc.
info@blood-tube.com
http://www.blood-tube.com/

古川智基　Tomoki Furukawa
SAFARI inc.
post@safari-design.com
http://www.safari-design.com/

細島雄一　Yuichi Hosojima
サンクディレクションズ　CINQ DIRECTIONS
〒 150-0033　東京都渋谷区猿楽町 29-9　ヒルサイドテラス D35
Tel. 03-6416-1975　Fax. 03-6416-1924
hoso@39d.co.jp
http://www.tottemoinc.com

奔保彰良　Akira Hombo
株式会社マイリアルビジョン　MY REAL VISION INC.
〒 153-0051　東京都目黒区上目黒 3-13-10
Tel. 03-3715-5411　Fax. 03-3715-5412
hombo@mrv.co.jp
http://mrv.co.jp/

間嶋龍臣　Tatsuomi Majima
間嶋デザイン事務所　MAJIMA TATSUOMI DESIGN Inc.
〒 771-0144　徳島県徳島市川内町榎瀬 846-6
Tel. 088-665-1243　Fax. 088-665-1243
majix@peach.ocn.ne.jp

松下 計　Kei Matsushita
有限会社松下計デザイン室　Kei Matsushita Design Room Inc.
153-0051　東京都目黒区上目黒 3-30-8　メゾン・ド・シノ S-1
Tel. 03-5721-0868　Fax. 03-5721-0670
staff@keimdr.com

松本弦人　Gento Matsumoto
SB
http:// bccks.jp/

三浦 遊　Yu Miura
株式会社資生堂 宣伝制作部　Advertising Division, Shiseido Co., Ltd.
〒 105-8310　東京都港区東新橋 1-6-2
Tel. 03-6218-6298　Fax. 03-6218-6329
miura@ad-shiseido.com

丸橋 桂　Katsura Marubashi
株式会社資生堂 宣伝制作室　Advertising Division, Shiseido Co., Ltd.
〒 104-0061　東京都中央区銀座 7-5-5
marubashikatsura@gmail.com

三木 健　Ken Miki
三木健デザイン事務所　Ken Miki & Associates
http://www.ken-miki.net/

水垣 淳　Jun Mizugaki
株式会社マッシーン　Machine Inc.
Tel. 03-3402-0459　Fax. 03-3402-0464
jun@machine.ne.jp
http://www.machine.ne.jp/

水谷孝次　Koji Mizutani
株式会社水谷事務所　Mizutani Studio
〒 106-0046　東京都港区元麻布 3-1-38　第五谷澤ビル 7BC
Tel. 03-3478-1931　Fax. 03-3478-2787
studio@mizutanistudio.com
http://www.mizutanistudio.com/

水野 学　Manabu Mizuno
株式会社グッドデザインカンパニー　good design company
contact@gooddesigncompany.com

宮田 識　Satoru Miyata
株式会社ドラフト　DRAFT Co., Ltd.
〒 150-0011　東京都渋谷区東 2-14-6
Tel. 03-3498-5281　Fax. 03-3498-5377
http://www.draft.jp/

宮田裕美詠　Yumiyo Miyata
STRIDE
〒 939-8081　富山県富山市堀川小泉町 657
Tel. 076-420-3035
s@stride.me
http://www.stride.me/

村松丈彦　Takehiko Muramatsu
muramatsu.takehiko@gmail.com
http://muramatsu-takehiko.com/

杢谷吉也　Yoshinari Mokutani
モクタニデザイン　Mokutani Design
mokutani_d@h05.itscom.net

森本千絵　Chie Morimoto
株式会社 goen°
〒 107-0062　東京都港区南青山 5-10-12 3F
Tel. 03-5774-1150　Fax. 03-5774-5025
goen@goen-goen.co.jp
http://www.goen-goen.co.jp/

安原和夫　Kazuo Yasuhara
YASUHARA DESIGN
〒 150-0001　東京都渋谷区神宮前 4-14-13　ハイシティ表参道 213
Tel. 03-3401-1564
yasuharadesign@yahoo.co.jp

矢野まさつぐ　Masatsugu Yano
株式会社オープンエンズ　OPENENDS Inc.
〒 451-0044　愛知県名古屋市西区菊井 2-8-15　DANP Bldg. 2F
Tel. 052-533-6316　Fax. 052-533-6326
yano@openends.org
http://www.openends.org/

山形季央　Toshio Yamagata
株式会社福原コーポレーション　Fukuhara Co., Ltd.
〒 105-0021　東京都港区東新橋 1-1-16　汐留 FS ビル
Tel. 03-6253-1469
yamagata@fkginza.co.jp

山口 馨　Kaoru Yamaguchi
有限会社バウ広告事務所　BAU Advertising Office
〒 106-0032　東京都港区六本木 3-16-35　イースト六本木ビル 4F
Tel. 03-3568-6711　Fax. 03-3568-6712
yamaguchi@bau-ad.co.jp
http://www.bau-ad.co.jp/
http://www.e-ykj.com/

山口至剛　Shigo Yamaguchi
有限会社山口至剛デザイン室　Shigo Yamaguchi Design Room Inc.
〒 150-0002　東京都渋谷区渋谷 4-3-13　常盤松葵マンション 906
Tel. 03-3486-1052　Fax. 03-3486-1053
ydr@gol.com

山崎晴太郎　Seitaro Yamazaki
株式会社セイタロウデザイン　Seitaro Design Inc.
〒 106-0031　東京都港区西麻布 3-13-15 パロマプラザ B2
Tel. 03-6434-0115　Fax. 03-6434-0116
s@seitaro-design.com
http://www.seitaro-design.com/

山本哲次　Tetsuji Yamamoto
株式会社山本哲次デザイン室　Tetsuji Yamamoto Design Office Co., Ltd.
〒 135-0034　東京都江東区永代 2-31-5　内田ビル 4F
Tel. 03-3643-9807　Fax. 03-3643-9808
tetsu@kc4.so-net.ne.jp

山本ヒロキ　Hiroki Yamamoto
マーヴィン　MARVIN
〒 150-0002　東京都渋谷区渋谷 2-6-9　カケイビル 2F
Tel. 03-6419-7766　Fax.03-6419-7776
info@marvin-ltd.com
http://marvin-ltd.com/

山本洋司　Yoji Yamamoto
株式会社ビジュアルメッセージ研究所　Visual Message Inc.
〒 102-0083　東京都千代田区麹町 4-8-26　ロイクラトン麹町 4F
Tel. 03-3234-7411　Fax. 03-3234-7466
yamamoto@visual2004.com
http://www.visual2004.com/

吉田直樹　Naoki Yoshida

米村 浩　Hiroshi Yonemura
ノープロブレム合同会社　no problem LLC.
http://www.noproblem.co.jp/

渡辺卓也　Takuya Watanabe
渡辺卓也デザイン室　Takuya Watanabe Design Room
〒 156-0043　東京都世田谷区松原 3-23-19 松原フラット B104 号
Tel. 03-3324-6495　Fax. 03-3324-6495
d.room01@m5.dion.ne.jp

Alexander Gelman [USA/Japan]
Design Machine
http://www.designmachine.net/

Benny Au [Hong Kong, China]
Amazing Angle Design Co., Ltd.
http://www.amazingangle.com/

John Maeda [USA]
Maeda Studio
http://www.maedastudio.com/

John Warwicker [UK/Australia]
tomato
http://www.tomato.co.uk/

Xu Wang [China]
Wang Xu & Associates Ltd.
Guangdong Museum of Art
http://www.wangxu.com.cn/

NPO法人　東京タイプディレクターズクラブ
〒160-0023　東京都新宿区西新宿 5-25-13-6A
Tel. 03-6276-5210　Fax. 03-6276-5211

Tokyo Type Directors Club Office
6A, 5-25-13 Nishi-shinjuku, Shinjuku-ku, Tokyo 160-0023 Japan
Tel. +81-3-6276-5210　Fax. +81-3-6276-5211
info@tdctokyo.org
http://tdctokyo.org/

ENTER

どうも。
サン・アドです。

さいきん、しごとや社内のもろもろを
ホームページでご紹介しております。
コツコツ更新しておりますので
おひまなときなど、おこしくださいませ。

www.sun-ad.co.jp

株式会社サン・アド　107-0061 東京都港区北青山 2-11-3 青山プラザビル　Tel.03-5785-6800

typography

paper
design &
technology

Arouse your Experimental Spirit!

All the challenging creations of Aleksandr Rodchenko;sculptures, architecture, interiors, furniture, graphics, and photography, were overflowing with experimental spirit. Still, after more than 90 years, the stimulating shards of his spirit intensely shake us to the core. It whispers to our hearts-urging us to arouse with confidence.

Exhibition design+Photography:Kijuro Yahagi

RODCHENKO Innovator of Russian avant-garde

公益財団法人DNP文化振興財団
DNP Foundation for Cultural Promotion

ggg ∫∫∫ CCGA

http://www.dnp.co.jp/foundation

目覚めよ、実験精神！

アレクサンドル・ロトチェンコの挑んだ、立体、建築、インテリア、家具、グラフィック、写真の作品全てが、実験精神の破片に満ち溢れていた。九〇年以上の歳月が流れた今でも、飛び込んでくるその実験精神の破片は、我々の心を激しく揺さぶりながら、確信を持って目覚めよとささやいてくる。

RODCHENKO Innovator of Russian avant-garde

アイデア、技術、企業家精神。私たちは3つの力でイノベーションをつくってゆく。 Good Innovation. dentsu

東京造形大学
〒192-0992 東京都八王子市宇津貫町1556
Tel. 042-637-8111 URL: http://www.zokei.ac.jp/

9代目学長
諏訪敦彦

Photo: Kaoru SUZUKI

デザインは爆発だ。

DESIGN SCHOOL

専門学校 桑沢デザイン研究所
〒150-0041 東京都渋谷区神南1-4-17
Tel. 03-3463-2431 URL: http://www.kds.ac.jp/

10代目所長
浅葉克己

桑沢学園には、東京造形大学と桑沢デザイン研究所の2校がある。理事長は小田一幸。常務理事は白澤宏規。東京造形大学9代目学長は映画監督の諏訪敦彦。巨大なキャンパスは八王子にある。桑沢デザイン研究所、10代目所長はアートディレクターの浅葉克己。渋谷の国立代々木競技場の前にある。2人とも現役の作家である。そして共に母校の出身者。創立者桑沢洋子は、1954年にドイツバウハウス学長だったヴァルター・グロピウスの訪問を受け、「桑沢こそバウハウスの精神がある」とサインをいただいた。2012年2人はデッサウのバウハウスを訪問した。

浅葉克己

MORISAWA F●NT

光朝で、プロに近づいた。
新ゴで、賞をとった。

タカハンドで、売上げが上がった。

タイプバンクゴシックで、意表をついた。

ゴシックMB101で、勝負に出た。

UD新丸ゴで、人にやさしくなれた。

太ミンA101で、プロポーズした。

プリティ桃で、辞表を書いた。

ヒラギノで、新境地を開いた。

黎ミンで、原点に返った。

MORISAWA PASSPORT

書体の美しさと品質の高さ、そして種類の豊富さから、出版やデザインにおける
業界スタンダードとなったMORISAWA PASSPORT。ジャンルを超えて、メディアを超えて、
時代のニーズにマッチした、豊かな文字環境を提供します。

MORISAWA PASSPORT　¥52,500 （税込み）
MORISAWA PASSPORT ONE　¥52,500 （税込み）

製品に関する詳しい情報は **www.morisawa.co.jp**

※記載されている社名および商品名は、各社の登録商標または商標です。　※本仕様は、予告なく変更する場合があります。

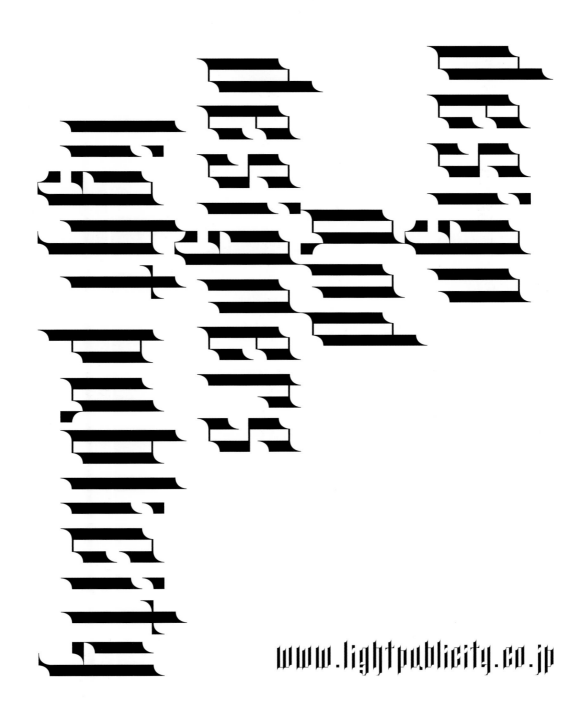

light publicity

design

designers design

graphic design

www.lightpublicity.co.jp

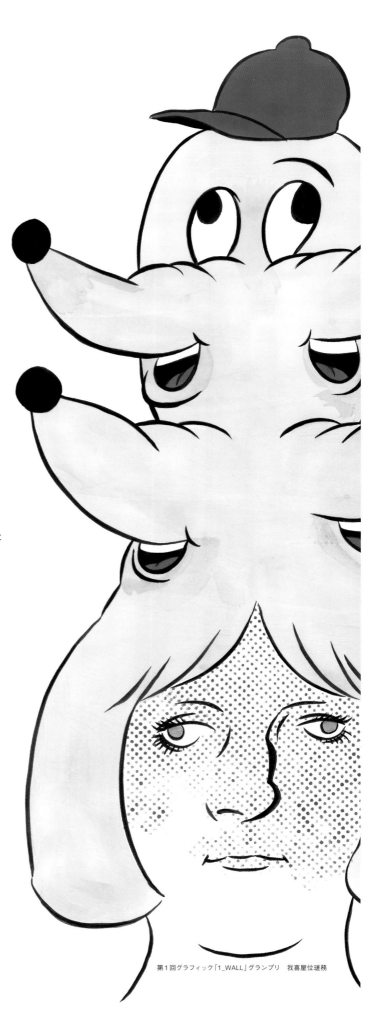

RECRUIT

見たいものは、
誰もまだ見たことないもの。

トップクリエイターの実験の場を目指す「クリエイションギャラリーG8」と
新人アーティストの表現活動を応援する「ガーディアン・ガーデン」。
創作する人も、才能を探している人も、表現を楽しみたい人も。
次の時代を担うクリエイションに、会いにきませんか。

リクルートの2つのギャラリー　http://rcc.recruit.co.jp/

Creation Gallery G8　クリエイションギャラリーG8
〒104-8001　東京都中央区銀座8-4-17 リクルートGINZA8ビル1F
TEL.03-6835-2260　11：00a.m.-7：00p.m.　日・祝休館　入場無料

Guardian Garden　ガーディアン・ガーデン
〒104-0061　東京都中央区銀座7-3-5 ヒューリック銀座7丁目ビルB1F
TEL.03-5568-8818　11：00a.m.-7：00p.m.　日・祝休館　入場無料

第1回グラフィック「1_WALL」グランプリ　我喜屋位瑳務

DATE DUE	RETURNED